Writing
in the
Margins

For Bobbi,

Thanks for your care
and friendship.

Fondly,
Marilyn

Writing in the Margins

The Ethics of Expatriation
from Lawrence to
Ondaatje

Marilyn Adler
Papayanis

Vanderbilt
University Press

NASHVILLE

THIS BOOK IS PRINTED ON ACID-FREE PAPER.

MANUFACTURED IN THE UNITED STATES OF AMERICA

DESIGN BY CAMERON POULTER

LIBRARY OF CONGRESS

CATALOGING-IN-PUBLICATION DATA

Papayanis, Marilyn Adler, 1953–
Writing in the margins : the ethics of expatriation, from
Lawrence to Ondaatje / Marilyn Adler Papayanis.—1st ed.
p. cm.
Includes bibliographical references and index.
ISBN 0-8265-1468-5 (cloth : alk. paper)—
ISBN 0-8265-1469-3 (pbk. : alk. paper)
1. English literature—Foreign influences. 2. Expatriation in literature.
3. Lawrence, D. H. (David Herbert), 1885–1930—Knowledge—
Mediterranean Region. 4. American literature—20th century—
History and criticism. 5. English literature—20th century—
History and criticism. 6. Americans—Foreign countries—History—
20th century. 7. British—Foreign countries—History—20th century.
8. Bowles, Paul, 1910—Knowledge—Morocco. 9. American literature—
Foreign influences. 10. Durrell, Lawrence—Knowledge—Greece.
I. Title.
PR125.P37 2004
820.9'358—dc22
2004017372

For Nick

Contents

Preface and Acknowledgments

"Guilty Pleasures"

I CONFESS THAT I FELL IN LOVE WITH *The Alexandria Quartet* upon first reading; I was mesmerized by the word painting, the evocative melancholia, the sheer exoticism of Durrell's "masterpiece." I was moved in ways I can't recapture now, but more than any other text, it was this one that drew me to the study of literature. I try to hold on to that now, when it seems difficult to cultivate the "ethics" of generosity that I advocate here.

I grew up folk dancing, international folk dancing; my mother taught it; folk dancing was—is—her passion. When most folks my age were getting high and listening to Jimmy Hendrix, Led Zeppelin, the Dead, I was hanging out in the Café Feenjon in New York's Greenwich Village, grooving to Greek, Turkish, Arabic, Israeli, and Yiddish music. Nothing seemed sexier or more exciting. That melding of musical cultures and styles, that community of musicians and aficionados, I now see, formed a kind of utopian horizon that haunts these pages, though one that I need to question now. The link with Durrell? *Being* exotic, as by doing or wearing exotic things, listening to exotic music, belly dancing, or hanging around with "foreigners," was fun. The charm, however, was proportional to my exteriority. I didn't have to live in Greece or the Middle East; I didn't have to wear a chadoor. I could shed my "exoticism" as easily as I could peel off a sweater or change a record. Being American insulated me from having to look at myself through "foreign" eyes. If it was "cool" to be a belly dancer here; it would be something else entirely "there." But I looked with condescension upon any "foreigner" who did not share my enlightened sense of what such things meant. Being exotic in that way was my own protest against "the modern moral order." The strange thing is, I find myself treating Durrell with the same condescension, and it gives me pause.

Reading Durrell critically, I have been forced to confront my own careless appropriations, my own cultural thefts: committing acts of cultural voyeurism, exploiting the Other's difference to enhance my own desirability. Certainly I've indulged in my own forms of "self-exoticization." It was my own form of expatriation. Ironically, it seems, I began doing the research for this project a long, long time ago, only I didn't know it. Not that I have stolen any precious artifacts or participated in the wholesale exploitation of a subjugated people. The only "epistemic violence" I have knowingly committed is taking pleasure in certain exoticist texts. And yet I'm compelled—correctly, I believe—to plead guilty as "situated" or, at any rate, to hold myself accountable for being born to middle-class parents in the richest and, arguably, the freest, country in the world. What does that mean? The "ethics of expatriation," a narrative about being "elsewhere" spun from diverse strands of literature, theory, and philosophy, have provided some provisional answers. This much is certain: one cannot be self-conscious enough when one leaves the "comfy liberalisms" of home, when one challenges the borders that both separate "the West" from—and join us to—the rest. It is true for literary expatriates and their fictional counterparts; it is true for the reader as well, for the reader travels with them, sees through their eyes, shares their wonder and dread. Hence the notion of "guilty pleasures."

But I wonder, now, about this guilt. Reading Jane Bennett's *The Enchantment of Modern Life*, I am more sensitive to the ethical possibilities inherent in certain kinds of pleasure. Enchantment, which is one species of pleasure, "is a feeling of being connected in an affirmative way to existence; it is to be under the momentary impression that the natural and cultural worlds offer gifts and, in so doing, remind us that it is good to be alive. This sense of fullness . . . encourages the finite human animal, in turn, to give away some of its own time and effort on behalf of other creatures" (156). *The Alexandria Quartet* was an important stop along my journey toward the ethics of expatriation. I think at first it was an affective attachment to a landscape made compelling through the sheer power of Durrell's color-drenched prose—reading, at times, like a Fauvist painting. In matters intellectual he's not, to me, all that interesting. After that, it seemed important somehow, to go further. I needed to acquire the tools. I went to graduate school. Through Durrell or, rather, on account of him and this project, I encountered other "exoticist" writers whom I could more readily embrace, writers like Paul Bowles, for whom the confrontation with alterity was not merely fodder for the literary imagination but the defining existential and *ethical* moment. And I read the lesser-known "Italian" novels of D. H. Lawrence, whose ambivalence toward the Italian peasantry took account of the common positionality of those who are carried forward on a relentless tide of progress and those whose resistance to progress carried them just as relentlessly backward.

Part of the challenge in writing about the ethics of expatriation is to learn to read generously, to try to avoid the inevitable, and perhaps natural, urge to act as arbiter and judge. At the same time we must, as Bruce Robbins suggests, "discriminate degrees of complicity." In attempting to read generously (and I'm thinking here of John McClure's admonition that to treat these writers in terms of a "normative" ethics would be to condemn them outright, and Robbins's assertion that negativity, by itself, is simply boring), I have tried to construct an "ethics" that takes account of the personal projects of each writer that is not accountable to a moral "system" and, more importantly, one that enabled me to temper, if not sidestep, my inclinations to pass judgment.

"Ascesis," my preferred term for the kind of ethical "work" practiced by these expatriates, is meant to suggest the seriousness, the arduousness, of their endeavors. While we may not always feel comfortable seeing through their eyes, we dare not disrespect the self-induced ordeals they suffer. While we may enjoy getting lost with them, we may not evade the accountability that only a later generation of expatriate protagonists will be forced to acknowledge. At the same time, such narratives are a part of the ascesis of their authors. While we cannot and should not assume that expatriate protagonists are stand-ins for their creators, we know that the expatriate experience provided fodder for the imagination, that it was a theme their creators returned to again and again in both fiction and nonfiction.

Often, memoir and correspondence seem consistent with the authorial presence in a given work. In the case of Lawrence, the substance of at least one of his letters finds its way into *The Lost Girl*. On the other hand, his autobiographical accounts of encounters with Italian peasants are far more self-reflective than his novels, where it seems representation is beholden to another set of demands. The juxtaposition of biography with fiction here reveals a tension or disjunction between the two. Similarly, when one listens to the musical compositions of Paul Bowles, it seems inconceivable that such charm and whimsy could have emerged from the imagination that produced "A Distant Episode" or *The*

Sheltering Sky. His life too, as documented in many sources, suggests nothing of the horror with which much of his fiction is imbued. On the other hand, his deep ties to Morocco are everywhere manifest, despite the troubling nature of his imaginative vision. What we learn from putting various types of texts into juxtaposition with one another is that the writer may be more self-conscious in his "own" voice than in the creation of his fiction. On the other hand, imaginative writings spring from a register that produces desires and contradictions not reducible to the simple—or even the complex—assertion. The ethics of expatriation are the offspring of both writerly impulses, and we need to be careful not to collapse the two.

Part of one's responsible participation in that estrangement which expatriate narrative calls upon us to share is acknowledging the degree to which the Other is there to facilitate various forms of self-dismantling rather than to become a partner in dialogue. Getting lost with Alvina Houghton means accepting the objectification of Ciccio; getting lost with Kit Moresby depends upon our assent to Abdelquassim's inhumanity and the absolute incommensurability of cultures. These seductive persecutors become the necessary guides to other planes of experience and self-knowledge. We, too, are susceptible to being seduced. We, too, want to get lost despite the risks and appalling potentiality for self-degradation. Bowles's Professor is paradigmatic. Indeed, it's both good and bad to get lost. The texts attest to that, and it's infinitely more exciting and satisfying to get lost where people look and sound different; where the tropes and fixtures of Orientalist and exoticist discourse provide the sole but unstable signposts within an impossibly strange and disorienting landscape. When we think of our positioning in this scenario through Bauman's concept of aesthetic space, however, we take our pleasures far more self-consciously, resisting, even, the notion of pleasure. Guilty pleasures.

The work, then, my own "ascesis" in the study of expatriate narrative and the ethics of expatriation, is something I can describe with reference to William Connolly's relational arts of the self. Literature, because it attacks in the visceral register, seems an especially potent instrument for the type of self-artistry Connolly has in mind: "Working on yourself in relation to the cultural differences through which you have acquired definition. Doing so to render yourself more open to responsive engagement with alternative faiths, sensualities, gender practices, ethnicities, and so on."[1]

Martha Nussbaum, against objections to reading literature in terms of ethics, asserts that "our relation to the books we love is already messy, complex, erotic." And she argues strenuously that novels can be read as a "philosophical investigation into the good of a human being," citing their "their rich exploration of the noncommensurability of the valuable things, their concern for particular context-sensitive judgments and for particular loves, their allegiance to the emotions as sources of insight as evidence of their "Aristotelian" workings.[2] If Nussbaum seeks to draw from certain literary texts some ethical universals, however, this study of the ethics of expatriation offers no such sweeping lessons. Nonetheless, what Nussbaum's Aristotelian emotion and Connolly's viscerals do seem to share is the clear sense that reason alone cannot be relied upon to induce the work of the self.

Expatriate fictions can take us to the edge of what we are and what we are not. The point of fissure is a matrix. As Lawrence's Gilbert Noon says: "One will come to the crack again and madly fight to get a further glimpse, madly and frenziedly struggle with the dear old infinite. And thus rip just a little wider gap in it, just a little wider: after tearing oneself considerably."[3]

As I note in the last chapter, postmodern expatriate texts suggest to us that staying home may well be the only way a Westerner can be ethical. I don't really believe that; nor do I believe the texts themselves require us to draw that conclusion. While *The Names* and *The English Patient* point in that direction, they also resist that sort of closure. Their energies flow too generously in favor of making connections, dissolving boundaries. It's hard to do that within the confines of home. The interest in colonial and postcolonial literatures and theory is itself evidence that the desire to be elsewhere and the desire to be ethical are not incompatible. As Bruce Robbins reminds us, there is no site of perfect purity where differentials of power and privilege do not exist.[4] Privilege alone, therefore, does not compromise the footfalls of those who enjoy its blessings, but neither does it render them exempt from accountability. In our "messy, complex, erotic" relations to these texts, we acknowledge our complicities without thereby forfeiting our right to voyage out. Guilty pleasures.

In a certain sense, however, the questions posed by these expatriate narratives are moot. Center and periphery, while still valid designations in economic terms, are now less and less characterized by radical difference. Consumer capitalism on a global scale and economic immigration have hybridized both. While portions of many Western cities look and sound like the native towns from which their immigrants flock, blue jeans, Nikes, Coke, and McDonald's have transformed the cultural (and architectural) landscape of many far-flung places. Fortunately, however, the world has not yet been wholly homogenized. I hope it never will be. So long as there are pockets where people are different from oneself, places whose radical strangeness or singularity beckons, and individuals with the means to voyage out, there will be refugees from home whose search for the good will take them there.

I wish to thank the members of my dissertation committee at Rutgers: my advisor, John McClure, and readers, Bruce Robbins, Marc Manganaro, and Asha Varadharajan, for their challenging insights, constructive criticism, and—perhaps even more importantly—for treating my project not merely as a dissertation, but as the book it has now become. Their continued support, above and beyond the dissertation process, is greatly appreciated. I owe a particular debt of gratitude to John McClure who, with wisdom, patience, humanity, and good humor, wandered through imaginative geographies with me, helping me to navigate the rigors of critical thought, find my way to the sources of illumination, and rein in that torrent of words, thoughts, and ideas out of which this book has emerged. I couldn't have wished for a better or more generous intellectual guide.

I also wish to thank Barry Blose, who read and commented on portions of the manuscript. Thanks also to the anonymous readers at Vanderbilt University Press and to Michael Ames, Director of the Press, for his strong interest in my project, and also to Bobbe Needham, my copyeditor, and the Vanderbilt University Press staff for their kindness and efficiency.

Special thanks go to Frank Adler for pointing me toward and helping me negotiate key texts in ethical theory and to Renate Bridenthal for casually suggesting that I take a look at Paul Bowles. Thanks also to family and friends who watched my growth from lawyer to scholar to author, lending love and support all along the way. I especially want to acknowledge my mother, whose intellectual passion has been a lifelong inspiration, and my father, who passed away in 2002, for making ethics matter.

I want, also, to acknowledge Dr. Robert Fine and Dr. Stephen Schreibman, whose brilliance and humanity touched my life in miraculous ways.

My greatest debt I owe to my husband, Nick Papayanis, for his willingness to read draft after draft after draft, his acute questions and kind praise, his eagerness to help me work through the intellectual conundrums of theory and its application, and his ready ear and always open heart. In his passion for intellectual and scholarly endeavor, he is both an inspiration and an exemplar.

*Writing
in the
Margins*

I

The Ethics of Expatriation

WE ARE MOVED BY THE PLIGHT OF EXILES, refugees, and immigrants, whose often wrenching departures from home bespeak the horrors of political persecution, economic deprivation, various degrees of unfreedom. We are fascinated by nomads and intrigued by the idea of hybridity and diaspora. We are, on the other hand, suspicious of—we condescend to—the expatriate. Indeed, the term "expatriate" itself, like the figure, seems fatally comprised through association with yet another term, "privilege," a shorthand way of referring to the collective entitlements attached to membership in an elite class, including mobility, relative prosperity, and the unquestioned right to go anywhere and call anywhere home. Particularly stigmatized is the metropolitan expatriate who, for whatever reason, chooses to relocate to relatively underdeveloped parts of the world. D. H. Lawrence, Lawrence Durrell, and Paul Bowles were just such figures, expatriates who spent significant periods of time living and writing at a remove from the cosmopolitan centers of the West. It was the voluntary and unmotivated *flight* from the cities of modernism to marginalized or colonized domains that shaped their work and their search for the good life, as each of them appears to have defined it. These "ex-centric" expatriates were caught up in a life project that was at the same time an aesthetic and also an ethical one, producing an "ethics of expatriation." That is to say, the question, how should I live? led invariably to the rejection of a life lived within the confines of modern industrial society. By the term "ethics" I mean to comprehend the multiple and often contradictory answers to that question. By the term "ethics of expatriation" I mean to suggest a variety of discursive and life strategies, constellations of motivations, desires, and responses in which expatriation, as an ethical practice, is a significant mode of apprehending some important life good.

Colonial discourse theory teaches us, quite correctly, to question the ethical claims of such writers; but it also can serve to short-circuit an analysis of their existential projects. Frequently, metropolitan expatriates bear the "taint" of privilege; sometimes they are also implicated in a wide range of predatory and exploitative practices, yoking aesthetic production to acts which, in today's critical terminology, translate as Orientalism or "epistemic violence."[1] At the same time, however, the desire to "decenter" oneself is not inevitably dishonorable, and it has a broad and varied narrative record. While the expatriate's story can be thought of or framed variously as a quest, a spiritual autobiography, an exoticist fantasy, or an imperial romance, I choose to view the expatriate's story in terms of ethics, or the apprehension of some significant life good. My object, then, is to explore that project which colonial discourse theory has at once illuminated and obscured, an undertaking that entails, among other things, taking these expatriates seriously when they attempt to articulate an ethics of expatriation: a justification of their departures from metropolitan homes; their decisions to take up residence in a colony or marginalized zone— or to keep moving; and the relations they established with members of the communities in which they dwelt. Expatriate narrative is this project's discursive form.

This study of expatriate narrative cuts across British and U.S. literary traditions, literary genres, and a good part of the twentieth century. The principal writers whom I study form an eclectic trio. D. H. Lawrence, of course, is a pillar of modern British literature. Lawrence Durrell, born in India, was a colonial son who never really lived in England. Although he is a "British" writer, one of his greatest literary mentors was the U.S. iconoclast Henry Miller. Paul Bowles, first and foremost a composer and musician, was an American. I conclude with a study of two contemporary examples of expatriate narrative, *The Names*, by Don DeLillo, and *The English Patient*, by Michael Ondaatje, that I read as "post" modern responses to or revisions of the earlier discourse of expatriation. Of the two, DeLillo is not an expatriate at all, and Ondaatje, who writes about a European expatriate in love with the deserts of North Africa, emigrated from Sri Lanka to Canada by way of England (a geographic twist that in itself adds an intriguing dimension to the Western expatriate's story). As to generic focus, this study is concerned primarily with novels, but it also attends to travel literature, biographical material, and correspondence, as I'm interested in exploring the interplay between expatriate narrative and the "ethical" subject who produces it—or through which it is produced. My intent is not to present thoroughgoing readings of the texts in question, but rather to pursue the ethical questions embedded within them.

The critical interventions of postcolonial theorists have called our attention to the discursive schemes that organize the experience of alterity through which much expatriate narrative is filtered. In their efforts to expose the multiple ways in which Orientalist discourse is imbricated in Western regimes of power and authority, they have crafted a vocabulary and a set of theoretical strategies that have transformed not only the way we read significant portions of the canon but also the canon itself. Indeed, any Western writer who has ever ventured into these now critically contested waters must answer to the charges leveled (correctly, I believe) by Edward Said and postcolonial critics who have both followed and challenged him in productive ways. One critic, Dennis Porter, takes Said to task for failing to make adequate qualitative distinctions among texts that he categorizes as Orientalist. It is Porter's contention that literary texts, by which he means "all texts—traditionally literary, philosophical, historical, etc.—which are of sufficient complexity to throw ideological practices into relief and raise questions about their own fictionalizing processes" need to be distinguished from those "offering no internal resistance to the ideologies they reproduce."[2] Porter shows how aesthetic considerations can sometimes subvert the logic of hegemonic presuppositions, especially in the domain of the erotic. Lisa Lowe argues, too, that "the logic of a discourse that seeks to stabilize domination is necessarily one that makes possible allegories of counterhegemonies and resistances to that domination."[3] These complications of the Orientalist paradigm suggest ways in which more nuanced readings of so-called compromised texts might proceed. It's important, though, to note that Lawrence, Durrell, and Bowles were not "colonials." Even Durrell, who worked for the British colonial administration when economic need dictated, was not truly embedded in the system. As far as Lawrence is concerned, issues related to colonialism do not, for the most part, arise here, as the texts we will be dealing with concern Italy. Their somewhat anomalous status in relation to colonial discourse and postcolonial criticism is precisely what makes them interesting.

The work of James Clifford, Mary Louise Pratt, and Caren Kaplan intersects with that of the postcolonial critics and interrogates the discourses of travel and the deployment of metaphors related to location and *dis*location. Kaplan's work on displacement is an important theoretical intervention into the critical discourse that seeks to understand, problematize, and historicize the polarities of home and not-home that animate both the modernist and postmodernist aesthetic. For Kaplan, who seeks both to demystify the trope of exile as it is deployed in modern and postmodern aesthetic discourses and to deconstruct the opposition between aesthetics and politics that underlies the privileging of "displacement" as a critical term,

> all displacements are not the same. Yet the occidental ethnographer, the modernist expatriate poet, the writer of popular travel accounts, and the tourist may all participate in the mythologized narrativizations of displacement without questioning the cultural, political, and economic grounds of their different professions, privileges, means, and limitations.[4]

To some degree, of course, Lawrence, Durrell, and Bowles have all helped perpetuate—even nurture—this displacement myth, but *not*, as I show, without productively complicating Kaplan's assertion in the process. That they do so unevenly and fitfully—and with varying degrees of self-reflectivity—does not therefore render them hopelessly compromised. What comes forward in a study of expatriate narratives is the profound particularity of each displacement. This particularized account, more often than not, is characterized by a high degree of experimentation, disenchantment, and a range of negotiation between the "displaced subject" and the site of displacement. That is to say, many expatriate narratives revolve around the definition or realization of an ethos, including the ethical possibilities and problems of expatriate existence, through dialectical explorations of center and periphery, north and south, east and west, self and Other.

I show that many expatriate fictions, far from representing "mythologized narrativizations of displacement," actually call into question those mythologies and the modes of thought which inspire them. They often reference, implicitly or explicitly, an idealized expatriate narrative only to expose its contradictions, deflating its suggestive power. Like Chris Bongie's forlorn exoticist for whom "the exotic necessarily becomes, for those who persist in search of it, the sign of an aporia—of a constitutional absence at the heart of what had been projected as a possible alternative to modernity," the expatriate often finds himself suspended somewhere between desire and disillusionment.[5] What begins as a narrative of anticipated deliverance ends as a narrative of disenfranchisement and disenchantment. In the process, the "ethics of expatriation" that sponsor such projects—the recuperation of an organic community, or an instinctual, "primitive" connection with nature or the cosmos; the mastery of some radically unfamiliar geographical or cultural condition; the quest for the exotic, the realization of a condition of absolute freedom or nonresponsibility—are interrogated and often undermined. At the same time, however, such narratives of disenchantment often produce qualified successes in ways that are both paradoxical and unseemly—the Bowlesian protagonist finds his or her bliss on the far side of consciousness; Lawrence's "lost girl" achieves psychic autonomy through passional surrender to a coarse and uneducated peasant. We can better understand these moments within the context of an ethical project whose nature will become clear as we proceed.

Many diverse values underlie the choice of an expatriate lifestyle. Missionaries, adventurers, soldiers of fortune, and diplomats are all motivated by already articulated ethics of expatriation. For the writers considered here, the impetus to leave home was bound up, at least in part, with the cultural phenomenon of modernism, a phenomenon characterized, as much as anything, by voluntary geographic dislocation sponsored by a variety of inclinations and disinclinations. Prominent among these, perhaps, was a desire to protest against, in Charles Taylor's words, both "a world dominated by technology, standardization, the decay of community, mass society, and vulgarization"[6] and what he calls the "modern moral order," a term meant to designate the spiritually impoverished but highly disciplinary system of values that remains after God, the sacred, and other "external" moral sources, such as "nature," and "civilization," have been "subtracted" out.[7] What began as an essentially Christian worldview, in other words, devolved over time into a "non-transcendental, purely humanist mode" of understanding the human condition. Here is Jane Bennett's succinct distillation of Rousseau, Hegel, Marx, and Weber on the story of the world's disenchantment:

> There was once a time when Nature was purposive, God was active in the details of human affairs, human and other creatures were defined by a preexisting web of relations, social life was characterized by face-to-face relations, and political order took the form of organic community. Then, this premodern world gave way to forces of scientific and instrumental rationality, secularism, individualism, and the bureaucratic state—all of which, combined, disenchant the world.[8]

This "antimodernity" is reflected in a familiar series of binaries—reason versus instinct or the irrational; mechanism versus organicism; discipline versus liberation; rationalized, administered space versus the metaphorical richness and plenitude of places associated with premodernity, and the like—that evoke a specific imaginative geography. In modernist cartography, the industrial West is the domain of disenchantment. The places of expatriation—Italy, Greece, North Africa—promise an amelioration of the modern condition. They are the domain of the passional, the instinctual, the organic, the sensual; of sun and light; and, of course, of the exotic. This is the familiar story.

I open up the modernist treatment of expatriation to a broader interpretive analysis by reading these texts from the perspective of a range of iconoclastic and innovative ethical thinkers whose own work tends to resist or complicate the categorical "isms," such as organicism, primitivism, exoticism, and hedonism, associated with modernist tropes and figures. Indeed, the imposition of such received categories tends to obscure rather than illuminate the richness of the ethical debates these narratives rehearse. Instead of "hedonism," therefore, we can speak of the ethics of expatriation in terms of "asceticism," in the tradition of Foucault's practices of the self, on the one hand, and the more complicated term "eroticism" on the other. Instead of a retrograde "organicism," we can invoke Nietzsche's philosopher of the future. Instead of a primitivist "escapism," we can follow Bataille to the extreme limit of the possible or the schizos and nomads of Deleuze and Guattari. Instead of "exoticism," we can work with Fredric Jameson's concept of the "sensorium," and instead of the romance of place, we can build upon Zygmunt Bauman's formulation of social space. I do not mean to suggest that my "counter-"terms represent discrete experiential domains or that they themselves do not bleed into that which I am seeking to redefine or re-vision. For just as the "isms" of modernism are like the prismatic surfaces of a core discontent—or better, a palimpsest of rhetorical response—so my categorizations represent a constellation of ideas that collect around the same core issue: the articulation of value in a "disenchanted" world. While part of my project inevitably entails working with the familiar tropes and figures associated with modernism's "antimodernity," I aim to pry the texts loose from such categories with a different set of interpretive strategies. I show the extent to which the ethics of expatriation are produced through experimentation and the subject's passionate desire to remake—or unmake—himself in the interstices of the modern administered world. And, of course, their projects are enabled by privilege. Read against the grain, however, these fictions of expatriation acquire a sense of timeliness and even integrity.

I also call into question the notion that expatriate fiction is indifferent to the relations of inequality that inevitably attend—that enable—the practices it depicts by looking at the problem of self and Other. To explore the periphery as a contact zone, "where disparate cultures meet, clash, and grapple with each other, often in highly asymmetrical relations of domination and subordination," rather than a counter-zone to modernity, is to allow the relations between expatriates and "natives" to reveal themselves in all their ambivalence and complexity.[9] The representation of a subject's acute immersion in the "foreign" brings to light problems of heterogeneity, polyphony, and incommensurability on a scale far in excess of the more "intramural" displacements associated with modernist cosmopolitanism. In their confrontation with radical alterity, whether as servants of empire or as private individuals, the metropolitan expatriates I study are forced to negotiate identity and privilege in spaces transformed by their strategic importance to the West both economically and militarily. Indeed, the degree to which certain expatriate narratives seriously and self-reflectively attend to issues of power and difference is startling. The subjects of this study, then, were not mere postlapsarian pastoralists at loose in a rapidly dissolving Arcadia, nor were they immune from or indifferent to the volatile nature of social relations in these contested spaces of the Western periphery. Their work reveals a greater range of "intersubjectivities" and a more responsible engagement with alterity than, as readers of postcolonial theory, we are generally predisposed to see, and we will discover perhaps, a kind of ethical wisdom that contradicts the narrative design, making the familiar story strange. A word about organization. If my argument rests upon the necessity of taking the metropolitan expatriate seriously, it does not thereby follow that one (or that I) cannot or should not discriminate among the ethical projects of Lawrence, Durrell, and Bowles. I offer, then, what I believe to be a scheme of developing complication, beginning with Durrell and ending with Bowles, rather than a chronology.

Last, I explore the movement from a modernist to a postmodernist ethics of expatriation. I do not undertake a comprehensive

analysis of the cultural and historical factors that produced or contributed to the qualitatively different register of aesthetic and lived
experience that postmodernism represents, which, in any case,
has been amply documented. I am interested, as I have said, in the
ethical sensibility that animates the impulse to become an expatriate. Although I argue for the ethical seriousness of modernist
expatriate fiction, their work reflects—to varying degrees, it is
true—that these expatriate writers came of age in a culture that
did not need to confront seriously the claims of the "Other." If
Lawrence, Bowles, and Durrell wrote about a world whose construction was not wholly impermeable to the claims of the colonized, of minorities, and of women, these voices from the margin
were, nevertheless, far from constitutive. In much the same way,
their texts of expatriation hint at, from time to time, but cannot
fully comprehend the extent to which the expatriate figure is himself implicated in the twin forces of production and oppression
through which the periphery would be transformed—forces that
these writers, themselves, sought to flee. That comes later, with the
postmodern turn. Through my readings of *The Names* and *The
English Patient* I uncover postmodern developments in my genre of
expatriate fiction that foreground positionality rather than the
commitment to an "elsewhere," and the situated—as opposed to
liberated or autonomous—status of the expatriate protagonist.

Rethinking the Categories of Antimodernism

There are thinkers whose body of work provides a source of insight
into and a theoretical context for an analysis of the representation
of expatriate experience that takes us beyond the familiar binaries
of aesthetic modernism. Friedrich Nietzsche, Georges Bataille,
Gilles Deleuze and Félix Guattari, and Michel Foucault do not concern themselves with expatriation per se, but when read alongside
certain expatriate narratives, their writings illuminate not only the
spirit but also the motivations, energies, and desires that power
the impulse to be "elsewhere." Indeed, these philosophers and the
expatriate writers who are the subject of this study comprise something of a tradition—a tradition of "externality"—at the heart of
which is a deep resistance to the propensity of reason to draw all
phenomena into a system of representation and cognition that
purports to be universal but that, in fact, follows the historical trajectory of capitalism, whose own virulent growth it serves and
naturalizes. Of course, this is a gross oversimplification of the

complexity and essential irreducibility of an immense—and immensely varied—body of work; taken collectively, nevertheless, its informing spirit yearns toward multiplicity, heterogeneity, decentralization, contingency, and freedom. Their writings offer points of connection, departure, and mutual complication that illuminate and enrich our understanding of the ethics of expatriation.

We begin with the idea of ascesis. Thinking of expatriation as an ascetical practice is, perhaps, counterintuitive. Our received ideas about expatriate experience, derived from such sources as Malcolm Cowley's *Exile's Return* or Norman Douglas's fictional *South Wind*, not to mention sensationalistic representations of the expatriate community in Tangier, Morocco, lead us to associate expatriation with hedonism, decadence, and a life of relative privilege. An ethics of expatriation is of course an ethics of personal liberation, but personal liberation can take a variety of forms. The ethics of expatriation I examine here are not inconsistent with the notion of ascesis, where asceticism can denote, as Harpham writes, "any act of self-denial undertaken as a strategy of empowerment or gratification," *even* the paradoxical route through violence and excess preferred by such artistic and philosophical rebels as Rimbaud, Nietzsche, and, to varying extents, the expatriates who are the subject of this study. Harpham takes Saint Anthony as paradigmatic:

> A Holy Man such as Anthony spent his life in a studied rejection of the familial and indeed all of the social, engaging . . . "in a long drawn out, solemn ritual of dissociation—of becoming the total stranger." . . . The eremite rejected human culture not merely by leaving it but by existing at the extremities of human capacity.[10]

At the same time, the ascesis I associate with a modernist ethics of expatriation is indebted both to hermetic/monastic Christian models and to "technologies" of the self in the pre-Christian period, the subject Michel Foucault takes on in *The Care of the Self*. Foucault describes the "care of the self" as the practice of taking oneself "as an object of knowledge and a field of action, so as to transform, correct, and purify oneself" (42). Care of the self does not signify mere solipsism or narcissistic self-involvement, but rather "a sort of work, an activity; it implies attention, knowledge, technique."[11] In antiquity, he writes, the work of the self

> is not imposed on the individual by means of civil law or religious obligation, but is a choice about existence made by the individual. People decide whether or not to care about themselves. . . . they acted

so as to give their life certain values (reproduce certain examples, leave behind them an exalted reputation, give the maximum possible brilliance to their lives). It was a question of making one's life into an object for a sort of knowledge, for a *techne*—for an art. (GE, 361–62.)

These "pagan" ethics are focused upon "the kind of relationship you ought to have with yourself . . . and which determines how the individual is supposed to constitute himself as a moral subject of his own actions" (352). There are four aspects to this process: the "ethical substance," or that aspect of oneself that is to be "worked over"; the mode of subjection, or "the way in which people are invited to recognize their moral obligations"; the self-forming activity itself, which Foucault calls "*l'ascétisme*"; and, finally, the telos or object of such self-transformation (purity, immortality, freedom, or self-mastery, for example) (354–55). What is clear is that the ethical work of the self is not in the service of any over-arching moral scheme, as in Christianity. There is, however, an important aesthetic dimension to this "pagan" asceticism. Foucault's "arts of existence" are also about making one's life "into an *oeuvre* that carries certain aesthetic values and meets certain stylistic criteria."[12] This concept of pagan asceticism can help us articulate the link between expatriation and ethics. There is a work of the self that expatriate protagonists perform; it is, first of all, about becoming free. But the freedom itself is attained in the service of a larger project, which may be linked to self-transformation or self-making, as for Durrell and Lawrence, or to more austere rituals of self-purification or self-dismantling, as for Bowles. I would go so far as to suggest that expatriate narratives are somewhat analogous to the *hypomnemata*, or notebooks, that attained popularity in the time of Plato and in which individuals would record "quotations, fragments of works, examples, and actions to which one had been witness or of which one had read the account, reflections or reasonings which one had heard or which had come to mind" (GE, 364). The notebooks, or the fact of writing them, came to be a significant component of the care of the self. In a similar way, the writing of expatriate narrative can itself be a form of ascesis, not in the nature of confessional or spiritual autobiography, which Foucault forcefully distinguishes from the *hypomnemata*, but rather a working through, a reflection on received wisdom, an imaginative rendering of and meditation upon experience.

Alexander Nehamas speaks of the arts of the self in terms of Nietzsche's injunction to "become what one is." He argues that for

Nietzsche and Foucault, among others, the practice of philosophy and the art of living are one and the same thing. While the subjects of my study are not "professional" philosophers, like Nietzsche and Foucault, they "make the articulation of a mode of life their central topic." Performed in the interstitial and (from the perspective of modernity) unadministered spaces of the periphery, the expatriate practice of self-artistry, like that of Nehamas's self-creating philosopher, seems to insist upon its own singularity, inimitability, and risk. "As in the acknowledged arts," Nehamas writes, "there are no rules for producing new and exciting works. As in the acknowledged arts, there is no better work—no best life—by which all others can be judged."[13] Nietzsche suggests that only an entirely new type of being can "redeem" man from the "bad conscience" bred of original sin, of "man's will to find himself guilty, and unredeemably so." For in order to revalue the "good" itself, one needs to cultivate a certain "strictness and dignity." One must, in a sense, hold oneself apart from "all the comfortable, resigned, vain, moony, weary people." What is required, Nietzsche affirms, are "minds strengthened by struggle and victories, for whom conquest, adventure, danger, even pain, have become second nature. Minds accustomed to the keen atmosphere of high altitudes, to wintry walks, to ice and mountains in every sense."[14] Becoming who one is, then, must be seen in terms of an ascesis, a self-overcoming that is brutally iconoclastic, that represents the abandonment of everything that is homely, secure, and settled. Expatriate ascesis approaches, at times, this type of heroism, especially in the work of Paul Bowles, where danger and the promise of pain are courted at every turn. Indeed, the Bowlesian ethics of expatriation involve a technique of the self that pushes human experience to the limits of individual consciousness itself, beyond will, beyond the injunction to "become what one is."

In *The Romantic Agony*, Mario Praz explores the aesthetic tradition to which my expatriate narratives are linked in spirit, if not by verifiable influence (although it is relatively certain that both Durrell and Bowles were familiar with the late Romantics). From Milton's Satan through Sade, Baudelaire, Poe, Flaubert, and Wilde, to name only a few of the most familiar, the preoccupation with horror, death, ugliness, cruelty, and perversion left its distinctive mark on a body of work that revalued the beautiful and the good and made a virtue of excess. Nietzsche was of their party. Writing against a tradition in which evil is synonymous with novelty, he affirmed that "the highest evil belongs to the highest goodness."[15] Of the late Romantics he wrote:

> All of them were great discoverers in the realm of the sublime, also of the ugly and the horrifying; even greater discoverers of new effects. . . . All of them had talents far surpassing their genius; they were thoroughgoing virtuosos, with uncanny entry into anything seductive, alluring, compelling, and upsetting. They were born enemies of logic and straight lines, greedy for things foreign, for the exotic, the monstrous, the crooked, the self-contradictory.[16]

Nietzschean affirmation runs counter to the "bait of dependence that lies hidden in honors or money or offices or sensuous enthusiasm."[17] And so he celebrates the endeavors of those who reject duty, safety, comfort, and the paltry rewards of material success in favor of a continual self-overcoming that demands the constant violation of structure. The "ascetical" practices of such "experimenters," based as they were upon violence, deviance, and the transgression of boundaries, opened out into a realm that can be described only in terms of Bataille's "extreme limit of the possible." Embracing the abject, the useless, the "heteronomous," they sought access to a divinity rooted in excess, in that which exceeds the self but finds its articulation only in the throes of anguish as consciousness faces its erasure in death.

It is Bataille, however, rather than Nietzsche, who best illuminates such an ethics, though he freely acknowledges their common unorthodoxies:

> That in the path of inner experience, he only advanced inspired, undecided, does not stop me—if it is true that, as a philosopher he had as a goal not knowledge but, without separating its operations, life, its *extreme limit*, in a word experience itself, *Dionysos philosophos*. It is from a feeling of community binding me to Nietzsche that the desire to communicate arises in me, not from an isolated originality. No doubt I have tended more than Nietzsche toward the night of non-knowledge. He doesn't linger in those swamps where I spend time, as if enmired. But I hesitate no longer: Nietzsche himself would be misunderstood if one didn't go to this depth. [Bataille's emphasis][18]

No doubt we will find Bowles lingering in those very swamps, for he, and at times Lawrence too, projects an ethics of expatriation that is responsive to the lure of the abyss, the lure of an object, perhaps experience itself, that is religious in its intensity and yet "incommensurable with the moral ends" assigned to religious practice."[19] If Nietzsche's goal of self-fashioning is a courageous response to the groundlessness and contingency of human existence, Bataille wants to recuperate a sense of the human collectivity. This is not a gesture toward the oceanic, however, but an acknowledgment of the essentially social—as opposed to individualistic—nature of the human condition. His concept of "inner experience" is, in some sense, an internalization of the Dionysian principle where the individual subject and all his projects, discourses, and investments collapse into human totality. Bataille's writings touch upon excess, rupture, eroticism, and the extremes of human anguish and endeavor. While this is scripted as a journey "inward," the Bowlesian expatriate's "voyage out" often traverses similar spiritual, psychological, and moral terrain.

Bataille's "ascesis" tends toward a form of self-dismantling that challenges the limits of human reason and intelligibility. Inner experience, he writes,

> responds to the necessity in which I find myself—human existence with me—of challenging everything (of putting everything into question) without permissible rest. . . . Dogmatic presuppositions have provided experience with undue limits: he who already knows cannot go beyond a known horizon. I wanted experience to lead where it would, not to lead it to some end point given in advance; And I say at once that it leads to no harbor (but, to a place of bewilderment, of nonsense).[20]

At the same time, however, the subject is paradoxically affirmed. In experience, the subject "loses its way; it loses itself in the object, which itself is dissolved. It could not, however, become dissolved to this point, if its nature didn't allow it this change; the subject in experience in spite of everything remains."[21] We can, perhaps, better understand this type of "inner" experience, in which interiority itself is emptied out, by reading Bataille from a post-Romantic perspective. As Charles Taylor explains:

> a turn inward, to experience or subjectivity, didn't mean a turn to a *self* to be articulated, where this is understood as an alignment of nature and reason, or instinct and creative power. On the contrary, the turn inward may take us beyond the self as usually understood, to a fragmentation of experience which calls our ordinary notions of identity into question.[22]

And so, inner experience, rather than marking the place of individual essence, leads instead to "the extreme limit of the 'possible,'" the place "where, despite the unintelligible position which it has for him in being, man, having stripped himself of enticement and fear, advances so far that one cannot conceive of the possibility of going further" (Bataille, *IE*, 39). If the human condition is everywhere defined by its limits—death, discourse, discontinuity—then knowledge itself cannot exceed its own limits without in some sense turning into its opposite, nonknowledge. This liminal space between knowledge and nonknowledge is the narrative terrain of Paul Bowles, and its graphic embodiment is North Africa. Indeed, the antihumanism of Bataille's concept of community seems to be mirrored in the Bowlesian texts: their energies move relentlessly toward the abyss but their attention is at the same time focused upon the Moroccan Other, whose presence the texts insist upon even as his relationship to the Western expatriate is shrouded in ambivalence. The Bowlesian protagonist, suspended between alienation and totality, is the very embodiment, in fictional terms, of Bataillian "sovereignty."

Bataille's term evokes the Nietzschean *Übermensch* and, like that figure, denotes a condition of radical freedom from the regimes of production and reproduction into which and out of which the subject is woven. But Bataille's concept, which he describes as "life *beyond utility*," freedom from all productive social activity, parts company with Nietzsche to the extent that project itself, any project, renders the subject subservient.[23] It would suggest a sense of pure existence, a living in the moment, and, at the same time, a realization of the sacred. When man is no longer a thing, a tool in the service of project, he realizes freedom. Bataille's freedom is not political, but it is transformative. Sovereignty points toward a state of absolute self-overcoming, just as unimaginable, just as unrepresentable, as the future in which the *Übermensch* will come into his own, but as an end in itself rather than in the service of self-artistry or individuation. Bataille's atheistic asceticism engages with the categories of organicism and primitivism but is beholden to a contrary impulse. Part of modernism's flirtation with the primitive was the desire to tap into the energies of premodern culture, seen as more "authentic," more vital, and more passional than bourgeois civilization; but thinking in terms of risk rather than recuperation, of self-dispersal rather than homecoming, we are better able to grasp the heroism—not a term that readily comes to mind here—of the expatriate's quest. The work of Paul Bowles continues this tradition, sharing Bataille's preoccupation with violence, excess, rupture, and eroticism, and recounts the subject's radical rebellion against the Symbolic itself that structures its identity, its isolate individualism. Even the far less risky (in existential terms) narrative output of Durrell can be seen as a kind of useless expenditure—both in its purple prose and the pursuit of unproductive, sensual pastimes—in the Bataillian tradition.

Jeffrey Weeks puts the idea of a non- or anti-Symbolic realm in terms of an opposition between Althusser and Gilles Deleuze and Félix Guattari. For the former, entry into the symbolic is precisely what makes us human; for thinkers like Deleuze and Guattari, and probably Bataille too, "it was precisely this human (and patriarchal) order that was an imposition. For these, leaving the world of flux that preceded 'oedipalization' and acculturation is the real human tragedy, for in that flux desire was polymorphous and hence 'revolutionary.' "[24] Foucault describes Deleuze and Guattari's *Anti-Oedipus* as an "art of living" that "carries with it a number of essential principles." He summarizes one of them in the following manner:

> Withdraw allegiance from the old categories of the Negative (law, limit, castration, lack, lacuna), which Western thought has so long held sacred as a form of power and an access to reality. Prefer what is positive and multiple, difference over uniformity, flows over unities, mobile arrangements over systems. Believe that what is productive is not sedentary but nomadic.[25]

The figure best able to carry out the injunctions of *Anti-Oedipus* is the "schizo" in whose mind the codes get scrambled. "The prime function incumbent upon the socius," Deleuze and Guattari write, "has always been to codify the flows of desire, to inscribe them, to record them, to see that no flow exists that is not properly dammed up, channeled, regulated."[26] Whereas the neurotic is "trapped within the residual or artificial territorialities of our society, and reduces all of them . . . to Oedipus as the ultimate territoriality," the schizo, "continually wandering about, migrating here, there, and everywhere as best he can, . . . plunges further and further into the realm of deterritorialization" (35). If the law of Oedipus requires that we be one thing and not the other, the schizo stands for "disjunctive synthesis; . . . a synthesis that remains disjunctive, and that still affirms the disjointed terms" (76). The schizo is the one that "follows the *lines of escape* of desire" (277). The process of "schizoanalysis," which Deleuze and Guattari juxtapose to psychoanalysis, is another form of care of the self: "Destroy, destroy.

The task of schizoanalysis goes by the way of destruction—a whole scouring of the unconscious, a complete curettage. Destroy Oedipus, the illusion of the ego, the puppet of the superego, guilt, the law, castration" (311). If, as we will see, Lawrence's expatriate characters become "unEnglished," so too do they become "de-oedipalized."

Living beyond Oedipus means, among other things, becoming nomad, resisting the centralizing power of the dominant institutions. Nomadic notions, "becoming, heterogeneity, infinitesimal, passage to the limit, continuous variation," write Deleuze and Guattari, juxtapose themselves to order and stability. The "State-form,"as a form of interiority, has a tendency to reproduce itself, remaining identical to itself across its variations." The figure of the nomad stands for one who refuses to be contained within the thought systems, identities, and narratives sanctioned by the "state." Nomad thought

> does not immure itself in the edifice of an ordered interiority; it moves freely in an element of exteriority. It does not repose on identity; it rides difference. It does not respect the artificial division between the three domains of representation, subject, concept and being; it replaces restrictive analogy with a conductivity that knows no bounds. [27]

Such rhetorical flights are more suggestive than literal, of course. But that, I guess, is the nature of nomad thought; it exceeds the pure functionality of conventional theoretical or philosophical expression, a quality which the writings of Nietzsche and Bataille also share. Expatriate narrative expression is, by contrast, much tamer, though the quality of experience represented is not. The nomadic impulse is inherent in the idea of expatriation, though not all expatriates are nomads. Lawrence was a nomad, and *Aaron's Rod* explores the tension between an expatriate style that values perpetual movement and one that seeks "the one true place." Bowles was a nomad during the early part of his life but "reterritorialized" in Tangier. Durrell was more sedentary; once he left England, his migrations were determined more by external events than by inclination. He reterritorialized in southern France.

To a great extent, expatriate desires are inimical to the laws of Oedipus. Expatriate desires are suffused with a kind of eroticism that is to be distinguished from "mere" hedonism. Eroticism is the prism through which intimacy between the expatriate and the native is most frequently represented, drawing together different modes of desire: the carnal, the spiritual, the destructive, the life affirming, the violent, the passive, the quotidian, the sublime, the transgressive, and the domestic, the exotic and the mundane. It is Bataille's definition of the term "eroticism"— "assenting to life up to the point of death"—and the body of writings through which it is elaborated that offer the most compelling articulation of eroticism's mysterious juxtapositions.[28]

> Death alone—or at least, the ruins of the isolated individual in search of happiness in time—introduces that break without which nothing reaches the state of ecstasy. And what we thereby regain is always both innocence and the intoxication of existence. The isolated being *loses himself* in something other than himself. What the "other thing" represents is of no importance. [Bataille's emphasis][29]

Eroticism is thus beyond intimacy. And so often we will find that the eroticism of expatriate literature is less a function of human sexuality than a desire to lose oneself in a landscape, to surrender oneself to a place. The desiring machines of Deleuze and Guattari seek their satisfactions at the margins of the domain of Oedipus, at once the law of the father and of the fatherland. Homoeroticism, sadism, promiscuity, obsession, and the like are nodal points of a desire whose excess is both incommensurate and incompatible with both bourgeois models of production and reproduction and the modern moral order. I do not mean to suggest that eroticism cannot comprehend "normative" modes of sexual expression, but rather that expatriate models of eroticism—which often, but not always, contain elements of the abject—seem somehow more fully invested in exploring eroticism's potentialities, in decoding the flows that Oedipus seeks to domesticate. Expatriate eroticism tends to inhabit the domain of nonreproductive sexuality. There are few live births in the expatriate fiction under discussion here. For the expatriate, eroticism may promise the moment when he asserts his possession of, or dominion over, the native, or the moment when he himself is fatally undone. It may express the expatriate's inexplicable longing for contact with something outside himself, or the moment of crisis when the consciousness is wrenched from its moorings in the fragile edifice of the self.

Bataille writes that "the principle of classical morality is connected with the *survival* of being: that of sovereignty (or of sanctity) with the being whose beauty is composed of indifference to survival, of attraction, we might almost say, to death" (183, Bataille's emphasis). Expatriate eroticism is steeped in the contemplation of such beauty; it inclines toward the negative pole of being, the point where being and nonbeing merge. Within a framework of good and evil wherein the good is always rational, always conditioned upon common interest and survival (23), eroticism takes its stand on the side of evil. In Lawrence's *Aaron's Rod* and *The Lost Girl*, for example, bourgeois marriage, the institution of reproduction, is seen as offering no outlet for eroticism. In the former, heterosexual relations are equated with death, while Florence, "a city of men," is life enhancing to the extent its protagonist maintains a position of exteriority to it. Aaron's "rod" is destroyed there, and he is at the same time drawn to the curative seductions of his nomadic countryman Rawdon Lilly. In *The Lost Girl*, eroticism defines the very contours of its heroine's enigmatic union with an Italian peasant, a union that comes very close to epitomizing Bataille's formulation. In Bowles's *Sheltering Sky*, as well, bourgeois marriage, as a paradigm of failed intimacy, is repudiated in favor of the dangerous pursuit of paid-for sex with the native woman and the violence of rape. In Durrell's *Alexandria Quartet*, the city of Alexandria is the very sign of eros and death, while in DeLillo's *The Names* eroticism is parodied and then, in Ondaatje's *English Patient*, recuperated.

By the same token, however, the life-affirming aspects of eroticism, to the extent they confirm one's humanity, open the door to communication. If the gulf that separates discontinuous beings is infinite, we can, at any rate, "experience its dizziness together."[30] Eroticism is a human condition. Bataille would say it is *the* human condition. Embedded as it is in the relation between self and Other, eroticism is the ground upon which ethics falters, contradicts itself, strives to remain true to itself. Indeed, the constellation of practices and ideas that I have called the ethics of expatriation is itself a function of the tension between incommensurable and often incompatible ethical models, those that are directed toward the self and those that are directed toward the Other. Eroticism, as Jane Bennett writes, is a "fugitive" of rationalization, for "even where rationalization has achieved its widest scope, there remain aspects of experience that elude it, incalculable bits that float in and out of the iron cage, and inexplicable compulsions and convictions that make camp in the rationalized self." Such bits become "fugitives; they become targets of attempts to close them in a rational scheme."[31]

Turning from eroticism to exoticism, we can tap the work of Fredric Jameson for fresh sources of insight. Jameson uses the term "sensorium" to characterize Conrad's aestheticizing strategy, but we can also use it to redescribe expatriate exoticism. The sensorium signifies "a Utopian compensation for everything lost in the process of the development of capitalism—the place of quality in an increasingly quantified world, the place of the archaic and of feeling amid the desacralization of the market system, the place of sheer color and intensity within the grayness of measurable extension and geometrical abstraction."[32] With its exoticist, primitivist, and organicist underpinnings, the term resonates powerfully within expatriate narrative as a whole. In particular, however, Jameson's discussion helps us tease out an ethics of expatriation in Durrell's *Alexandria Quartet* that emerges, *precisely*, at the level of form. This is important, because the text's silences tend to speak louder than its rhetoric in terms of the articulation of such an ethics. Indeed, the failure or refusal of his narrators to "worry" over their expatriate status is a clearer articulation of their ethical predispositions than any assertion could be. Durrell's work is troubling because, among other things, it conforms rather unapologetically to Abdul JanMohamed's schematization of colonial literature. JanMohamed argues that colonial literature is driven by a Manichean economy that casts the colonizer and the colonized in a flexible and even contradictory range of binary positions in which the colonized is always the negative reflection of the colonizer. This is particularly so of the "imaginary" category of colonial literature in which the "representation of indigenous people tends to coalesce the signifier with the signified. In describing the attributes or actions of the native, issues such as intention, causality, extenuating circumstances, and so forth are completely ignored."[33] While the substance of Durrell's work might be consistent with JanMohamed's formulation, we might complicate his exoticising aesthetic by attempting to understand it in terms of a sensorium. As an aesthetic and cultural response to the drabness and moral rectitude of England and English society, Durrell's purple prose is like a cry of protest, an excess of color, light, texture, and physicality. At the same time, its redundancies are curious. A more "transparent" language would, presumably, remain just as truthful to the Orientalist aesthetic, but Durrell's *re*aestheticization or overaestheticization of the Orient must be seen as its reinvention, evidence that it is only in Durrell's fevered imagination, rather than abroad, that value may be said to inhere. If the object of his transformative vision were London or Paris rather than

Alexandria, perhaps we might continue to celebrate him; but that is, perhaps, because he is their cultural offspring. The integrity of the artist as truth teller, even in its guise as reinvention, cannot, it seems to me, be separated from the idea of intimacy, a connection of both identity and difference with the object. And even if the object has no claim upon the artist, and the artist no claim upon it, passionate interest or deep sympathy might yet charge the imagination with emotional honestly, if not responsibility. Place, as we know, is never neutral.

And so, finally, we need to rethink the category of place, which is never a simple "objective" rendering of expatriate destination, but rather a complex and unstable interweaving of desire, promise, expectation, and materiality. Within the same text, place might at once reinforce the state of alienation that the expatriate subject, in some sense, incarnates, and the solution to the subject's alienation. As I suggested earlier, the periphery tends to be seen—and valued—in terms of its difference from the industrial West. Whether the site of an organic peasant society or a quasi-mystical landscape imbued with pagan energies, as in Lawrence, or an absolute alterity associated with the desert or the vertiginous pathways of the native quarter, as in Bowles, the places of expatriation promise both an escape from the constraints of "civilization" and a testing ground for new forms of experience that often push the limits of what it means to be a subject at all. Often, however, the promise turns out to be illusory: the space of the Other turns out to be quite inhospitable or unliberating, or the promised alterity is itself rendered by the forces of industrialization into "forlorn" landscapes of the same.

There are other ways to think about the idea of place, however, and Zygmunt Bauman's concern for social space renders him attentive to the intersubjective relations between selves that must inevitably constitute a part of the ethics of expatriation. His "postmodern ethics" represents a critique of both universalist ethical norms and moral codes generally. The former mask the operation of power and suppress heterogeneity, while the latter are, of necessity, unresponsive to the essential ambivalence that lies at the heart of most human relations. "Given the primary structure of human togetherness," he writes, "a non-ambivalent morality is an existential impossibility."[34] Bauman is sensitive to the way the condition of modernity necessitates a constant negotiation among subjects and their Others in physical spaces that often share no coordinates with the social spaces he delineates. While the city represents for Bauman the paradigmatic social space in which unlike selves interact, the colony or other spaces of the periphery may produce similar types of spacings.

Social space, Bauman says, which through much of history was closely aligned or correlated with physical space, has become heterogeneous and chaotic. He argues that "modern" social space is constituted through the complex and multilayered interaction of three related but distinct "spacings": the cognitive, the aesthetic, and the moral (*PE*, 145). These spatial "fields" answer to different perceptual modes. In terms of human relationships, cognitive space is a function of how much or how little one knows about the Other; aesthetic space is a function of the Other's entertainment value; moral space is a function of how responsible one feels for the Other. If the strategies associated with such spacings provide a way to navigate the modern world, the juxtaposition of relative strangers in social space has become exacerbated in postmodernity, where metaphors of travel, dislocation, and displacement have shaken the settled dualities of center/periphery, home/abroad, and self/Other, at least in theoretical terms. Whereas postmodern space may be constitutively and inescapably plural and heterogeneous, the modernist expatriate in the periphery was, in a sense, a precursor of the postmodern subject, experiencing microcosmically the spatial discontinuities that several decades hence would epitomize postmodernity. Hence, Bauman may have something to tell us about the construction and negotiation of social space in expatriate narrative.

Bauman explains cognitive space as mapped along a continuum of knowledge about the Other that ranges from intimacy to anonymity. In the cognitive mode, for example, the extreme Other, or the stranger, about whom nothing may be known, may be excluded from social space altogether and relegated to a socially impoverished "realm of non-engagement, of emotional void, inhospitable to either sympathy or hostility; an uncharted territory, stripped of signposts; a wild reserve inside the life-world" (154). Bauman's "stranger" is the Other within physical but not social reach— neither neighbor nor alien. Bauman refers to the technique of living with such strangers as the "art of mismeeting." Mismeetings "'desocializ[e]' the potentially social space around, . . . preventing the physical space in which one moves from turning into a social one— a space with rules of engagement and rules of interaction" (155).

Where cognitive space constitutes itself through laws and rules of engagement, mismeetings, when they occur, have something of the random event about them; they are episodic, producing anxiety and fear. They represent the Other's interruption of the orderliness and predictability of cognitive space and forcible intervention into the hegemonic subject's sphere of attention. When cognitive space shrinks to the size of a colony or an enclave in the otherwise discontinuous and baffling geographic space of the Other, however, the "subject of reason" must attend to the nearly overwhelming anxiety of mismeeting, where mismeeting becomes the norm rather than a mere episode in daily life. In the narratives of expatriation, then, mismeetings abound. We will experience the discomfort of Lawrence's Aaron Sisson, who must confront a surly Italian peasant in the crowded third-class compartment of an Italian train. We will follow Paul Bowles's Port Moresby as he wanders into the native quarter and discovers that he is ill prepared for what he finds there. In *The Alexandria Quartet,* on the other hand, we will find that the stranger—who is invariably the Arab—is, for the most part, consigned to a social wilderness.

Unlike cognitive space, aesthetic space is valued precisely in terms of its unpredictability or "the uneven distribution of interest, curiosity, capacity to arouse amusement and enjoyment" (168). Indeed, the quintessential denizen of aesthetic space, the flaneur, is as at home in the bazaars of Marrakesh and Cairo as he is in the arcades of Paris. Aesthetic spacing, in Bauman's formulation, relies upon zones of safety that are well administered and policed but nevertheless produce effects that mime the contingencies and risks of the contact zone. "Play" is the operative word. Rooted in play, aesthetic spacing seems to speak to the condition of expatriation: "Being gratuitous and being free is what sets play apart from the 'normal,' 'ordinary,' proper,' 'real life' (170). "Play does not spill over, contaminate, reach the parts one would wish to or has to keep clean; it can be isolated, confined in limits so that it does not affect or disturb what it should not. . . . And thanks to the clarity (and conventionality) of borders, one may enter and leave the play, a feat which cannot be accomplished in 'reality' " (170–71). We will see that it is precisely in these terms that Durrell will characterize his expatriate lifestyle in Corfu, and the sense of play carries over into his fiction as well. Not surprisingly, the texts under analysis in this study tend to foreground the processes associated with aesthetic space, but they do so in diverse ways. *The Alexandria Quartet* and Bowles's *Sheltering Sky*, for example, engage in a certain flânerie characteristic of aesthetic spatial practices; at the same time, however, the two texts differ from one another in their willingness to see particularity, and, of course, in their capacity to maintain the structural boundaries of play. The *Quartet* rarely, if ever, surrenders its safety net; Durrell's "game," so to speak, is virtually leakproof. *The Sheltering Sky*, on the other hand, is risky both for its protagonists and for its reader; its transparency, for lack of a better word, allows the reader no "shelter" from the visceral impact of its characters' psychic disintegration. In addition to constituting a kind of spatial practice in and of themselves, the texts also represent and comment on the spatial practices of their expatriate characters. Mismeetings are common in the work of Lawrence and Bowles and draw attention to characters' anxieties concerning rules of engagement with the Other. Durrell, on the other hand, creates characters who rarely venture out of the neighborhoods, hotels, cafes, and villas associated with the European class. When they do, the text tends to become highly stylized. Hence, Durrell's "cognitive" spaces contrast starkly with the novel's "aesthetic" spaces, the domain of exotic festivals and lurid houses of child prostitution, which Durrell neutralizes—by means of a kind of ritualized staging—rather than explores.

If cognitive and aesthetic spacings are structured upon principles of identity and difference, Bauman's third category, moral space, is distinguished by its inattention to both. Indeed, moral space exists independently of knowledge and knowledge production; it engages, Bauman writes, "no human intellectual capacities —such as examination, comparison, calculation, evaluation" and flows, quite simply, from the recognition of particularity:

> As residents of moral space [the others we live *for* as opposed to *with*] remain forever specific and irreplaceable; they are not specimens of categories, and most certainly do not enter the moral space in virtue of being members of a category which *entitles* them to be objects of moral concern. They become objects of a moral stance solely by virtue of having been targeted directly, as those concrete others out there, by moral concern. (*PE*, 165, Bauman's emphasis)

Of course, moral space often coincides with cognitive space, and sometimes with aesthetic space as well, but even when this is the case, the underlying impulse is radically different. Moral spacing is "un-reasonable, wayward and erratic" (166) and, therefore, potentially subversive, while cognitive space is concerned with boundaries and the maintenance of a status quo. Indeed, Bauman argues that cognitively based social spacing strives to contain moral responsibility where its eruption might be counterproductive to desired social ends. Aesthetic space, on the contrary, is deeply invested in the novel, the fleeting, the exciting, at the expense of the care and attention that are incumbent upon the moral subject: "The moral stance, with its noxious proclivity to forge its own fetters in the form of responsibility for the other (which turns the Other from an object of satisfaction into a demanding Face), is a sworn enemy of drift—that essence of aesthetic spacing. . . . In other words, responsibility is a lasting sediment; the consequence of attention" (180). To render aesthetic space moral, Bauman argues, its inhabitant must "accept the limits and constraints which aesthetic spacing is bent on sweeping away" (181). This is one of the challenges of expatriate narrative, and the results are highly uneven, as we will see.

Gender

The ethics of expatriation are intimately bound up with issues that relate to masculinity, and not simply because most ex-centric expatriate writers are or have been men. As it turns out, masculine "privilege," that which enables such figures to wander with relative impunity across the globe, is precisely what is at issue in nearly all the narratives I've looked at. Kaja Silverman, who takes as her topic masculine *in*sufficiency, uses the term "dominant fiction" to describe the "ideological reality" that places the paternal function at the center of the symbolic and domestic order. It does so through the mechanism of Oedipus. "The Name-of-the-Father," she writes, "is . . . lived by the boy as the paternal legacy which will be his if he renounces the mother, and identifies with the father. It is lived by the girl as the experience of anatomical and cultural 'lack'; as a compensatory desire for the father and his surrogates; as a forced identification with a devalued mother."[35] Our dominant fiction

> calls upon the male subject to see himself, and the female subject to recognize and desire him, only through the mediation of images of an unimpaired masculinity. It urges both the male and the female subject, that is, to deny all knowledge of male castration by believing in the commensurability of the penis and phallus, actual and symbolic father. (43)

Only female subjectivity, Silverman argues, can safely accommodate the condition of lack and submission that is a structuring element of both female and male subjectivity. The dominant fiction sustains the legacy of Oedipus and is a way of theorizing the ways patriarchy is inscribed within our psychic and cultural economy. At the same time, its fictional nature tends to belie its efficacy. The fiction must be maintained against a host of enemies. As she goes on to state: "The male subject's aspirations to mastery and sufficiency are undermined from many directions—by the Law of Language, which founds subjectivity on a void; by the castration crisis; by sexual, economic, and racial oppression; and by the traumatically unassimilable nature of certain historical events" (52). Sometimes, this vulnerability cannot be overcome. During certain periods, as a result of war or other types of social turmoil (she cites, for example, the fin-de-siècle period in England when, among other salient cultural phenomena, the figure of the New Woman emerged), large numbers of men are unable to sustain their belief in the dominant fiction. Silverman is interested in this idea of "ideological fatigue," and she looks at masculine subjectivities that escape or repudiate the ideal of masculine sufficiency to "embrace castration, alterity, and specularity," tropes that tend to "feature prominently only within the conscious existence of the female subject" (3). To refuse one's share in the dominant fiction is, at the same time, to embrace those positions culturally aligned with femininity. It will become apparent that the expatriate subjectivities that emerge in my reading of expatriate narratives are, like those Silverman has chosen to focus upon, "marginal." That is to say, they are inadequate to the paternal legacy that nonetheless binds them. Thus, for example, *The Alexandria Quartet's* Darley will struggle to assert his masculine privilege in the sexual phantasmagoria that is Alexandria, the protagonist of *Aaron's Rod* will have his "flute" blown up, while Bowles's hapless expatriates will seek solace from the demands of productive and reproductive labor that are the cost of patriarchal privilege.

Jessica Benjamin sheds further light on the mechanics of oedipal identification and the psychological underpinnings of the "voyage out." Writing about the infant boy's early experience of individuation, she argues that

> [s]eparation takes precedence over connection, and constructing boundaries becomes more important than insuring attachment. The two central elements of recognition—being like and being distinct— are split apart. Instead of recognizing the other who is different, the boy either identifies or disidentifies. Recognition is thus reduced to a

one-dimensional identification with likeness; and as distinct from early childhood, where any likeness will do, this likeness is sexually defined.[36]

At the same time, the boy's disidentification with the mother has negative consequences, stimulating "a new kind of helplessness, one which has to be countered by a still greater idealization of control and self-sufficiency" (174.) More importantly: "The inaccessibility of the mother who has been projected outside lends to the image of the reunion—whether utopian return to nature or irrational regression—the qualities of an absolute, a journey away from civilization with no return ticket" (174). This key notion links the construction of gender difference to a particular imaginative geography, that of the primitive or premodern, and is richly suggestive in terms of the ethics of expatriation. A fascinating inversion of this trope is to be found in Lawrence's *Lost Girl* and Bowles's *Sheltering Sky*, in which female characters who are "rational" and "modern" surrender themselves to dark and exotic foreign men who embody an "anti-bourgeois" ideal of male sexuality that is both atavistic and irrational.

The anomalousness of this inversion will become even more salient when we consider the relationship between masculinity and modernity. Benjamin argues that the vocabulary of the Enlightenment—our legacy—is gendered; she writes that "the rationality that reduces the social world to objects of exchange, calculation and control is in fact a male rationality (184). Victor Seidler's study *Rediscovering Masculinity* argues similarly that the construction of masculinity in the West, indeed of modern civilization itself, is beholden to Enlightenment concepts of reason:

> [b]ecause society has taken as its self-conception since the Enlightenment a version of itself as a 'rational' society, and because reason is taken to be the exclusive property of men, this means that the mechanisms of the development of masculinity are in crucial ways the mechanisms of the development of the broader culture. (3–4)

The "modern" world and the dominant image of masculinity in that world are thus mutually reinforcing. Seidler has written extensively of the relationship between modernity and a "masculinist form of rationalism that is built around a categorical distinction between reason and nature," to the great impoverishment of masculine subjectivities. He argues for a "recovery" of a mascu-

line self through the refusal of this dichotomy and an acknowledgment of "the inner nature of emotions, feelings, and desires so
often despised within a secularized Protestantism able to recognize reason alone as the voice of conscience."[37] His argument suggests to me that a masculine self that has been "recovered" is, in
some respects, analogous to Silverman's "marginal" masculine
subjectivities.

The ethics of expatriation that I uncover here respond to particularly masculine anxieties, for expatriate protagonists tend to
live and desire in counterpoint to the dominant fiction. Not only
do they leave home as a result of an incapacity or refusal to
embrace their paternal legacy within a productive domestic and
capital economy, but also they live out their expatriate lives in a
condition of lack, submission, and self-loss. Expatriates tend not
to be married, and if they are, their marital relations are unorthodox by bourgeois standards. By the same token, expatriate domiciles resist identification with domestic space; they are often hotels
or "single-occupancy" dwellings. Sometimes, as in *The Lost Girl*, they
are identified by their very antithesis to bourgeois space. Expatriates
do not work, or at least not the way they do or would at home; they
are not part of a "domestic" economy. Expatriates tend to value
experience over reason and seek their bliss where discourse cannot follow; they chafe under the boundedness of the law of language. They are ex*patria*tes, then, not only because they leave their
fatherlands behind but because they abandon the Name-of-the-
Father as well, opting out of a phallic regime that is both symbolic
and real, a regime that Deleuze and Guattari call the "imperialism
of Oedipus."[38] In doing so, they repudiate that which has come to
represent our highest ethical good. And they do so in the name of
an imagined plenitude. Deleuze and Guattari write that "sexuality
and love do not live in the bedroom of Oedipus, they dream instead
of wide-open spaces, and cause strange flows to circulate that do
not let themselves be stocked within an established order" (116).
The expatriate, as I suggested earlier, is like the schizo, who

> follows the *lines of escape* of desire; breaches the wall and causes
> flows to move; assembles its machines and its groups-in-fusion in
> the enclaves or at the periphery—proceeding in an inverse fashion
> from that of the other [paranoiac fascisizing] pole: I am not your
> kind, I belong eternally to the inferior race, I am a beast, a black.
> Good people say that we must not flee, that to escape is not good,
> that it isn't effective, and that one must work for reforms. But the

revolutionary knows that escape is revolutionary—*withdrawal, freaks*—provided one sweeps away the social cover on leaving, or causes a piece of the system to get lost in the shuffle. (277, Deleuze and Guattari's emphasis)

If the acknowledgment of lack and castration seems to run counter to the spirit of *Anti-Oedipus,* there is nevertheless the sense that disidentification with the paternal figure, because it signifies a piercing of the ideological net, is the beginning of the system's dismantling. Expatriate writers, whose fictions of expatriation tend to "work over" their lived experiences as expatriates, are no less ex-centric to the dominant fiction than are their characters. One could argue that Lawrence, Durrell, and Bowles represent "marginal" masculinities to varying extents—Lawrence because of his class identity, Durrell because of his status as an Anglo-Indian, and Bowles because of his homosexuality. As artists, moreover, their externality to the system was integral to their vision. Expatriate fiction projects a world where the dominant fiction could be replaced by other kinds of human relations, where the burdens of selfhood could give way to a loss of self, where masculine privileges could be exchanged for marginal subjectivities.

If there seems to be something inherently masochistic about expatriate experience as represented in the body of work that is the subject of this book, Roy Baumeister, in *Masochism and the Self,* makes explicit the link between masochism and modernity. He argues that masochism involves an escape from the self, broadly defined to include not only one's physical body, but also one's "social and interpersonal roles, commitments and obligations, memberships in groups and institutions, personal values and goals, personal history, concepts of one's own personality, and conceptions of one's potential identity" (26). He links what he calls the "burdens" of selfhood—autonomy, agency, productivity—to bourgeois individualism and claims that in the West, at least, "masochism must be recognized as essentially a modern phenomenon. It appeared and spread during the early modern period and has been around ever since" (6). The burdens of selfhood, like the capacity for reason, may be linked to a role that is historically male. In this rather shorthand way, Baumeister recapitulates and condenses the story of the modern subject who comes into being with the convergence of social, political, and economic forces that give birth to the nation-state, a subject characterized, on the one hand, by his own subjection to the disciplinary regimes associated with the forces of production and reproduction in a capitalist society and, on the other, his interpellation as a free and autonomous agent. Kaja Silverman argues that through identification with the feminine the male masochist repudiates a dominant fiction that puts the burdens of selfhood squarely upon his shoulders. Practices of self-dismantling associated with masochism—and with certain forms of expatriate experience—are ways of refusing both subjugation and the demands associated with agency. Expatriate narratives written by women seem to follow a different internal logic, and, where relevant, I will touch upon the work of Isak Dinesen, Jane Bowles, Esther Freud, and Nadine Gordimer, in order to foreground some significant differences between male- and female-authored texts.

Self and Other

Contemporary criticism in the tradition of Said's *Orientalism* has sensitized us to the discourses of "othering" that inform textual representations of alterity, bringing to light the Manichean economies inherent in much colonial fiction and imperial romance. But the metropolitan expatriate does not stand in the shoes of the colonizer. Indeed, the sheer unpredictability, the unstructured quality, the unmotivated nature of expatriate existence renders the representation of moral space in expatriate narrative extremely complex. Even Lawrence Durrell, whose political sentiments and occupational ties position him well within the penumbra of the colonial enterprise, retains an alternative space—an aesthetic one, to be sure— within which to organize experience. The spaces of expatriation often present problems and challenges that exceed the capacities of the expatriate's own discursive structures to order and control, opening up a range of possibilities and dangers. If, as Charles Taylor asserts, one becomes a self "only in relation to certain interlocutors: in one way in relation to those conversation partners who were essential to my achieving self-definition, in another in relation to those who are now crucial to my continuing grasp of languages of self-understanding" (*Sources of the Self*, 36), expatriate texts invariably explore the rupture, by linguistic and cultural difference, of such self-sustaining interlocutory relationships. At the same time, they might also reflect something akin to the "density of overlapping allegiances" that Bruce Robbins in "Comparative Cosmopolitans" calls "situatedness-in-displacement" (173), a term meant to contrast with the "abstract emptiness of non-allegiance" associated with the ideas of homelessness and cosmopolitanism, terms that share a great deal with expatriation. In fact, expatriate narratives exhibit a broad range of sensitivity to the Other and, read with certain ethical concepts in mind—William Connolly's "relational arts of the self," Richard Rorty's "redescription," Seyla Benhabib's discussion of the ethics of care, for example —reveal the workings of expatriate "intersubjectivities."

William Connolly writes of the "visceral register" on which a "host of historically contingent routines, traumas, joys, and conversion experiences leave imprints . . . and these thought-imbued, often intersubjective intensities also exert effects on linguistically refined patterns of discourse and judgment."[39] Attending to Nietzsche's pronouncements about "instinct," Connolly recuperates the term from its association with "a brutish, biologically fixed force" and makes of it instead a "protothought . . . situated in culturally formed moods, affects, and situations." He argues that "this 'invisible' set of intensive appraisals forms . . . an infrasensible subtext from which conscious thoughts, feelings, and discursive judgements draw part of their sustenance" (27). Through the visceral register new possibilities of thinking and being can be produced, including new relations between self and Other, through "relational arts of the self." By the relational arts of the self, Connolly means to suggest a type of self-artistry that is a process less of self-making than of self-reflectivity. It involves

> working on yourself in relation to the cultural differences through which you have acquired definition. Doing so to render yourself more open to responsive engagement with alternative faiths, sensualities, gender practices, ethnicities, and so on. . . . Self-artistry is not a 'subjectivist' practice, then, if that means simply expressing what you already are, or more dramatically, treating what you purport to be as the universal standard to which everyone else must conform. Such artistry, rather, involves *the selective desanctification of elements in your own identity.* (145–46, Connolly's emphasis)

Connolly's relational arts of the self are a suggestive frame of reference for talking about the ethicality of certain expatriate experiences and narratives. For might not the act of expatriation itself be seen as precisely that form of self-artistry Connolly describes? And where is expatriate narrative born, if not in the visceral register of the novelist's psychic apparatus?

If "selective desanctification" begins with an acknowledgment of the contingency of self-definition, so too does Rorty's term "redescription," "the power of language to make new and different things possible and important."[40] For Rorty, all systems of meaning are linguistic in nature; they are vocabularies subject to revision and redescription, with no basis in "reality" and no relation to "truth." Rorty's "ironist," practicing another kind of self-artistry, invents and reinvents herself and the world through redescription. In the spirit of the Nietzschean self-overcoming subject, or the nomad thinker of Deleuze and Guattari, her search for

> a better final . . . vocabulary is dominated by metaphors of making rather than finding, of diversification and novelty rather than convergence to the antecedently present. She thinks of final vocabularies as poetic achievements rather than as fruits of diligent inquiry according to antecedently formulated criteria. (77)

The expatriate learns a lot about contingency in the periphery, where the confrontation with alterity redounds upon him in unpredictable ways. Like Rorty's liberal ironist, he often learns to redescribe himself, making new relationships possible—in theory, if not always in practice. Rorty is a great champion of solidarity; he wants us to notice suffering, our common vulnerability as mortal creatures. His liberal ironist's attention to the Other—"her hope that she will not be limited by her own final vocabulary when faced with the possibility of humiliating someone with a quite different final vocabulary" (93)—like the relational arts of the self, engages the visceral register through such practices as "imaginative identification." At the same time, however, Rorty acknowledges that the practice of self-artistry is often beholden to an impulse contrary to the liberal desire for a universal amelioration of, or even sensitivity to, pain and suffering. Writing of Deleuzian thought, Weeks argues similarly: "Its main axis of speculation is the body and its apparently unbounded possibilities and pleasures, not the processes of language, while its relationship to the real world of exploitation and material hardship remains unspecified." This "latent naturalism," he writes, "produces a strong displacement of all ethical and moral systems."[41] This split returns us to the conflictual relationship between the aesthetic and moral dimensions of social space that Bauman elucidates and to the textual object that these ethical orientations cohabit uneasily, if at all.

An ethics of care, when it emerges, flows out of personal rather than abstract concerns, and it is nearly always rooted in the visceral. Seyla Benhabib distinguishes from that field of duties and responsibilities governed by "right, obligation and entitlement" an ethics of care "whose moral categories . . . are those of responsibility, bonding and sharing," and whose "corresponding moral feelings are those of love, care, and sympathy and solidarity."[42] Her discussion flows out of Carol Gilligan's groundbreaking study of the gendered nature of moral judgment. Women's moral development, Gilligan found, is more situational, more dialogic; "it shows a greater propensity to take the standpoint of the 'particular other,' and women appear more adept at revealing feelings of empathy and sympathy required by this" (149). The ethics of care, then, grow out of concern for the *concrete* Other rather than the *generalized* Other whose putative universalizability and reversibility (which inevitably, Benhabib argues, fall back on patriarchal, phallocentric models) form the basis for contract-driven models of social justice. While the "justice" model of morality relies upon our common identity, the ethics of care require us to see particularity, require us to acknowledge that "our differences . . . complement rather than exclude one another" (159). Seeing particularity is one of the greatest challenges in the attempt to render social space moral.

More than anything else, it is the ghost of Emmanuel Levinas that hovers over my attempts to articulate an ethical language. He asks:

> Can the Same welcome the Other, not by giving the Other to itself as a theme (that is to say, as being) but by putting itself in question? Does not this putting in question occur precisely when the Other has nothing in common with me, when the Other is wholly other, that is to say a human other . . . ? When, through the nakedness and destitution of his defenseless eyes, he forbids murder and paralyzes my impetuous freedom?[43]

This key concept of putting the I in question is meant to counter the imperialism of the Same in Western thought, shifting the balance of power between self and Other in radically innovative ways. Putting the I in question is the "other-directed" telos of expatriate technologies of the self, the ethical imperative. As Levinas explains:

> The absolutely Other is the human Other. . . . And the putting into question of the Same by the Other is a summons to respond. The I is not simply conscious of this necessity to respond, as if it were a matter of an obligation or a duty about which a decision could be made; rather the I is, by its very position, responsibility through and through. . . . Hence to be I signifies not being able to escape

responsibility. . . . Putting into question is a new tension within the I. Instead of annihilating the I, putting into question binds it to the Other in an incomparable and unique way.[44]

How does one become predisposed to this kind of ethicality? And what does this have to do with expatriation? Jane Bennett suggests that the mood of enchantment is an essential part of ethics. Enchantment involves a state of wonder, of being "transfixed," or "spellbound." Unlike the sublime, however, enchantment is not coercive; it does not produce dread. On the contrary, enchantment is pleasurable, producing a mood of "fullness, plenitude, or liveliness." In the mood of enchantment, "you notice new colors, discern details previously ignored, hear extraordinary sounds, as familiar landscapes of sense sharpen and intensify. The world comes alive as a collection of singularities."[45] And this state of mind is conducive to an ethics of care. For however one situates oneself in moral space, whatever rules or moral obligations one will be guided by, "one needs an aesthetic disposition hospitable to them, the perceptual refinement to apply them to particular cases, the energy or will to live them out, and the generous mood that enables one to reconsider them in the face of new and surprising developments" (29). "Presumptive generosity, as well as the will to social justice," Bennett writes, "are sustained by bouts of being enamored with existence" (12). In a disenchanted world, it's hard to generate this kind of affective attachment to one's surroundings, so part of one's "care of the self" would be to seek out sites of enchantment, to cultivate "a discerning and meticulous attentiveness to the singular specificity of things" (37). The mood of enchantment may become a source of redescription; it may stimulate the visceral register; it may promote feelings of generosity and empathy. If expatriates are in flight from a disenchanted world, it stands to reason that the voyage out is, in some important sense, a quest for enchantment. One cannot, of course, speak of enchantment and ethics in terms of cause and effect. In their encounters with novelty, expatriate characters are often enchanted, and sometimes it goes no further. But sometimes their mood of enchantment is represented as a positive interruption of habitual ways of thinking and seeing, even as the logic of the text works to reconfirm or recuperate a less ethically "vigorous" disposition toward the Other. I hope to illuminate those textual moments when, despite the narrative "argument" to the contrary, the moral energy of the text stakes its claim.

Postmodern Expatriate Narrative

Some twenty years or so separate *Clea,* the fourth volume of Durrell's *Alexandria Quartet* and the most recent of the "modernist" expatriate narratives under consideration here, from Delillo's *Names.* Ondaatje's *English Patient* came out some ten years after that. In the interim, the social and political transformations associated with the struggle for national liberation in the periphery—the civil rights movement, the war in Vietnam, the events of 1968, and feminism, to name just a few of the more salient—dramatically altered the cultural and philosophical landscape. The centrality of Western ways came into question; the voices of the colonized became insistently audible; and the subject of privilege was called to account. Expatriate narratives continue to be written, but not without significant revision. In moving from the consideration of modernist to postmodernist ethics of expatriation, then, we see the emergence of a new cultural agenda: the transformation of "individualist" selves into situated subjects, and the interrogation of the expatriate's positionality in a postcolonial world. The shift is not categorical; it is, rather, an alteration in the "structure of feeling" to which the ethics of expatriation are responsive.

When we look at postmodern expatriate narratives such as *The Names* and *The English Patient,* we can identify characters who embody aspects of the modernist expatriate figure—Owen Brademas in *The Names* and Almásy in *The English Patient*—but their projects are far more radically called into question than in the earlier texts. Postmodern expatriates go home, confounded by an inescapable "positionality" that, now transparent, cloaks their expatriate projects in a mantle of dishonor. The modernist expatriate figure, who in these novels is associated with quasi-scientific disciplines devoted to the acquisition or production of knowledge about the periphery, is, as Mary Louise Pratt has argued, no longer an innocent figure; he carries too much baggage. What is more, he is a self whose construction, predicated, arguably, upon philosophy's now problematized "unencumbered self," is inadequate to the demands of a postmodern, postcolonial world. The postmodern expatriate narrative is far more self-conscious about its Western protagonists' "situatedness" and holds them accountable. In these novels, global capital and global warfare provide a context in which every potential subject comes to the table fully invested in the social and structural machinery of home. At the same time, paradoxically, the idea of "homeland," which modernity has dictated should take the form of the nation-state, is itself destabilized by global markets, massive economic immigration, and technological cross-communication and cultural exchange. But we are not thereby rendered homeless. We are, rather, aligned: north versus south, east versus west; first world versus third world.

Just as the postmodern ethics of expatriation foreground the expatriate's positionality, they strive toward the articulation of some greater sense of individual responsibility: an ethics of care, of global feeling, of solidarity—whose achievement is to be worked out in a register of human endeavor that is at once parallel and wholly antithetical to that in which the apparatuses of economic and military domination operate. In the process, certain values associated with the modernist expatriate project are recuperated. Through the character of Kathryn Axton, for example, *The Names* suggests a form of responsible, if provisional, expatriate attachment to place and community that is at odds with the "deterritorialized " community of global capitalism. While Axton demonstrates his "deliverance" from the machinery of state power by making a pilgrimage to the Acropolis, where he comes to appreciate the immediacy of communicative solidarity through the medium—or prayer—of language, it is Kathryn, his wife, who is more fully vested in "moral space." *The English Patient's* Almásy, on the other hand, not only renounces his profession of mapmaking, he comes to embrace an ethos of radical communality. Paradoxically, it is his spirit alone that is able to transcend the positionality that disperses the postmodern generation of expatriates, suggesting that from the crimes and excesses of the modernist expatriate project come the means to surmount them as well.

The Chapters

In Chapter One I explore Lawrence Durrell's early travel books, *Prospero's Cell*, *Reflections on a Marine Venus*, and *Bitter Lemons*, and his most well-known work of fiction, *The Alexandria Quartet*, in order to illuminate the ethical projects of this once celebrated novelist and poet. The most "compromised" of the three figures, Durrell left England for the island of Corfu in his early twenties. An "economic" expatriate, he intended to live cheaply and hone his literary craft. While Durrell represents his early years in the Mediterranean in terms of a regime dedicated to sensual pleasure, intellectual camaraderie, and writing, once World War II broke out, he was never again able to achieve the same degree of relative freedom from care. Durrell's vocational projects demanded, on the one hand, that he perform the work of empire, and on the other, that he achieve autonomy as an artist. In both these capacities, moreover, he seemed intent upon subduing the doughy mass of colonial politics and the landscapes and cultures of the Mediterranean into policy statements and aesthetic forms. Taking my cue from Fredric Jameson's *Political Unconscious*, I explore the way form and content work together to articulate an imperial ethics of expatriation that celebrates the periphery as both a source of aesthetic gratification and a "space of containment" where the expatriate's work—aesthetic self-fashioning, forging an imperium of the imagination—can be performed. Both in the real world and outside it, Alexandria is at once the stage upon which the *Quartet* can enact its "investigation of modern love" without regard to material relations of production and reproduction and the site of imperial power in which those processes are implicated and advanced. Central to this narrative is the tension between politics and private artistic endeavor and the subsequent eruption of colonial politics into the apolitical practices associated with self-liberation and literary creativity.

Chapter Two examines D. H. Lawrence's Italian experience through a reading of *Aaron's Rod* and *The Lost Girl*, with attention as well to the travel essays contained in *Twilight in Italy*. I show the extent to which these texts invoke both the idealized South of the Romantic imagination and the metropolitan expatriate's idealized experience of it only to interrogate and undercut these expatriate "mythologies." In my reading, therefore, Lawrence's narratives of expatriation represent not so much a reactionary or retrograde paean to the premodern as a Nietzschean project of self-overcoming that looks both forward and backward. I begin with the idea that expatriation is, for Lawrence, a means of exploring that part of the self not accommodated or exhausted by the social forms and narratives available at home. Expatriation makes possible the practice of "redescription." I go on to trace the emergence in these works of a multiple and sometimes contradictory ethics of expatriation, each locating value in a different mode of apprehending the relation of the self to the world. Using Deleuze and Guattari, for example, I read *Aaron's Rod* in terms of the tension between a "nomadic" and a "migrant" mode of expatriate experience. I read *The Lost Girl*'s ethics of expatriation, on the other hand, in terms of the link between expatriation and the ambivalent desire for selfdismantlement. On one level these texts rehearse the belief that traditional societies offer an organic solution to the inorganic constitution of the world of modernity; on another, they represent the failure of traditional culture to live up to these imagined riches. Nevertheless, the experience of expatriation remains an enabling one, though often in unseemly and counterintuitive ways, revealing both the contingent nature of received interpretations and experiential modes unavailable at home.

Chapter Three looks at Paul Bowles in North Africa through a primary concentration on *The Sheltering Sky, Let It Come Down,* and *The Spider's House.* The productive tension in these texts between a radically antihumanist ethos and one that is animated by imaginative identification and engagement with the Other is enacted in a variety of ways, but always with obsessive concern for the inevitably complex, inevitably conflicted encounter between the Western subject and his North African interlocutor. In this chapter, the work of Georges Bataille is of signal importance in providing a language—a discourse—of existential experimentation that brings to the fore the radical risk and reward invoked by Bowles in these narratives of expatriation. I use Bataillian concepts of "inner experience," "the extreme limit of the possible," "sovereignty," and "eroticism" to grasp the ethics of expatriation that Bowles's work reflects and to illuminate the extreme forms of psychic dismantling that they repeatedly enact. A quintessentially metropolitan figure, Paul Bowles was not at all interested in the project of redescription, but rather in the possibilities of pushing the self so far that it ceased to be a self at all. While his experiments in self-dismantling are far more severe and unforgiving than those of Lawrence, his capacity for imaginative identification and social engagement with the native inhabitants of Morocco is also more compelling. The ethics of expatriation articulated by Bowles suggest that expatriation offers a means both to undo the culturally determined structural apparatus of consciousness altogether and to explore different modes of being, of perception, and of social intercourse, again through profound attention to the local and the locale.

Chapter Four considers two novels, Don DeLillo's *The Names* and Michael Ondaatje's *The English Patient,* as late-century revisions of the concerns and ethical preoccupations of the earlier expatriate texts. Where the high- and late-modernist narratives of expatriate experience tended to focus on problems of the self and its presumed—or desired—autonomy from the social machinery of home, producing a "modernist" ethics of expatriation, the "post-modern" narrative interrogates this problematic by revealing the self as "always already," situated, trailing the institutional baggage of capitalism and imperialism in its wake. Both *The Names* and *The English Patient* articulate a "postmodern" ethics of expatriation through the juxtaposition of two generations of expatriates. The older, "modernist" expatriates pursue a doomed project of personal redemption. They languish or die in the periphery. The postmodern expatriates, on the other hand, are driven home once their positionality and complicity are revealed. At the same time, however, these works keep the project of expatriation alive by pointing toward a more fully "ethical" ethics of expatriation that cannot yet be realized.

2

Lawrence Durrell
and the Poet(h)ics of Imperialism

In a way he reminds me of a pearl oyster cultured by himself, for the purpose of carrying out the objectives he has staked out for himself: in contrast to such 'uncultured' but natural pearls, as Proust, or Kafka, or Joyce. The natural pearl is the product of a diseased oyster, the cultured one is the result of deliberate infection.

Alfred Perlès

LAWRENCE DURRELL was the quintessential "imperial expatriate." Born in India to first- and second-generation British settlers, he also worked on and off as a colonial administrator in the eastern Mediterranean. The antithesis of an expatriate self who faces outward to confront a world perceived as either a miracle of diversity or an abyss of terror, Durrell suggests an expatriate self who turns himself inside out. His vision of the periphery is essentially a *re*-vision. Having already "internalized" the periphery, so to speak, Durrell sees it through the prism of an imaginative geography forged in early childhood. His identity, a design in the weave of colonial history and personal biography, is dispersed through affiliation with disparate homelands: India, England, and Greece, the "spiritual" birthplace. Durrell's existential crisis occurs when he leaves India at the age of eleven; he returns to the periphery to get put back together. But because the work of self-repair goes hand in hand with Durrell's development as an artist, the periphery serves another function as well. It is a place where he can live cheaply, devoting himself to his art without giving up any of the natural pleasures of life: sunshine, sea, fresh food, good fellowship. Durrell went to the periphery in search of color and sensual pleasures and a place conducive to artistic and existential experimentation. But his colonial investments complicate, even as they illuminate, the story. Imperial politics and imperial aesthetics, proceeding apace, orient him away, invariably, from "global" feeling and toward England, though often ambivalently. His profound desire for liberation from the cultural machinery of England made of him an "enfant terrible" even as he served the Foreign Office with an at times baffling sense of enthusiasm. On the other hand, the very bohemianism that drove him from England was itself tempered by a generally bourgeois desire for artistic acceptance and certain material conveniences. At the most basic level, his desire to write was complicated by the need to earn a living and support wives, ex-wives, and children, and his need to earn a living forced him to assume a public role which he seemed to repudiate in an art dedicated to a purely private vision. Durrell, in other words, was both a hedonist and a civil servant. He was both a bohemian and a *bon bourgeois,* and he may well be the epitome of those writers whose "mythologized narrations of displacement" Caren Kaplan has attempted to situate. But because we think we know these now critically suspect figures so well, it may be time for a second look, not to redeem but to complicate, to read the work *precisely* in terms of an ethics of expatriation.

Durrell's flight from England was motivated, in part, by many of the same antimodern sympathies that led both Lawrence and Bowles to leave the metropolitan West. These include, of course, a deep aversion to bourgeois conventions and values, a contempt for bourgeois sexuality, a profound discomfort with the spiritual barrenness and monotony of a mechanized world, and a desire to escape the pressures of conformity. Durrell sought liberation from what he called "the English death," a kind of somatic and spiritual impoverishment that was inimical to his artistic growth. Another motivation he shared with Lawrence and Bowles was the desire to live cheaply in a sunny place, what he has described as "a perfectly honourable passion for sunlight and low income tax."[1] Both Durrell and Lawrence before him forged an aesthetic in which the periphery looms large as a source of myth, symbol, and sensual wisdom. Like Lawrence, Durrell implies in his work that this search for an "elsewhere" is doomed to failure. Unlike Lawrence, however, Durrell is a colonial; he belongs to a world whose contours were firmly and unapologetically fixed by the imaginative geography of the British Empire, and his search for an elsewhere nearly always implicated him in the slough of British colonial politics. Also unlike Lawrence, there is a sense of belatedness about Durrell and not only because of his colonial outlook. As Reed Dasenbrock has noted, *The Alexandria Quartet* fits squarely within the tradition of modernism in terms of its thematic of sexuality, its experimental form, and its self-conscious attitude toward art and the artist.[2] However, the historical and social conditions that contributed to the development and vitality of the modernist movement had, by the time Durrell begins writing, given way to a different aesthetic, at least insofar as English literature is concerned. For the Thirties generation, stunned by the Great Depression and the rising tide of fascism, politics, rather than art, promised some escape from the nightmare of history. Literature, therefore, turned to a "'diagnostic' or 'psychological' response to the strangenesses, terrors and irrationality of the historical world."[3] Durrell's adherence to a modernist "religion" of art, like his reactionary politics, is an important component of his ethics of expatriation.

Durrell's "imperial aesthetic" is embodied in his concept of the "Heraldic Universe," his "special signature and preoccupation with a mystical unity resting behind phenomena and lives, which he delineates through a confluence of Eastern metaphysics and Western physics."[4] Writing to Henry Miller in 1936, Durrell proclaims: "All great art of every kind and degree is this struggle to impose the inner on the outer, to transform the material, the social, to the psychic. The Heraldic Universe is just a name for that element in which that queer fish the artist swims."[5] A sublimated imperial poetics, if ever there was one, the Heraldic Universe, with its "struggle to impose," suggests an empire of the imagination where all that is Other is appropriated and transformed into consumable literary goods after a productive detour through the literary consciousness. This is, as Molly Hite says in *Ideas of Order and the Novels of Thomas Pynchon,* a common modernist ontology, articulated by Wallace Stevens and others. As the *Quartet*'s Pursewarden puts it: "[T]he so-called act of living is really an act of the imagination. The world—which we always visualize as 'the outside' World—yields only to self-exploration!"[6] The self, for Durrell, was all-important, and Richard Pine notes:

> In this insistence on *self* as the only knowable entity, and the
> elucidation of worlds in which the self is at once king and only
> inhabitant, we see a quite different approach to the novel than that
> of Proust or Joyce whose concern is with the outer world and with
> history. In . . . Durrell . . . the elements of time and place, whatever
> form they take, have no meaning unless they can be first measured
> against the yardstick of pure self.[7]

What I call Durrell's "heraldic reality," then, is the substitution of Durrell's aesthetic "truth" for what we can refer to as "history."

Leo Bersani's discussion of Baudelaire's aestheticism, which he links to Freud's concept of primary narcissism, is instructive here. The Baudelairean artist, in his desire to be penetrated by otherness, at the same time extracts from the other an idealized form that emerges from the artist himself, from

> the internally inscribed history of the self's relations with the world. Very strangely, then, the penetration of the artist by "the picture of external life" is also a turning away from all such real scenes; it is a going out of oneself, indeed an uncontrollable breakdown of the very boundaries of selfhood, which is also an exceptional self-expansion, a kind of celebration of the self-as-world, in short, a narcissistic jouissance.[8]

Durrell's heraldic aesthetic complicates Edmund Keeley's assertion that he was "the first important British writer to have approached contemporary Greece not with the idea of bringing to it more wisdom than he supposed he would take away, as appears to have been the case with Byron, but to enter "'the dark crystal' of Greece. . . . and drink of what wisdom he found there."[9] For Durrell would later assert to a friend attempting to write a travel book: "Invent some people, peasants and so on—and treat them quite boldly. Put them in and forget them just as you feel inclined."[10] It is not surprising, therefore, that early on in *Prospero's Cell,* the first of Durrell's Greek travel narratives, he asserts: "Other countries may offer you discoveries in manners or lore or landscape; Greece offers you something harder—the discovery of yourself" (11)—a paradoxical statement in that he subtitled his work "A Guide to the Landscape and Manners of the Island of Corcyra." If, to some extent, Italy functions in a similar fashion for Lawrence, it is because Italy provides another perspective, loosens the hold of received interpretations. Durrell's project is a different one.

Indeed, Durrell's rearticulation of "the spirit of place"—a term he borrows from D. H. Lawrence—owes much to "heraldic" poetics rather than to Rorty's redescription, "the power of language to make new and different things possible and important."[11] Elaborating upon this notion in an essay titled "Landscape and Character," Durrell writes that "human beings are expressions of their landscape." But, for Durrell, that does not make them unreadable or inaccessible, for "in order to touch the secret springs of a national essence you need a few moments of quiet with yourself" (157):

> It is there if you just close your eyes and breathe softly through your
> nose; you will hear the whispered message, for all landscapes ask the
> same question in the same whisper. "I am watching you—are you
> watching yourself in me?" . . . Ten minutes of this sort of quiet inner
> identification will give you the notion of the Greek landscape which
> you could not get in twenty years of studying ancient Greek texts.
> (158)

It militates against any sense of "thick" description, of course, to
ascribe deep understanding of a foreign culture to such self-
reflexivity. Indeed, this sublimely egotistical recipe for cultural
wisdom not only turns the site into an aesthetic object awaiting
penetration and expurgation, but also, paradoxically, tends to train
attention on the self rather than the Other in a dialogic fashion.
Nevertheless, the injunction to turn inward is characteristic of
Durrell's idiosyncratic style of knowledge, which infuses the
imperium of the imagination with gnosticism and Eastern philoso-
phies such as Buddhism and Taoism.

Since Durrell is attempting to make Lawrence's term his own,
we should, perhaps, take a look at Lawrence's essay, "The Spirit of
Place," which opens the volume entitled *Studies in Classic American
Literature.* The interesting thing about this essay is that it is all
about expatriation and Lawrence's understanding of why Europeans left the Old World in search of the new. He seems to be
exploring the relationship between the American classics, the
American "art-speech" of Hawthorne, Poe, Cooper, and the like,
and the American "spirit of place." He writes: "Every continent has
its own great spirit of place. Every people is polarized in some
particular locality, which is home, the homeland."[12] Lawrence is
attempting to read the American classics in terms of the "novelty"
of American experience. Not surprisingly, he characterizes new
experiences in terms of displacement and pain. A new experience
"displaces so many" old ones; it "hurts horribly" (11). He notes:
"There is a 'different' feeling in the old American classics. It is the
shifting over from the old psyche to something new, a displacement. And displacements hurt. . . . It is a cut, too. Cutting away the
old emotions and consciousness. Don't ask what is left" (12). It is,
perhaps, the "unspeakable" nature of what is left that is at the
heart of expatriate self-disciplinary practices, the desire to mor-
tify, purify, extinguish. Lawrence takes the spirit of place seriously;
he is concerned that America's spirit of place is as yet unrevealed
even to itself. The questions at stake are large ones having to do

with the legitimacy of American freedom and democracy, relations between European settlers and indigenous peoples, the nature of a homeland. Although we can, perhaps, learn a lot about Lawrence's own motivations for leaving England in reading what he has to say about the Pilgrim fathers, we know little about the American spirit of place; there is little sense that Lawrence's spirit of place will yield up its secrets as facilely as Durrell's. If America's spirit of place may be lodged deep within the breast of its inhabitants, no amount of deep breathing will make it accessible to Lawrence!

Nevertheless, Durrell experiences the periphery in a more complicated relation to himself than does Lawrence, even if his response is less intellectually and emotionally complex. The latter stages the often disturbing work of the self in dramatic confrontations with alterity in ways that suggest rupture, tearing, and disequilibrium. Writing suggestively of the Pilgrim fathers, Lawrence asserts, "They didn't come for freedom," but rather "[t]o get away. Away from what? In the long run, away from themselves. Away from everything. . . . To get away from everything they are and have been" (13–14). On the subject of Poe's "disintegrative vibration," he writes that "old things need to die and disintegrate, because the old white psyche has to be gradually broken down before anything else can come to pass. Man must be stripped even of himself. And it is a painful, sometimes a ghastly process" (74). Where "home" is represented, alternately, as a negative center of gravity and as the place of domestic responsibility, of production and reproduction—Nietzsche's "hairshirt of duties"—expatriation opens the door to another kind of labor.[13] Durrell's project is, by contrast, more conventionally vocational. He is searching for his artistic voice and, finding it, he also solves the riddle of his identity. That is the work of *The Alexandria Quartet*.

We find, moreover, when we compare the *Quartet* with the expatriate narratives of Lawrence and Bowles, that Durrell's hero and the narratives in which he is embedded do not worry over the facts of expatriation—motivations for departure, the psychology of displacement, relations with the natives—revealing an ethical orientation quite antithetical to that of the other two writers. To be fair, Durrell's relationship with Egypt was far different than that of Lawrence with Italy or Bowles with Morocco. Durrell chose Greece, but the outbreak of World War II forced him to flee to Egypt, where he was compelled to wait out the war. Indeed, we can more readily understand Durrell's predicament if we think of it as a "potent negative centre," a term Lawrence's protagonist in *The Lost Girl* (314) uses to describe her response to rural Italy:

> It seems there are places which resist us, which have the power to overthrow our psychic being. It seems as if every country has its potent negative centres, localities which savagely and triumphantly refuse our living culture. And Alvina had struck one of these, here on the edge of the Abruzzi.

And if we add to this the exigencies of war, we should not be surprised at the ethics of expatriation that emerge from *The Alexandria Quartet*—an ethics that emerges from the text's silences or its peculiarities of style rather than through explicit representation. This is not to say that the formal detachment of Bowles's prose does not also articulate an ethics of expatriation. In his "egoless" prose we see, perhaps, the impulse to be invisible, to have no impact. The stylistic qualities of the Durrellean narrative, however, intrude upon—are, indeed constitutive of—narrative itself. They suggest, in contradistinction to the "narrative ethics" of Bowles, that the materiality of place is infinitely malleable, and this is wholly consistent with Durrell's aesthetic theory and with the absence of "worry" the texts reflect. Fredric Jameson's term "sensorium," which he uses to describe the aesthetic practice of Joseph Conrad, will help us decode the ethical underpinnings of Durrell's purple prose.

Beyond that, *The Alexandria Quartet* shows rather than tells the reader that the periphery is where the work of the self can be performed without the "deforming" realities of material life, what Bataille might call the world of "practice." Hence Alexandria may be thought of as a site of "useless expenditure," a status bound up, of course, with the politics and psychology of colonialism. On the other hand, as an outpost of European culture, Alexandria is not "peripheral" at all. It is exotic and at the same time cosmopolitan in a very European sense. Other aspects of Durrell's ethics of expatriation are more explicit. His text celebrates diversity and Levantine cosmopolitanism, even as it indulges in the coarsest of Orientalisms. Its narrator seems to advocate an ethics of simple care even as the *Quartet's* aesthetic spacings objectify and caricature its subjects. Hence, we will find certain ethical stances explored, sometimes to endorse, sometimes to repudiate, but always in a fragmentary, unsystematic fashion. What emerges, then, is less an ethical "outlook" than a series of local endorsements and repudiations.

In what follows I first provide a biographical context to flesh out Durrell's imperial outlook and background. I then turn to a discussion of the travel books, *Prospero's Cell, Reflections on a Marine Venus,* and *Bitter Lemons,* to consider the themes of economic expatriation, Durrell's "treatment" of the native, and his emerging persona as a diplomat. In the last section, I explore the ethics of expatriation articulated in *The Alexandria Quartet,* focusing on its "heraldic" poetics and the idea of "sensorium."

A Detour through Biography

Durrell's biography provides many insights into the ethical predispositions that inform the expatriate project. His childhood in India, for example, provided a context in which the Other took his place within the Manichean dualities of colonialism. His departure for England at an early age represented a trauma for which the imagination provided the sole antidote. His departure *from* England, on the other hand, provided a means to both recuperate a sense of colonial privilege and to carve out a space in which to realize his artistic vision, but the complicating necessity of earning a living often frustrated his aesthetic pursuits. More than either Lawrence or Bowles, Durrell remains captive to the systems and ideologies that formed him.

Durrell was born in 1912 in Jullunder, India, and it is empire—rather than England—that formed the horizon of his national identity. Durrell's Indian childhood distinguishes him immediately from Lawrence and Bowles, both of whom were born in the West. Ian MacNiven's comprehensive biography supplies many of the details of the Durrell family's colonial existence. We learn, for example, that Durrell was raised by a series of native "ayahs" and actually learned the local dialects. His father was, apparently, a forward-thinking individual when it came to matters of the "color bar," having nominated an Indian doctor for membership in his club. When the other members blackballed him, Durrell senior apparently resigned his own membership. People of mixed Indian and English blood, often shunned by both societies, were welcome in the Durrell home.

Durrell's formal education began with his enrollment in St Joseph's College, a Jesuit-run school in Darjeeling with a diverse student body that included Catholics and non-Catholics alike (Durrell's family were Protestants). Darjeeling lay on the Tibetan frontier, and the sight of the Himalayas created a lasting impression on the young Durrell, as did his early confrontation with Catholic iconography in the form of a " 'life-size figure of Christ crucified hanging over the alter, liberally blotched with blood and perfectly pig-sticked and thorn-hatted.' " According to MacNiven, Durrell's horror, exacerbated by the shadowy gloom of the school's small chapel into which he had wandered, confirmed Durrell in "his early rejection of Christianity."[14]

At the age of eleven, Durrell was sent to England with his younger brother, Leslie, to continue his education. He has described his arrival there as culture shock, "Tarzan thrown head-first into the constricted world of the English!"[15] His identification with Tarzan is a telling one. In *Gone Primitive: Savage Intellectuals, Modern Lives,* Marianna Torgovnick convincingly argues that the figure of Tarzan provided English society with an imaginary alternative, rooted in the primitive at the same time as it rejects the "native" in favor of its binary superior, the white, European male subject. Like Kipling's Kim, the figure of Tarzan functions as a cultural hybrid; his distance from English culture allows him to serve both as a cultural critic and, as Torgovnick points out, an exemplar of the constructedness of identity, while his biological markers evidence his innate superiority and difference from the "true" primitive. Durrell's sense of estrangement from English culture is further exemplified by his identification with the Irish side of his family (his mother's), additionally complicating his already diffuse and conflicted sense of identity. In his writings, his Irish ancestry represents a sense of rootedness otherwise lacking. Paradoxically, however, he never visited Ireland. It may be that his privileging of the maternal embodies a response to an early deprivation: a colonial childhood of freedom, happiness, and privilege riven by the paternal mandate to "return" to the center to become properly British. Durrell's father, an engineer who had been involved in the construction of the Darjeeling railway, had hopes that his son would return to India one day, following in his footsteps as a loyal servant of Empire, and young Durrell proved himself very much his father's son in some important respects.

By all accounts, Durrell did not thrive in the English public school system, although he did cultivate an abiding interest in the Elizabethans. In lieu of attending the university, Durrell led a bohemian existence in Bloomsbury; there he met his first wife, Nancy, an aspiring painter. To supplement a small income left by his father following his early death in India, Durrell worked at a variety of jobs that included playing piano in a jazz club. In 1935, at age twenty-three and recently married, he succeeded in convincing his mother, who had returned to England a number of years earlier with her remaining two children, to move the entire clan to Corfu, where his intent was to find "a good base of operations with a cheap exchange and pit out our existence for a year or two until our stock as artists goes up."[16] The original impulse to expatriate, then, is unabashedly economic. The year or two, however, stretched to fifteen—the approximate time it took for Durrell's artistic stock to rise. Not all that time was spent in Corfu, of course; the war effectively ended Durrell's utopian expatriate existence, and he thereafter circulated throughout the eastern Mediterranean, working on and off for the British Foreign Office. True to his original intentions, however, the success of *Justine* enabled him to return to Western Europe, albeit to the south of France and *not* to England. Thus, for Durrell the ethics of expatriation are indexed to his vocation as an artist. The question, How should I live? is always considered in the light of Durrell's artistic aspirations: the periphery as apprenticeship, then, or as the liminal stage between neophyte and mature artist. Lawrence and Bowles also viewed the periphery as a cheap and sunny alternative to a hand-to-mouth existence in some urban bohemia; but, as their writings attest, their deep engagement with the places in which they lived caused them to reflect upon their own lives as expatriates, a theme they explored thematically in their work over and over again. Not so Durrell, as we will see.

After Durrell left England for Corfu in 1935, he never again called England his home. At the outbreak of the Second World War, he and his wife left Corfu for Athens. There he found work briefly at the British Legation gathering information about Greek opinion and feeding British propaganda to the Greek press: "eavesdropping on conversations at cafes, having clandestine meetings at street corners, and skulking in taxis."[17] During this period, he was introduced to life in the British expatriate community, which included a number of writers who would, like him, spend the war years in Egypt. He also cultivated the friendship of important Greek writers, such as the Nobel Prize–winning poet George Seferis, and George Katsimbalis, memorialized by Henry Miller in his own travel narrative about Greece, *The Colossus of Marousi*. After the German invasion, Durrell, his wife, and their infant daughter fled Athens for Crete, where they boarded one of the last passenger steamers leaving for Egypt. Durrell remained there for the duration of the war.[18]

During the war years in Egypt, Durrell's wife left him, and he became involved with Eve Cohen, an Alexandrian Jew, whom he eventually married. She would become the model for Justine. Ever anxious to escape the desert winds and sultry heat of Egypt, it was in Alexandria that Durrell recreated, in *Prospero's Cell*, his idyllic experience of life on the island of Corfu. After the war, Durrell wasted no time getting back to Greece. The Dodecanese Islands, having been captured by Italy during the war, were governed by the British during the period before their return to Greece. Durrell was appointed public information officer with headquarters in Rhodes. Now that he has official duties and is part of a vast colonial machine, the economic motives of expatriation are linked explicitly to employment. In December 1945 he wrote to Sir Walter Smart in response to the latter's apparent praise for *Prospero's Cell*, "I'm afraid though that the life it tries to depict is impossible under a military dispensation however humane and liberal."[19]

Durrell's tenure in Rhodes expired with the return of the islands to Greece in early 1947, and he returned briefly to England before accepting a two-year appointment as lecturer with the British Council in Argentina. Bored and depressed there, Durrell broke his contract and returned to England. By April 1949 he was appointed to the relatively lucrative post of press attaché to the British Embassy in Belgrade, where he developed a strong aversion to communism. He abandoned this position in 1952, hoping to find in Cyprus a lifestyle more conducive to his artistic endeavors. He was now in the midst of work on *Justine* and eager to recapture the utopian experience enabled by economic expatriation. In October he wrote to Henry Miller: "No money. No prospects. A tent. A small car. I feel twenty years younger. Heaven knows how we'll keep alive but I'm so excited I can hardly wait to begin starving."[20] But Eve Cohen, now married to Durrell, was beginning to experience symptoms of severe mental illness, what Durrell describes to Miller as "a bout of Judeo mystical schizophrenia," and he has their young daughter, Sappho, to contend with.[21] Eventually, he and Eve separated, and Durrell's mother came out to stay with Durrell and his daughter in the Turkish villa that he renovated in the village of Bellapaix. He wrote to Miller: "This island has only been discovered in the last year—or else it's me arriving—but lots of writers and artists are beginning to settle here. It's not as lovely as Greece, but very exotic—a voluptuary's island, *Aphrodite*."[22] Durrell's attempt to recreate the idyllic Corfu experience, an experience enabled by financial self-sufficiency, was frustrated by economic need. The costs of maintaining the home in Cyprus and supporting Eve in England forced him back to work, first as an English teacher in a Greek school and then, when the political crisis broke out, as director of information services for the Crown. When Durrell's contract expired in the spring of 1956, he left Cyprus. With the success of *The Alexandria Quartet*, however, Durrell finally became a self-supporting writer, and he was able to settle permanently in the south of France, on the "right" side of the Mediterranean, as the Durrellean character Darley muses from an Alexandrian café. Henceforth Greece and the eastern Mediterranean would be little more than occasional vacation destinations.[23]

Durrell's personal biography, then, strangely triangulated by a childhood in India, an adolescence in England, and an early adulthood spent almost entirely in Greece and the eastern Mediterranean, was shaped not by its continuities but by its fissures. His dispersed identity as a colonial and an Irishman made the idea of a homeland, any homeland, a vexed one. As a colonial, of course, for him the spaces of his lived and imagined identities did not coincide. India was his birthplace and the birthplace of his parents, but India both was and was not home. England was the source of identity, the hub of empire—that greater imagined community which constituted him as its subject. Yet his insistent Irishness and colonial childhood alienated him from England even as they confirmed him as a colonial vis-à-vis the subjected population of India. England both was and was not home. A certain metaphysical discomfort manifested itself in an artistic awakening that could not reconcile the perceived Symbolic of London and the British Isles with an Imaginary inseparable from and identical with the Indian landscape. I use these Lacanian terms advisedly to delineate two qualities of imaginative geography: the one deeply invested in a prediscursive and image-driven understanding of the world, the other associated with the institutional, paternalistic, and discursive structures through which national identity is mediated.

Following Homi Bhabha, who takes from Foucault's *Discipline and Punish* the notion that "the most individuated are those subjects who are placed on the margins of the social," we can see that Durrell's Indian birth and childhood already position him as a sort of square peg; expatriation further "individuates" him.[24] For the

self is, from the start, both abject—thrust away from the "maternal bosom" of India—and dispersed, the crisis of individuation
amplified by the trauma of geographic dislocation. A letter to
Henry Miller underscores the theme of rupture around which
Durrell's childhood experiences seem to be organized:

> My life is like a chopped worm. Until eleven marvellous memories—
> white—white the Himalayas from the dormitory windows . . . the
> blue fissures in the hills. God what a dream, the *passes* into Lhasa—
> blue with ice and thawing softly towards the holy forbidden city. . . .
> I live on the edge of it with a kind of nursery-rhyme happiness.[25]

Elsewhere he has asserted that according to Eastern ways of thinking everyone has two birthplaces—the one where he was born and
the other where "he wakes up to reality." Durrell's second birthplace was Greece, eliding the symbolic of England to embrace once
more the pastoral Imaginary of the periphery. His discovery, moreover, "that the Greek philosophers had all taken their degrees
in India and that there had been a continuous message coming
through, on some sort of wavelength," enabled him to realize "that
what I was trying to do was find my way back to India and my personal life to restore the broken context."[26] It is surely this desire
for the impossible return, for the geography of the Imaginary, that
informs certain aspects of Durrell's quest. The broken context to
which Durrell refers also suggests a key to his search for meaning,
for a philosophical bridge between East and West that will color
and shape both his coming of age and the development of his artistic voice. So, while part of Durrell's ethics of expatriation is rooted
in the desire to liberate the self from a disenchanted and stultify-
ing world, another part is predicated upon irreparable geographical loss and abjection, the "geography" of the imagination his only
true home, the vocabulary of art his one true moral source.

When Durrell was asked during an interview in the early seventies whether his Indian childhood had any lasting influence
upon his outlook, he replied:

> I am, and I remain, an expatriate. That vague sense of exile has never
> quite left me. But at the same time it has meant that I can feel at ease
> anywhere, given a minimum of sunshine. The expatriate carries his
> country with him, inside him: *everywhere belongs to him*, because he
> belongs nowhere. [My emphasis][27]

One cannot quite imagine either Lawrence or Bowles assuming
such a proprietary stance toward the world. Quite to the contrary,

Bowles has asserted that "one *belongs to* the whole world, not to just one part of it" (my emphasis), a tacit acknowledgment of the world's claim upon him.[28] Durrell's interest is at once proprietary and detached, and such a point of departure informs not only Durrell's diplomatic outlook, but also his artistic one, and so imparts to his ethics of expatriation an imperial cast. Lugwig Pursewarden, one of Durrell's alter egos in *The Alexandria Quartet*, asserts, moreover: "I am always glad to get out of England to countries where I feel no moral responsibility."[29] If part of Durrell's own desire to leave England was to escape feeling morally responsible, his choice of domicile, often motivated by employment possibilities held out by empire, certainly complicated this imperative by involving him in colonial politics. So as a subject of empire, he is not speaking altogether figuratively in asserting that he belongs everywhere and not altogether truthfully in asserting that he belongs nowhere. Despite Durrell's assertion, therefore, that "the expatriate carries his country with him, inside him; everywhere belongs to him, because he belongs nowhere," it is significant that he never had to live just anywhere. The geography of empire— along with the expansive possibilities of art, of course—provides an imaginative force field within which the fragments of his identity will coalesce despite his predisposition against things English. No doubt his status as a colonial in England contributed to his sense of alienation. For one thing, he is unable to reproduce in England the status his family enjoyed as second-generation colonials in India, a status that was nevertheless to leave its political and cultural mark on him. Bowker's biography points out that in England, "'colonials' tended to be snubbed, and had no clear place in highly structured English society, with its subtle gradations and petty snobberies," a circumstance which would tend to exacerbate an already festering sense of rootlessness and abjection.[30]

The Travel Books

Durrell's Mediterranean domiciles allowed him to recuperate the imaginative geography of India and to "replay" his colonial childhood. But perhaps "play" is the operative word here. As pointed out by Marc Alyn in his interview with Durrell in the early seventies, Durrell chose to settle in Corfu, "in what can only be called the British Mediterranean." Durrell clarifies: "It wasn't the Englishness that mattered, but the communications, the postal service, the degree of civilization." Alyn wisely concludes: "When it comes down to it, you have always been concerned for your comfort. You like your wilderness in civilized surroundings."[31] Durrell was manifestly uninterested in the kind of radical existential experimentation undertaken by Lawrence and Bowles; he merely wanted a warm and sunny place in which to pursue his goal of becoming a writer.

A key to the informing "ideology" of Durrell's early years in the Mediterranean might be located in the pastoral aesthetic. In his book *Abroad* (209–10), Paul Fussell has suggested that travel books are displaced pastoral romances, for, he asserts:

> If William Empson is right to define traditional pastoral as a mode of presentation implying "a beautiful relation between rich and poor," then pastoral is a powerful element in most travel books, for, unless he's a *Wandervogel* or similar kind of layabout (few of whom write books), the traveler is almost always richer and freer than those he's among.

If England did not readily yield itself up to the kind of pastoral romance that Durrell's early childhood represented, there were places abroad highly susceptible to his projection of a pastoral aesthetic, places where he might live in "a beautiful relation" to the local peasantry, places where his outsider status could be turned to advantage and his social identity resolved. Thus, the aesthetic of the pastoral enables Durrell to resolve the problem of social status while at the same time both masking and perpetuating the relations of social and economic inequality that sustained his childhood Imaginary and his career as an artist. At the same time, he makes of "economic" expatriation a self-aestheticizing project. That is to say, in his attention to the material and sensual delights of a gracious and hospitable physical environment, he produces himself as the object of aestheticized experience.

Durrell's celebration of the senses—hyperstimulated by the physical splendor of the Mediterranean—was an important aspect of his rejection of Judeo-Christian orthodoxies and the cultural and material aesthetic of home. Durrellean prose replicates in discourse that sensual brilliance in which the body reveled. His verbal impressionism is of a piece with this attentiveness to physical sensation, which entails, in addition to visual alacrity, a sense of ambivalence and physical dissolution:

> Corcyra is all Venetian blue and gold—and utterly spoilt by the sun. Its richness cloys and enervates. The southern valleys are painted out

boldly in heavy brush-strokes of yellow and red while the Judas trees punctuate the roads with their dusty purple explosions.[32]

Durrell and his wife "bathe naked, and the sun and water make our skins feel old and rough, like precious lace" (23). Lying in the waters of the Ionian,

> It is like the heartbeat of the world itself. It is no longer a region or an ambiance where the conscious or subconscious mind can play its incessant games with itself; but penetrating to a lower level still, the sun numbs the source of ideas itself, and expands slowly into the physical body, spreading along the nerves and bones a gathering darkness, a weight, a power. So that each individual finger-bone, each individual arm and leg, expand to the full measure of their own animal consciousness in this beneficent and dangerous sun-darkness. . . . One is entangled and suffocated by this sense of physical merging into the elements around one. Blinded by this black sunlight, nothing remains of the known world, save the small sharp toothless kisses of fish on the hanging body—*now no longer owned;* . . . One could die like this and wonder if it was death. The density, the weight and richness of a body without a mind or ghost to trouble it. (100, my emphasis)

Durrell's preoccupation with the physical here shares with primitivism the desire to recover a sense of connectedness with the universe. Torgovnick writes: "Fascination with the primitive . . . can nurture forbidden desires to question or escape Western norms. Most of all, it can nourish intense desires to void the idea of the autonomous self and merge or connect with life sources." At the same time, however, this merging was perceived as perilous, "a danger to what Jung called 'the mature European self' "[33] The passage also calls to mind Bataille's dicey path to inner experience, but where the latter would be concerned with a tearing of the self, an opening out to a radical form of communication, Durrell's idea of continuity is evoked in more natural and harmonious terms, a Romantic rather than post-Romantic vision. Neither form of self-dissolution is, however, a typically Durrellean impulse insofar as, even here, the metaphor of ownership interjects itself. This is about as close as Durrell comes to the practices of self-dismantling that we will see in Lawrence and that will become even more severe and unforgiving in Bowles.

Imperial poetics aside, Durrell does practice certain "relational" arts of the self, albeit with other like-minded subjects. For the aesthetic is also an alternative means of forging community. By creating an intersubjective space of sensual enjoyment and apprecia-

tion, the aesthetic binds individuals together in terms of affiliations wholly discontinuous with nationalism, ethnicity, or other
"tribal" functions. Durrell's aesthetic communities, which were
largely though not exclusively comprised of fellow expatriates,
form a staple of his "travel books" and provide a model for the
close-knit group of Alexandrians and expatriates at the center of
The Alexandria Quartet; they were the medium within which his
attachments to the places about which he wrote took root. Indeed,
the larger imagined community of aesthetes extends backward and
forward in time:

> we artists form one of those pathetic human chains which human
> beings form to pass buckets of water up to a fire, or to bring in a
> lifeboat. An uninterrupted chain of humans born to explore the
> inward riches of the solitary life on behalf of the unheeding
> unforgiving community. (*Clea*, 168)

At the same time, though, the solipsistic nature of this artistic calling
—the Heraldic Universe is emblematic here—and its realization in
the particular aesthetic communities of which Durrell was a part
(the Greek literary circles in which he traveled were a significant
exception), rendered him immune from the kind of self-scrutiny
that would attend to the relations between expatriates and natives
or, for that matter, to the material grounding of aesthetic production itself. If the ideology of the aesthetic functions to isolate the
modern artist from the realm of value and accountability associated with politics and the market, how much more so for the expatriate artist in the periphery, whose flight insulates him from both
the petty indignities and material rigors of life in the industrial
world!

Durrell valorized the realm of useless expenditure, which we
can better understand through Bataille's observation that "humanity recognizes the right to acquire, to conserve and to consume
rationally, but it excludes in principle *non-productive expenditure*."[34]
He celebrated leisure and sensual enjoyment and enthusiastically
embraced the type of expatriate lifestyle pursued by Americans in
Paris during the Twenties that Malcolm Cowley has memorialized.
"The *real* island flavor," Durrell writes in *Prospero's Cell*, is embodied by "our existence here . . . in this delectable landscape, remote
from the responsibilities of an active life in Europe" which "have
[*sic*] given us this sense of detachment from the *real* world" (22, my
emphasis). Indeed, it is the quintessence of expatriate life itself
in the popular imagination! Where the flight from "responsibility"

or "project" that I trace in Lawrence and Bowles is a modernist ascesis of sorts, Durrell's characterization suggests a more conventional, more typically hedonistic mindset. He exudes a certain lightness of heart that makes his project seem somehow less legitimate. He's having fun. For that reason, among others, he seems more vulnerable to critical scrutiny and to the questions we now ask: for *whom*, exactly, is this the *real* island flavor? Certainly not for the peasants, artisans, and fisherman who people the "objective" landscape—Spiro the village idiot, Nick the douser—who must be presumed to partake of some other, "unreal" island way of life. We consider later, in contrast, the more troubling portraits drawn by D. H. Lawrence, whose "forlorn" Italian figures command our profound respect—and Lawrence's as well—despite his refusal to grant them full "spiritual parity," and Bowles's hybridized Moroccans, the immediacy of whose demand both seduces and threatens. Such figures are, moreover, embedded in a dynamic physical and cultural landscape whose very disenchantment resonates with a kind of emotional honesty. Indeed, it is in part Durrell's desire to escape from "the real world" and the moral responsibilities that attend it which prompts him to situate himself in a realm that *allows* him to play fast and loose with the—for him—unreal world of the Other. Not surprisingly, this desire also diminishes the ethical force of his project. As I suggested earlier, the artist's integrity as truth teller, even in its guise as reinvention, cannot be separated from the idea of intimacy, a connection of both identity and difference with the object. The Heraldic Universe, I would argue, can prove resistant to this kind of intimacy. Durrell's romantic view of a national essence, moreover, obscures the complexities we now take for granted in any discussion of so-called essentials in a way that Lawrence's and Bowles's views do not.

Reflections on a Marine Venus, Durrell's second Greek travel book, represents an aesthetic and sensual reengagement with Greece after four years of "exile" in Egypt during the war. It begins on a note of astonishing self-reflectivity concerning the quality of the Greek experience. Durrell wonders "whether it was still a reality based in the landscape and the people—or whether we had simply invented it for ourselves in the old days, living comfortably on foreign exchange, patronizing reality with our fancies and making bad literature with them."[35] In one stroke, he manages to interrogate the economic basis for expatriation, the efficacy of the Heraldic

Universe, and the value of such "compromised" literary production. But the text quickly affirms rather than disaffirms his earlier
vision with its aestheticizing *re*vision of the wartime landscape.
While the port of Mandriccio is littered with the detritus of war,
and starving civilians and German prisoners of war comb through
the ruins, these soon become minor blemishes against the vibrant
colors of a Rhodian sunset:

> The houses had begun to curl up at the edges, like burning paper, and
> with each sink of the sun upon the dark hill above us, the tones of
> pink and yellow curdled and ran from corner to corner, from gable to
> gable, until for a moment the darkening minarets of the mosques
> glowed into blue ignition, like the light glancing along a sheet of
> carbon paper. (*RMV*, 30)

Durrell's highly impressionistic renderings of landscape stand in
stark contrast to his representations of the Greek peasant. Indeed,
his propensity to typify and caricature, while often articulated in
sympathetic and affectionate tones, is seldom tempered by the
individual voices of his subjects. A notable but ambiguous exception occurs when Durrell purports to record a conversation between
himself and Manoli the fisherman. He writes of Manoli:

> His sixty-year-old body reminds me of some ancient boat, cankered
> and swollen at the seams from years of sea-work; yet his heart is in
> repair still, and with it that marvellous natural intelligence which is
> only to be found among the semi-literate. . . . His interest in world
> politics is a consuming passion and it is wonderful how clearly he
> reads between the lines of a conference or a speech to deduce at once
> its failure or success, its truth or intrinsic falsity. He is a much keener
> judge of affairs than his counterpart in England would be; yet a
> poorer judge of Greek matter than any child—domestic Rhodian
> affairs, that is. (49)

This passage reflects a mixture of condescension and respect.
While Manoli is individuated, he is at the same time subsumed by
his occupation: the ancient fisherman is translated into the ancient
vessel itself. His "marvellous natural intelligence" exceeds that of
his British counterpart yet cannot comprehend Rhodian politics.
On the subject of poverty, however, and Western efforts to relieve
it, he scoffs at Durrell's assertion that education and economic
improvement are unequivocal gains and queries, "Who can say
what I should gain—and what I should lose?" "Who indeed?"
muses Durrell. And while Manoli is cast as the interlocutory figure

who calls modernity and all of its supposed advances into question, it is from a position of security and relative prosperity that
Durrell can assert of Manoli's poverty that "the process of acceptance has given him a kind of joy—a water-tight happiness which
plays about his face and gestures, investing them with a strange
kinetic beauty" (50).

Then, as if to bring the point home, the text turns immediately
from Manoli to Durrell's discovery of the simple but idyllic dream
house which he will then occupy during his tenure on the island.
Quite simply, Manoli's gain would be Durrell's loss—the loss, that
is, of the ready availability of primitive experience: the rustic
charms of a beatified peasantry and a pristine landscape, the raw
materials of a certain aesthetic space, and, above all, the possibility
of its textualization. As we have just seen, part of Durrell's idyll is
the romanticization of the poor: the threadbare fisherman, the
poignant sea-scented prostitute named—what else?—Aphrodite
who embodies "the whole of Greece, its sunburnt airs, dazzling
bony islands, and the chaste and honourable poverty which the
people has converted into a golden generosity" (78). Durrell clearly
does not believe he is "patronizing reality with [his] fancies" here,
but we are left wondering whether Manoli and Aphrodite are realities or mere examples of Durrell's bold imaginary peasants.

Rhodes, like Egypt, exposes Durrell to the hybridity of Levantine
culture, and he continues to interpret the culture of the eastern
Mediterranean through the theoretical prism of the spirit of place.
While Corfu's culture and ambience seemed, in *Prospero's Cell*, to
reflect a kind of classical melding of the Greek and the Italian,
Rhodes had a significant Turkish population in addition to the
Greek and the Italian. Egypt, "with its swarming vermin, its population of Apes in nightgowns, its dirt, disease, and truncated beg-
gars on trolleys," had represented for Durrell "the suffocating
beastliness of Islam and all it stands for, bigotry, cruelty and ignorance," but on Rhodes, "all the jagged edges of the faith have been
filed away. . . . Rhodes has converted Islam and made it part of the
island's green and gentle self" (*RMV*, 42, 53). The spirit of place—its
essential nature—somehow subdues and appropriates all foreign
influences. Of the Crusaders, whose fortress dominates the old city
of Rhodes, he writes: "They burned with a self-dedication which
could withstand every temptation—save at last the languorous airs
of the Levantine landscape they dominated for so long" (135). Their
culture "never penetrated to the heart of the Mediterranean way-

of-life—that mixture of superstition, impulse and myth which so quickly grows up around whatever is imported, seeking to domesticate it" (141). I wonder, too, whether Durrell's more nuanced response to Islam in Rhodes reflects an "ethics of generosity" borne of enchantment, whether the experience of Rhodes's beauty and charm produced just those "fortuitous circumstances" by which "the good humor of enchantment spills over into critical consciousness and tempers it, thus rendering its judgments more generous and its claims less dogmatic."[36]

Cyprus is Durrell's next island paradise. With the incursion of Greek nationalism, however, the island ceases to enchant, and Durrell's ethics of generosity seem likewise attenuated. *Bitter Lemons* was written after Durrell's tenure as director of information services on the island of Cyprus expired in 1956. With that text, the ethics of expatriation, until now bound up with aesthetic self-interest, merge painfully with the ethics of imperialism. While it is true that Durrell experienced Rhodes from the perspective of an administrator, the politics of imperialism were not allowed to intrude upon his essentially dilettantish attitude toward his official duties. *Bitter Lemons* is a text about colonialism's last gasp and the attenuation of heraldic reality. Not surprisingly, the book begins with a theft—from an overturned book stand in Trieste—of a curious volume entitled *A Lady's Impressions of Cyprus:*

> I stopped guiltily, fearful of incurring the penalties of looting should the police return, and picked Mrs. Lewis up. Her faded green cover with its floral device promised me a Victorian travel-account which might introduce me in a most suitable manner to the Crown Colony of Cyprus. But something more than this. I felt she was a sort of omen.[37]

As with his other island books, Durrell will indulge in a certain amount of Orientalist quotation. So he is correct, I believe, to trust Mrs. Lewis as a guide to the Crown colony as opposed to the less decipherable register of lived experience, local custom, and native politics, "where weird enclaves of these Mediterranean folk lived a joyous, uproarious, muddled anarchic life of their own" (*BL*, 34). The failure of these spaces to conform to the represented space of its colonial administrators, the Orientalist version of Cypriot reality, and their failure to be so fully "joyous" and "uproarious" frustrate Durrell's desire to impose his own heraldic reality upon the island.

Durrell is at first annoyed by his cab driver, whose "biting air of laziness and superiority made one want to kick him. He answered my politenesses with grunts, gazing at me slyly in the mirror from time to time." (24). This surly gentleman is soon disarmed by the discovery of a book of Greek folk songs in Durrell's paraphernalia lying about in the back seat, and he "suddenly turned into a well-educated and not unhandsome young man, full of an amiable politeness" (25). Nevertheless, Durrell's tone of imperiousness and suspicion indicates the degree to which his pose has hardened into something approaching superciliousness and the degree to which he is discomfited by the sly gaze of his subject. It is during this cab ride, early on in *Bitter Lemons*, that the problem of Enosis is first introduced. Enosis, union with Greece, will prove to be the Greek Cypriot narrative of freedom whose intervention into Durrell's overarching heraldic scheme will effectively rob him of his Mediterranean paradise. It is Durrell's inability to see, or his ideological predilection to refuse to see, anything but love and regard for Britain in the eyes of its subjected Others that contributes to his disillusionment. In Cyprus, Durrell trusts "that the old sentimental tie was still alive, that it had not been killed by wooden administration and *bad manners*" (26, my emphasis).

It is in Cyprus, ironically, that Durrell will most fully attempt to integrate himself into native life. He does so deliberately, rejecting the typically colonial spaces where "the British colony lived what appeared to be a life of *blameless* monotony, rolling about in small cars, drinking at the yacht club, sailing a bit, going to church, and suffering agonies of apprehension at the thought of not being invited to Government House on the Queen's birthday" (35, my emphasis). Yet, says Durrell, his

> compatriots were decent, civil folk, who had been brought here, not by any desire to broaden minds cumbered only by the problems of indolence and trade, but by *a perfectly honourable passion for sunlight and low income tax.* How sad it is that so many of our national characteristics are misinterpreted! Our timidity and lack of imagination seem to foreigners to be churlishness, our taciturnity the deepest misanthropy. But are these choking suburbanisms with which we seem infused when we are abroad any worse than the tireless dissimulation and insincerity of the Mediterranean way of life? (35, my emphasis)

Durrell's irony here is tempered by affection. Never before has he so completely identified with his countrymen. His sympathetic rendering of their bland but honest nature (in contradistinction to the "tireless dissimulation and insincerity" of their hosts) is matched by an obsessive need to make them appear lovable to, and loved by, the standoffish Greeks, who, it is claimed, will exhibit undying devotion at the slightest condescension: the attempt, for example, to pronounce "potato in Greek." Perhaps his professional —and personal—stake in the machinery of colonialism militates against the possibility of achieving the critical distance from culturally determined truths that, for Lawrence and Bowles, was so fundamental to their ethics of expatriation. It's important, though, that despite this affectionate sympathy for his countrymen, Durrell pursued his inclination to live in a small Greek village, believing his "doubleness" rendered him an objective reader and interpreter of local culture and politics. Indeed, he takes his fellows to task for not learning so much as a simple "Good morning" in Greek or Turkish; he comments: "These things are trivial, of course, but in small communities they cut deep; while in revolutionary situations they can become the most powerful political determinant" (37). This is an interesting observation, for on the surface his words seem to plead for civility toward, even recognition of, the indigenous populations. In light of his position on the Enosis question, however, the words appear somewhat naive. In fact, what Durrell seems to be suggesting is that a few civilities here and there can stem the rising tide of nationalism in subjected territories. Durrell's naivete can, at least arguably, be linked to the "ideology" of the pastoral in its mystification of the relations between rich and poor (or colonizer and colonized). Indeed, in Cyprus he has little contact with the colonial centers, at least before the period of political unrest. He chose not to live with other expatriates, but rather undertook the exhaustive renovation of a Turkish villa in a small relatively remote Greek village from which he was required to travel a considerable distance to get to work.

Despite his affection for the locals, however, Durrell writes:

> Life in a small island would be *unbearable* for anyone *with sensibility* were it not enriched from time to time by visitants from other worlds, bringing with them the conversations of the great capitals, refreshing the quotidian life in small places by breaths of air which make one live once more, for a moment, in the airs of Paris or London. (96, my emphasis)

And so, like his other island books, much of *Bitter Lemon* is preoccupied with his aesthetic community: the various artists, writers, and other more or less professional wanderers who sooner or later make their way to the great expatriate centers of the Mediterranean.

The implication is, of course, that no native of Cyprus or, for that matter, no member of the diplomatic community, could possibly share his sensibility, his aestheticism.

Durrell writes that his friend, the architect and perfect aesthete Austen Harrison, "represented that forgotten world where style was not only a literary imperative but an inherent method of approaching the world of books, roses, statues and landscapes" (99). Other friends included the travel writers Freya Stark and Patrick Kinross, who, together with Harrison,

> travelling about as they all did . . . were able to indulge their taste, and bring back to Cyprus a bewildering medley of objects, from Egyptian *musarabiyas* to Turkish mosque-lamps. They were steadily stripping the Arab world of its chief treasures . . . and soon their houses in Cyprus would have everything, except the mosaics of St. Sophia. (100)

Durrell himself can't afford to participate in this practice of raiding, but he "enjoyed these treasures vicariously . . . and appreciated nothing more than one of the great palavers which went on when one or other of the friends had arrived back in Cyprus with something exotic. . . . triumphally stolen from Fez, Algiers or Istamboul" (100). Indeed, the phrase "triumphally stolen" should give us pause, suggesting on the one hand, a guilty act and, on the other, the sense that the precious artifacts of other cultures are merely awaiting heroic rescue by Western travelers.

All this comes to an end, however, when

> the *vagaries of fortune* and the *demons of ill-luck* dragged Cyprus into the stock-market of world affairs and destroyed not only the fortuitous happiness of these friendships but, more tragically and just as surely, the *old tried relationships* on which the life of the little village itself was founded. (101, my emphasis)

What intervenes as the "vagaries of fortune" and "demons of ill-luck" in Durrell's pastoral is political self-awakening: the narrative of Enosis forged by the Cypriot Greeks. His link to the villagers of Bellapaix, now undermined, is an important component of his island identity. He is anxious for their acceptance and approval as, perhaps, a validation of a certain wished-for hybridity. He would like, perhaps, to embody the categorical instability of a Kim without at the same time losing his aesthetic sensibilities—which are, finally, the point of absolute closure for him. Paradoxically, he seeks to be confirmed in his Englishness at the same time he seeks to distance himself from the Englishness of home by being, some-how, the Englishman who is more Greek than the Greeks!

In no situation does Durrell's relationship to the native popu-lations reveal the ambivalent nature of colonial discourse more than in the Enosis crisis, and it is the doubleness of Durrell's sense of the Cypriot desire for autonomy that most characterizes his response. Initially, he regards Enosis as an unwarranted intrusion into the pleasures of aesthetic contemplation and consumption:

> It was distasteful in such scenery and over a wine which if it was not exactly vintage was at least of a good yeoman pedigree, to have to turn one's mind to the shallow bickerings of nations. Besides, I had come to Cyprus as a private individual, and had no concern with policy. (117)

He finds it "disquieting" that his Athenian friends "should take the affair so seriously" (118). His concerns, at this point, are strictly selfish: "My purely personal angle of vision, limited as it was by the horizon of my village, denied me such troubling reflections [open insurrection], yet I could not help but take them seriously since a disturbed island would mean a disturbed personal existence there" (119–20). Moreover, despite his so-called limited horizon, his angle of vision was wide enough to fully embrace the British position:

> We were known and loved; belief in our fair-mindedness and political honesty was unshakable; and indeed it seemed to me that even a referendum held after an intervening period of self-government might result in something like a drawn match. . . . I felt that some frank and generous statement was the best way of disarming the Enotists. (120)

In his rhetoric he resembles (pace Edmund Keeley) none other than Lord Byron himself who, responding to the potential power vacuum created in wake of the crumbling Ottoman Empire, writes in the notes to *Childe Harold*: "The Greeks will never be indepen-dent: they will never be sovereigns as heretofore, and God forbid they ever should! but they may be subjects without being slaves. Our colonies are not independent, but they are free and industri-ous, and such may Greece be hereafter."[38]

In 1955 Durrell was approached by the colonial secretary of Cyprus, whom he met socially, to apply for the post of press advi-sor, for "[t]here was much that needed doing in the field of public relations and it was felt that someone knowing Greek and having a stake in the island's affairs might do better than a routine official"

(*BL*, 139). This seemed like "an unhoped-for stroke of luck," for Durrell needed funds to complete the renovation of the villa. And so he emerged from the purely private status of expatriate artist into that of public figure and colonial administrator. As someone able to see things from the point of view of London, Athens, and Nicosia, he writes: "I might certainly be of use to the Government and play a small part in bringing about the sort of solution which I felt, we all felt, must be round the corner" (140).

Meanwhile, Durrell must contend with the growing support for Enosis in the midst of his pastoral retreat. He blames outside agitators for attempting to stir things up among the villagers, who

> listened as uncomprehending children might listen to the roll of distant drums which competed with the gentleness and timidity of their hearts in their insistence on other values based in hate, in spite, in smallness. Who was the enemy, where was he to be found, the tyrant who had liberated Greece? (140)

Unable to reconcile the British role as liberator with that of colonial master, he perhaps projects his ambivalence onto the Cypriots themselves. He is fully conscious of the Other's gaze: "They watched me with speculative curiosity as I walked up the main street with the three small sons of my builders. . . . Try as they might, they could not marry the two images. Wherein did my tyranny lie, I who was so polite and who was teaching my daughter Greek?" (140). He tries to reason with his Cypriot friends in the language of a benign overseer. They ask:

> 'But if we have offered every facility for bases does that not satisfy England? Must she maintain sovereignty over Cyprus? Why? We say to her: take as much as you want, build what you like, stay for ever, but let us have our island. At least if not today, tomorrow, in twenty years.' (141)

And so Enosis produces, for Durrell, a splitting effect. Outside agitators, not the Greek Cypriots themselves, are responsible for the political unrest. Durrell admits, however, that "the question of sovereignty was always the basic complex and I had been forced to design a sophistry to meet it" (141). How were the natives to be made to understand that Cypress was of strategic importance to the commonwealth? The question was far greater than "mere" independence. He responds to their concerns with a parable:

> 'Your brother has a piece of land, Andreas. You love him. He loves you. He tells you to borrow it and build a house on it for your family.

"Build what you like," he says, "and it will remain yours for ever."
Now, while you love him and trust him—who knows? Strange things
happen in the world. Would it not be wiser to keep the title-deeds of
the land before spending your capital in building on it? That is what
England feels.' (141)

Because of its strategic position in the Mediterranean, because of
the involvement of Greece and the possible response of Turkey,
Cyprus was, according to Durrell, more than a strictly colonial
affair. To clamp down on the dissidents, to hold the island by force
rather than "guile," was not necessarily the right approach.

As the situation escalated into outright rebellion, it became
apparent that British intelligence was inadequate to the task of
coping with popular revolt where "even the non-combatant's door
was always open to shelter a bomb-thrower" (190). Durrell's famil-
iarity with the politics of greater Greece filled him with a certain
ambivalence. He was aware of the contradictions inherent in the
British position. He was also aware that the star of empire was fading, that Cyprus was, finally, "part of a fragile chain of telecom-
munication centres and ports, the skeletal backbone of an Empire
striving to resist the encroachments of time"; but, he queries,
"Must it not, then, be held at all costs?" (194).

Durrell leaves when his contract expires, for "most of the swal-
lows had gone, and the new times with their harsher climates were
not ours to endure." He had contemplated an earlier departure, but
was afraid of giving the Greek press "grounds for believing that I
had resigned on policy grounds, which would have been unfair to
my masters" (214). On his last visit to the village to collect his things
from the house, he is received coldly. Quite simply, "the sight of an
Englishman had become an obscenity on that clear money-gold
spring air" (249). He finds the wicker basket containing the fragmentary record of his stay on Cyprus, all the things collected and
saved with loving fidelity. These he throws away, and with them,
it seems, the "dark crystal" of Greece.

It makes for an interesting juxtaposition here to consider the
ethics of expatriation from a female perspective. Isak Dinesen, the
nom de plume of Baroness Karen Blixen, was born in Denmark in
1885, the year of D. H. Lawrence's birth. In 1913, she and her husband, Bror Blixen, traveled to Africa, where they purchased a coffee plantation. They divorced in 1923, but Dinesen stayed on to
manage the farm, remaining in Africa for a total of seventeen years.
She is best known for her memoirs of African life, *Out of Africa* and

Shadows on the Grass. Although Dinesen was a generation older than Durrell, her association with Africa suggests an interesting study in contrasts. Dinesen was not a novelist, and so it would be unfair to juxtapose her memoirs with novelistic renderings of expatriate experience. Nor are those memoirs comparable to the travel narratives produced by Durrell, Lawrence, or Bowles. While I have made it a point to distinguish those writers from "colonialist" writers, Dinesen belongs squarely within the canon of colonialist literature. Nevertheless, she is an expatriate writer and a woman, and so might have something interesting to add to the conversation. Dinesen's colonialist attitudes have been documented by such critics as Abdul JanMohamed and Susan R. Horton. Her African characters are as fanciful as Durrell's Greek peasants, her enchantment with landscape and difference as self-conscious as his. Nevertheless, there are significant differences between their self-representation.

One of the more interesting aspects of Dinesen's memoir is its mixture of "feminine" specularity and passivity, on the one hand, and mastery, on the other. The farmhouse, for example, is represented as a relatively porous structure. She writes: "The doors of my diningroom, to lee, were always open" to the cooling east wind.[39] For this reason, "the West side of the house was popular with the Natives; they laid their way around it, to keep in touch with what was going on inside" (*OA*, 48). Opening herself up or being opened to the gaze of the Other is something she takes quite for granted. Of the natives, she admits, "I reconciled myself to the fact that while I should never quite know or understand them, they knew me through and through" (21). There were limits, however. If young shepherd boys were accustomed to moving in and out of the farmhouse with impunity, they were nevertheless required to maintain a certain decorum: they could neither touch anything, sit down, nor "speak unless spoken to" (49).

Their presence, for Dinesen, provided a "link between the life of my civilized house and the life of the wild" (48). Of course this representation of the relationship between colonizer and native is Manichean, but Dinesen also complicates the Manichean allegory at times. She writes, for example, that the native is the "cosmopolitan" figure, while the colonizer is the provincial: "The Native is more of a man of the world than the suburban or provincial settler or missionary, who had grown up in a uniform community and with a set of stable values" (54). The natives' hybridity and cosmopolitanism belie the notion that they are the embodiment of an eternal African essence. Their "acquaintance with a variety of races and tribes, and to the lively human intercourse that was brought upon East Africa, first by the old traders of ivory and slaves, and in our days by the settlers and big game hunters," situates them in a dynamic process of cross-cultural exchange (54). By contrast, the colonizer is seen as timeless and unchanging.

There is also, in Dinesen's representation of the farm's "porosity," a sense of communication between the civilized and the wild. She pays homage, despite her obvious delight in lion hunting, to the community of human and nonhuman beings. Her charming vignette about Lulu, the baby antelope she rescued and raised, continues this theme. As a youngster, Lulu had the run of the farmhouse; even after she returned to the wild, she would return to the grounds, though not to the house itself, with her offspring. "The free union between my house and the antelope," Dinesen writes, "was a rare, honourable thing. Lulu came in from the wild world to show that we were on good terms with it, and she made my house one with the African landscape, so that nobody could tell where the one stopped and the other began" (80). Dinesen also resists the wild, where other, admittedly fictional, expatriate figures are seduced by it, asserting:

> But I was a European, and I had not lived long enough in the country to acquire the absolute passivity of the Native, as some Europeans will do, who live for many decennaries in Africa. I was young and by instinct of self-preservation, I had to collect my energy on something, if I were not to be whirled away with the dust on the farm-roads, or the smoke on the plain. (47).

She is, as Horton points out, "hardly a figure for woman's harmony with the landscape or a representation of the eternal feminine for which she advocated; . . . she can be seen instead as the figure for a very 'masculine' manipulation of people and landscape to the end of her own self-production."[40] If life at "home" meant a life of relative leisure, life in Africa was associated with work, and in this her experience of expatriation (and, perforce, its representation) is worlds apart from Durrell's Mediterranean playground. And because she ran a large coffee plantation with many natives in her employ, her very situatedness lent itself to attachments and intimacies that do not find their way into Durrell's narratives about his life in various Greek islands. She spins a "domestic" yarn, one that revolves around her farmhouse and her "maternal" preoccupations with those within her domain. Finally, the admixture of humility in the face of Africa's immense beauty and diversity and presumption in terms of colonialism's claim upon it makes *Out of Africa* a curious piece of expatriate writing. As Horton so aptly puts it, Dinesen is not European/not-*not* European, not African/not-*not* African, not colonial/not-*not* colonial, not male/not female and not-*not* male/not-*not* female.[41] Durrell, were we to describe him in such terms, was not colonial/not-*not* colonial, and this curious status/lack of status troubles many of his writings.

The Alexandria Quartet

The Alexandria Quartet, I will argue, represents Durrell's attempt to make aesthetic sense of expatriate experience. His greatest literary achievement, the *Quartet* is at once the culmination of his imperial poetics and his own "portrait of an artist." It can also, of course, be read as colonial fiction, and certainly its assumptions concerning East-West relations and its representations of Arab Alexandria would seem to support such an interpretation. However, by attending to both to the structural role of Alexandria in the novel cycle and the stylistic characteristics of the work itself, it is possible to develop a more interesting reading of the ethics of expatriation than its debt to colonialism would suggest. This is important because, as I suggested earlier, the text does not "worry" over the status of expatriation.

Unlike expatriate narratives that begin with a departure and/or an arrival, the *Quartet* begins in medias res, allowing us no clue to Darley's background other than pointing up his autobiographical relation to Durrell himself: Darley's initials, "LD," and his Irishness (distinguishing him, in *Justine*, as "a mental refugee"). And, of course, the other principal male protagonists, Pursewarden and Mountolive, also embody aspects of Durrell's biographical trajectory: Mountolive is a colonial son from India whose father remained behind after mother and son "returned" to England, while Pursewarden is a celebrated novelist and adjunct of the British Foreign Office. Even the absent character, Jacob Arnauti, who is Justine's former husband, authors the prototype of the *Quartet* itself. His novel, *Moeurs*, is characterized as a diary,

> well written indeed, in the first person singular, . . . of Alexandrian life as seen by a foreigner in the middle thirties. The author of the diary is engaged on research for a novel he proposes to do—and the day to day account of his life in Alexandria is accurate and

penetrating; but what arrested me was the portrait of a young Jewess he meets and marries: takes to Europe: divorces.[42]

The decision, then, to call upon biography in order to read the *Quartet* as an imperial expatriate narrative is not wholly arbitrary. There is also its informing spirit. The difference between the imperial expatriate's self-understanding and sensibility as reflected in *The Alexandria Quartet* and that reflected in the other expatriate fictions considered here is arguably attributable, or partly so, to Durrell's identity as a subject of empire rather than of nation. And we need to attend to the fact that Darley is, from the start, unmoored, suggesting that expatriate experience will deliver him *to* rather than *from* himself.

In *Justine,* the first volume of the *Quartet,* the impoverished expatriate schoolmaster and artist-in-the-making, Darley, seeks to reconstruct his love affairs with both the cabaret dancer\prostitute Melissa, and the eponymous Alexandrian siren. He supplements his own narrative with fragments from *Moeurs* and the letters, diaries, and extended soliloquies of other characters. In *Balthazar,* the second volume, the same narrator is forced to submit to another interpretation of events. Balthazar's "interlinear" account of Darley's narrative exposes the supposed truth of the affair: that Justine was really in love with the novelist Pursewarden, and merely used Darley as a decoy to mislead Nessim, her husband. In the third volume, *Mountolive,* these narratives are revealed as screens for a plot of political intrigue, which is effectively confirmed in *Clea,* the fourth volume, which moves the *Quartet* forward in time and tells the story of Darley's love affair with fellow artist (and expatriate) Clea.

The first two volumes of the *Quartet* are lushly impressionistic, their texts often discontinuous, juxtaposing past and present, landscape, interior monologue, and elements of plot. *Mountolive,* a straightforward third-person narrative in the spirit of Graham Greene or George Orwell, concerns itself with the Coptic plot. In *Clea,* which records, through Darley, the impact of World War II on Alexandria, the aftermath of the Coptic plot, and the waning of British influence in Egypt, the extreme aestheticism and privacy of vision of *Justine* and *Balthazar* reassert themselves. Indeed, the very anomalousness of *Mountolive,* in terms of both form and content, throws into relief the degree to which the *Quartet,* as a whole, juxtaposes "realism" or "naturalism," which it associates with "popular" literature, and aesthetic truth.

What emerges is the sense that the political or civic is incompatible with the aesthetic. This comes out in other ways as well, for example, in Justine's transformation from femme fatale to grotesque when she disappears from Alexandria and reappears in Palestine. She is reputed to be working on a kibbutz, having achieved "a new and perfect happiness through 'community-service.'" Here is Clea's description.

> She has gone a good deal fatter in the face and has chopped off her hair carelessly at the back so that it sticks out in rats' tails. I gather that for the most part she wears it done up in a cloth. No trace remains of the old elegance or *chic*. Her features seem to have broadened, become more classically Jewish, lip and nose inclining more towards each other. . . . I noticed that those once finely-tended hands were calloused and tough. (*Justine*, 241–42)

Nessim's mother, Leila, the formerly beautiful lover of David Mountolive scarred by smallpox, undergoes an even more unwholesome alteration, and even Alexandria is similarly transformed as it begins to shed its colonial trappings. Finally, the romance of empire itself is undermined by a failure of the "idea," that Conradian principle upon which the entire imperial enterprise could be legitimately maintained.

The *Quartet*'s ethics of expatriation, then, have a great deal to do with the gestation of the artist. They are, moreover, enunciated in a different register of narrative production and evoke a different structure of feeling than do the other expatriate narratives we will consider. As I suggested earlier, this may be due, in part, to Durrell's own problematic relationship to Egypt. Egypt is not the chosen site, although, in fact, for David Mountolive, the eponymous hero of the *Quartet*'s third volume, Egypt is—or at least is believed to be—"the one true place." Far from being a place of enchantment, Egypt is like purgatory, a liminal place where he must wait out the war. Another distinction might be the way value itself is represented. If Lawrence and Bowles saw expatriation as, in some sense, a means of getting lost, they valued the periphery in terms of its capacity to facilitate this. In *The Alexandria Quartet*, value inheres in Alexandria's capacity to deliver the artist to himself. Alexandria is, on the one hand, an object of aesthetic contemplation and re-invention whose articulation is stylistically continuous with Conrad's "sensorium," or "the place of sheer color and intensity within the grayness of measurable extension and geometrical abstraction."[43] On the other, it is a marginal or colonial domain;

hence the ideal site for the work of the self that the *Quartet* enacts structurally: the imposition of an imperial poetics that is closely indexed to the subject's rebirth as artist. Just as colonialism manages its subjected territories and peoples, so Durrell manages their aestheticization. The *Quartet*'s thematic of epistemological uncertainty, "the fleeting image of truth in all its gruesome multiplicity" is resolved in favor of an artistic vision in which "poetic or transcendental knowledge somehow cancels out purely relative knowledge" (*Clea*, 127, 167). Indeed, Darley can discard his glasses when, no longer "blind as a mole," he can cease "digging about in the graveyard of relative fact piling up data, more information, and completely missing the mythopoeic reference which underlies fact" (167). In other words, he has accessed the Heraldic Universe. As Darley himself states:

> Our common actions in reality are simply the sackcloth covering which hides the cloth-of-gold—the meaning of the pattern. For us artists there waits the joyous compromise through art with all that wounded or defeated us in daily life; in this way, not to evade destiny, as the ordinary people try to do, but to fulfill it in its true potential— the imagination (*Justine*, 17).

The redemptive possibilities of literature, a belief "that the work of art has the authority to master the presumed raw material of experience in a manner that uniquely gives value to, perhaps even redeems, that material," is an important part of the heritage of modern literature, as well as being Darley's credo.[44]

If history appears to get short shrift in *The Alexandria Quartet*, this would appear to confirm Bersani's argument that the aestheticization of experience in its redemptive mode goes hand in hand with the devaluation of history. He writes: "The catastrophes of history matter much less if they are somehow compensated for in art, and art itself gets reduced to a kind of superior patching function, is enslaved to those very materials to which it presumably imparts value."[45] The *Quartet*'s version of historical becoming, the fanciful Coptic plot, is just such a devaluation. An early critic of Durrell, and a native Alexandrian to boot, writes that "no one before Durrell had thought of the grotesque notion of a Copt who thinks that the creation of Israel is a boon to Middle Eastern Christians. . . . The only thing that saves [the Coptic plot] from being insulting, my Coptic friends agree, is that it is too far away from reality to be worth fraying one's temper over."[46] Revealed, moreover, through the distorting lens of Orientalism, history itself is narrowly defined. Alexandria, under Islamic rule, is ahistorical, reduced to "a thousand years of silence and neglect."[47] As a palliative, we might contrast Ammiel Alcalay's more complicated view of Islamic history. In place of the reductionist view of Islam "as an all-embracing, pervasive, and conquering force subsuming everything in its vaguely imagined and frightening trail," Alcalay finds

> the very complex phenomenon of the old meeting the new, a process that was both characteristic and pervasive as Islam negotiated an identity with and through its new constituents. The ensuing synthesis and relations developing from that encounter are of utmost importance in any accurate assessment of life within Islamic society, particularly the lives of "minorities."[48]

Indeed, Alcalay illustrates the extent to which, on the one hand, Levantine cosmopolitanism and economic vitality thrived throughout the period of Arab and Islamic ascendency and, on the other, pan-Arabism is itself a response to Western imperialism.

When historicity, in the form of postcoloniality, does erupt into the political design of the Quartet, not to mention expatriate consciousness, its narrative assumes the "degraded" form of popular literature, the novel of espionage and political intrigue, *Mountolive* as opposed to the high literary aspirations of, say, *Justine*. Because of its omniscient narration, *Mountolive* is also the only book of the *Quartet* to speak in a kind of public voice, as opposed to the intensely personal and perspectival vision of the other books. Taken as a whole, then, the *Quartet* implicitly contrasts the failed endeavors of David Mountolive, the young and idealistic ambassador to Egypt, and Nessim Hosnani, the Coptic heir to a huge banking enterprise—characters whose dreams of action in the world are undone by political events they themselves have set in motion—with the successful artistic endeavor that need look no farther than the imagination. Durrell's Cyprus experience gave him an insider's view of the colonizer's political impotence in the face of a changing global ethic, confirming for him, perhaps, that true mastery could be realized only in another realm. The *Quartet*'s true hero, Darley, strives for a higher form of conquest, or the redemption of a degraded reality, in the Heraldic Universe.

In terms of the ethics of expatriation, the *Quartet* is full of anomalies. Its repudiation of the totalizing moral systems embodied by Islam and Christianity sits uneasily with its blatant Orientalisms. It is stridently anti-Arab at the same time it endorses a vibrant pan-

Levantine cosmopolitanism, a kind of narrowly construed culture of diversity. Durrell's imperial expatriate, astride two political moments, seems to find the limit of his "global" feeling in the face of the concrete Other. The Arab is either reduced to a stock figure, "one-eyed Hamid," or consigned to a social wilderness. We will see a similar strategy at work in Lawrence's *Aaron's Rod*, although in the latter, the meeting—or mismeeting—between the Englishman and the Italian is foregrounded. Durrell's figures do not, in the same way, cause the expatriate to reflect upon his own anomalousness. They do not practice Connolly's relational arts of the self.

How else does the relationship between the imperial expatriate and the margin inflect the fictional imagination? We might begin with the obvious: colonial or marginal domains, as I suggested earlier, offer enhanced social status and mobility, a way to recuperate the loss of colonial privilege. Edward Said distinguishes *Kim*, a colonialist text, from the works of other early modernist writers such as, for example, Flaubert, Zola, the later George Eliot, and James, whose works

> are essentially novels of disillusion and disenchantment. . . . Almost without exception the protagonist of the late-nineteenth-century novel is someone who has realized that his or her life's project—the wish to be great, rich, or distinguished—is mere fancy, illusion, dream; . . . the figure is a young man or woman bitterly awakened from a fancy dream of accomplishment, action, or glory, forced instead to come to terms with a reduced status, betrayed love, and a hideously bourgeois world, crass and philistine. This awakening is not to be found in *Kim*.[49]

And Said attributes the difference of *Kim* to the condition of its possibility: colonialism:

> How very different [the world of *Kim*] is from the lusterless world of the European bourgeoisie, whose ambiance as every novelist of importance renders it reconfirms the debasement of contemporary life, the extinction of all dreams of passion, success, and exotic adventure. Kipling's fiction offers an antithesis: his world, *because it is set in an India dominated by Britain, holds nothing back from the expatriate European. Kim* shows how a white Sahib can enjoy life in this lush complexity; and, I would argue, *the absence of resistance to European intervention in it*—symbolized by Kim's abilities to move relatively unscarred through India—is due to its *imperial vision*. For what one cannot accomplish in one's own Western environment—where trying to live out the grand dream of a successful quest means coming

up against one's own mediocrity and the world's corruption and degradation—one can do abroad. [My emphasis][50]

This is not to suggest that the period of high modernism that separates *Kim* from *Justine* does not itself affect the shape and preoccupations of fiction in ways that tend to complicate the applicability of Said's assertion, or that *The Alexandria Quartet*'s protagonist is immune to disillusionment and disenchantment. On the contrary, Darley's artistic coming of age is predicated upon his ability to embrace the degradation of his illusion and spin gold from the dross of disenchantment, to "redeem" experience. Nevertheless, his ability to move fluidly among the social and diplomatic elite of Alexandria, despite his being an impoverished teacher and would-be writer, is enhanced, if not enabled, by the imaginative possibilities associated with colonial life. At home, it's safe to say, he would be a Bloomsbury knockabout, à la the "pre-expatriate" Durrell.

One aspect of Darley's "quest" is the attainment of a sexually empowered masculinity, and he is able to do this by negotiating the carnivalesque eroticism that Alexandria represents. As Joseph Boone argues: "Engaging with libidinal fantasy through this mechanism of displacement, not coincidentally, frees Darley to emerge as mature novelist and successful lover at the end of the fourth volume."[51] He claims that the anxieties concerning masculine insufficiency reflected in *The Alexandria Quartet* are "intimately related to a crisis of authority in masculine and feminine self-fashioning in the postwar period" (361). Contributing to this crisis was the emerging sexual liberation movement, the fallout from which resulted in, among other things, a tension between an idealized domestic space in the suburbs and an intensification of sexual agency among both genders. Citing Linda Kaufman, Boone points to the "contradictory constructions of masculinity proliferating in the period and performed with a heightened intensity as both men and women jockeyed for position in a world striving to return . . . to 'normality' after the devastations of World War II and the separation of the sexes" (363). Durrell's Darley, he writes, "epitomizes the male fear of being 'unmanned,' rendered ineffectual and impotent, that accompanies men's sense, however imaginary, of women in charge—or, in the case of Justine and Darley, of women 'on top'" (364). For

> up to the final pages of the last volume, Darley remains a pitiably blocked writer, a deluded lover, and as a consequence of both, a

> confused sexual subject for whom issues of erotic perception,
> masculine subjectivity, and narrative authority are fatally linked.
> The result is a knot of sexual and textual anxieties that it takes, with
> no exaggeration, four volumes and nearly one thousand pages of
> writing to allay. (365)

Boone's project is to uncover the degree to which the text is threatened by the specter of homosexual desire, which it must struggle
to contain at all costs to project the conjoined image of heterosexual
virility and narrative authority. While Boone's hypothesis concerning the source of masculine anxiety makes sense, the question
of influence is a troubling one. The fact is, Durrell left England at the
age of twenty-one and never returned for any significant period of
time. Except in a highly mediated fashion, it seems unlikely that
the cultural climate of postwar Europe and the United States
would have extended as far as the eastern Mediterranean.

I believe the anxieties concerning masculine heterosexual sufficiency (and authorial competence) that underscore *The Alexandria
Quartet* can be better illuminated with reference to Kaja Silverman's
discussion of the ways in which historical trauma can erode belief
in the "dominant fiction." The dominant fiction, we recall, is a
fiction of unimpaired masculinity that places the paternal function
at the center of the symbolic and domestic bourgeois order. The
dominant fiction upholds this function "by fostering normative
desires and identifications" which, in turn, uphold the gendered
structure of power relations upon which patriarchy rests. The ideal
of masculine sufficiency, however, is under perpetual siege from
a variety of sources and is particularly vulnerable to historical
trauma, described as

> a historically precipitated but psychoanalytically specific disruption,
> with ramifications extending far beyond the individual psyche, . . .
> any historical event, whether socially engineered or of natural
> occurrence, which brings a large group of male subjects into such
> an intimate relation with lack that they are at least for the moment
> unable to sustain an imaginary relation with the phallus, and so
> withdraw their belief from the dominant fiction.[52]

Silverman identifies the period of World War II and its aftermath
as a time in which the "fiction" of masculine sufficiency can no
longer be maintained, and she points to a number of Hollywood
films, such as *The Lost Weekend* and *The Best Years of Our Lives,* that
reflect this "ideological fatigue." *The Alexandria Quartet* explores the

idea of masculine lack but in the end recuperates the dominant fiction precisely because, as Boone persuasively argues, such anxieties are displaced onto an Orientalist screen that empowers its Western subject. The structure of imperialism, in other words, masks the insufficiency at the heart of the dominant fiction itself.

Despite the flow of libidinal energy that permeates the *Quartet*'s unconscious and which it seeks to contain and redirect into normative channels, the quantity and variety of sexuality—or sexualities—greatly exceed the *quality* of eroticism. If we end with a catalogue of polymorphous sexual forms and predilections, we have little sense of erotic intensity except in the sense of its exotic coding. I would argue that the text is at its best not as a narrative of sexual adventure, but rather when it gives itself over to the charm of hybridity, the hybridity of the Alexandrians. Indeed, the colorful and evocative names of the Alexandrians, which, like a liturgy of diversity, are recited from time to time in the text, function not only as markers of its cosmopolitanism but as integral components of the sensorium effect:

> This was Alexandria, the unconsciously poetical mother-city exemplified in the names and faces which made up her history. Listen. Tony Umbada, Baldassaro Trivizani, Claude Amaril, Paul Capodistria, Dmitri Randidi, Onouphrios Papas, Count Banubula, Jacques de Guéry, Athena Trasha, Djamboulat Bey, Delphine de Francueil, General Cervoni, Ahmed Hassan Pacha, Pozzo di Borgo, Pierre Balbz, Gaston Phipps, Haddad Fahmy Amin, Mehmet Adm, Wilmot Pierrefeu, Toto de Brunel, Colonel Neguib, Dante Borromeo, Benedict Dangeau, Pia dei Tolomei, Gilda Ambron. . . . The poetry and history of commerce, the rhyme-schemes of the Levant which had swallowed Venice and Genoa.[53]

Even street names assume the status of incantation: "Rue Bab-el-Mandeb, Rue Abou-el-Dardar, Minet-el-Barrol (streets slippery with discarded fluff from the cotton marts) Nouzha (the rose-garden, some remembered kisses) or bus stops with haunted names like Saba Pacha, Mazloum, Zizinia Bacos, Schutz, Gianaclis (*Justine*, 63). In this environment Durrell's European expatriates travel fluidly and naturally, and it is against this vivid cosmopolitan palette that we must read Durrell's strenuous anti-Arabism and his aversion to the "burning airless spaces and . . . unrealized vastness—the grotesque granite monuments to dead Pharoahs, the tombs which became cities" of Arab Cairo—as opposed to European Alexandria (*Mountolive*, 145):

The city, inhabited by these memories of mine, moves not only backwards into our history, studded by the great names which mark every station of recorded time, but also back and forth in the living present, so to speak—among its contemporary faiths and races; the hundred little spheres which religion or lore creates and which cohere softly together like cells to form the great sprawling jellyfish which is Alexandria to-day. Joined in this fortuitous way by the city's own act of will . . . the communities still live and communicate—Turks with Jews, Arabs and Copts and Syrians with Armenians and Italians and Greeks. The shudders of monetary transactions ripple through them like wind in a wheatfield; ceremonies, marriages and pacts join and divide them. Even the place-names on the old tram-routes with their sandy grooves of rail echo the unforgotten names of their founders—and the names of the dead captains who first landed here, from Alexander to Amr; founders of this anarchy of flesh and fever, of money-love and mysticism. Where else on earth will you find such a mixture? (*Balthazar*, 151–52)

Durrell's "true" Alexandrians are, like him, expatriates, and they are oriented toward Europe:

The Alexandrians themselves were strangers and exiles to the Egypt which existed below the glittering surface of their dreams, ringed by the hot deserts and fanned by the bleakness of a faith which renounced worldly pleasure: the Egypt of rags and sores, of beauty and desperation. Alexandria was still Europe—the capital of Asiatic Europe, if such a thing could exist. (*Mountolive*, 130)

Politically, the text works to champion Alexandrian cosmopolitanism against Arab nationalism. Hence, Pursewarden's policy pronouncements regarding Arab "xenophobia" and the fate of the non-Arab communities in the postcolonial, post-European era:

Have I explained that one of the major characteristics of Egyptian nationalism is the gradually growing envy and hate of the "foreigners" —the half-million or so of non-Moslems here? And that the moment full Egyptian sovereignty was declared the Moslems started in to bully and expropriate them? The brains of Egypt, as you know, is its foreign community. The capital which flowed into the land while it was safe under our suzerainty, is now at the mercy of these paunchy pashas. The Armenians, Greeks, Copts, Jews—they are all feeling the sharpening edge of this hate; many are wisely leaving, but most cannot. . . . They are trying to save their industries, their lifework from the gradual encroachment of the pashas. (*Mountolive*, 93)

Durrell's non-Arab Alexandrians are seen as the direct descendants of the Ptolemies, the *rightful* heirs to modern Alexandria, "the Hellenistic capital of the bankers and cotton-visionaries," which was rescued by "all those European bagmen whose enterprise had reignited and ratified Alexander's dream of conquest after the centuries of dust and silence which Amr had imposed upon it" (*Clea*, 27). And it's interesting to take note of a number of present-day accounts of Cairo and Alexandria during the period about which Durrell writes. In his memoir *Out of Egypt*, André Aciman writes about growing up Jewish in cosmopolitan Alexandria. In large part, his account supports Durrell's representation of the city's ethnic and political scene. What accounts for Arab xenophobia, however, is an incident that postdates the period of time represented in the *Quartet* and Durrell's residence in Egypt, namely, the 1956 invasion of Suez by British, French, and Israeli troops. Aciman's family was strongly identified with the Europeans; contacts with Arabs seemed to be limited to servants. His uncle is heard to retort at one point: "Just wait for this war to be over, and we'll show these savages. I've suffered their nationalistic claptrap long enough" (164). A more ambivalent, more complicated response to the destruction of cosmopolitan Alexandria comes from Leila Ahmed, whose memoir *A Border Passage* reflects her postcolonial sensibilities, even as her family, part of the intellectual and professional elite of Egypt, deeply admired European culture and suffered greatly at the hands of Nasser. In Ahmed's home, Arabic, French, and English were spoken. Where Aciman's family hired Arabs as servants, Ahmed's family employs a European Christian as her nanny. Her memoir, moreover, attests to the historic cosmopolitanism of Egypt itself and weighs both the positive and negative aspects of becoming "Arab" in the wake of the Egyptian revolution. Durrell's Levantine cosmopolitanism, by contrast, is far more showy, but far shallower.

One way to approach Durrell's rendering of Alexandria and expatriate experience might be to attend more to the formal qualities of his prose. Fredric Jameson's discussion of Joseph Conrad suggests that a comparison between Conrad and Durrell might yield interesting results. While I do not attempt to offer either a "Jamesonian" or a Marxist reading of Durrell, I would like to build upon one of Jameson's insights—the idea of sensorium—to explore the ethics of expatriation that emerge from the conjunction of form and content. Jameson argues that the sensorium is, in effect, a by-product of the rationalizing forces of capitalism:

The very activity of sense perception has nowhere to go in a world in which science deals with ideal quantities, and comes to have little enough exchange value in a money economy dominated by considerations of calculation, measurement, profit, and the like. This unused surplus capacity of sense perception can only reorganize itself into a new and semi-autonomous activity, one which produces its own specific objects, new objects that are themselves the result of a process of abstraction and reificiation, such that older concrete unities are now sundered into measurable dimensions on one side, say, and pure color (or the experience of purely abstract color) on the other.[54]

Just as the sea in Conrad mediates between the worlds of work and nonwork, his stylistic practice mediates between aesthetic reality and "the organization and existence of daily life during the imperialist heyday of industrial capitalism" (226). The sensorium, as I noted earlier, is an aestheticizing strategy that "for whatever reason seeks to recode or rewrite the world and its own data in terms of perception as a semi-autonomous activity" (230). Not quite sheer textuality, but the accretion of adjective upon adjective, image upon image, a proliferation of language that straddles the border of the real and the imaginary, the sensorium represents both antidote to and utopian compensation for the processes of rationalization under capitalism. And it can be disruptive. Referring to Conrad's *Typhoon*, for example, Jameson writes:

In that stealthy struggle between ideology and representation, each secretly trying to use and appropriate the other for its own designs and purposes, the ideological allegory of the ship as the civilized world on its way to doom is subverted by the unfamiliar sensorium, which, like some new planet in the night sky, suggests senses and forms of libidinal gratification as unimaginable to us as the possession of additional senses, or the presence of nonearthly colors in the spectrum. (231)

Putting together Jameson and Bataille, we might say that the sensorium undermines and subverts the instrumentality of discourse insofar as discourse is itself implicated in "project." This cuts both ways. The sensorium is at once a compensatory diversion and a kind of scrambler of signals. Libidinal energy, as Boone has shown, is notoriously hard to canalize. And so the moment of postcoloniality, or what Roger Bowen describes as "the tension between a European 'possession' of the Middle East, its 'version' of the Orient, and the winds of change which will in time dispossess the European," is at once dramatized and derealized.[55]

One thing that gets recoded is landscape. This has significant implications, since Durrell believes that "human beings are expressions of their landscape." Messing with the landscape, he plays God, so to speak. That is the poet(h)ics of the Heraldic Universe. Against the grayness and boredom of a remembered England *and* the aesthetic shortcomings of Alexandria itself (Durrell, as I noted earlier, was no fan of Egypt), Durrell asserts his own domain, the sensorium, the place of the "archaic and of sensation."[56] The Durrellean sensorium might also represent an attempt to recuperate some sense of India, that long lost but never forgotten domain of childhood. In Durrell's first novel, *Pied Piper of Lovers*, he records the protagonist's first impressions of London. The son of an Anglo-Indian engineer, he has just left India and arrived in England, where he is to pursue his education.

> They were bundled into a taxi which jerked its unsteady way out of the station in the direction of Russell Square, while the two of them sat back on the seat like frightened children and gazed out disappointedly upon the slushy streets. The air was heavy and poisoned, a kind of dust-fog that was irritating to the throat and the nose. Hyde Park, of which they had read so much, turned out to be, on first sight, a foggy sector of threadbare grass, fringed by a line of damp green chairs. (180–81)

This shabby, down-at-heel quality applies as well to the "real" Alexandria. In a letter to Henry Miller, Durrell refers to it as a "smashed up broken down shabby Neopolitan town, with its Levantine mounds of houses peeling in the sun."[57] In *The Alexandria Quartet*, however, the essence of the city is transformed:

> Light filtered through the essence of lemons. An air full of brick-dust—sweet-smelling brick-dust and the odour of hot pavements slaked with water. Light damp clouds, earth-bound, yet seldom bringing rain. Upon this squirt dust-red, dust-green, chalk-mauve and watered crimson-lake. In summer the sea-damp lightly varnished the air. (*Justine*, 14).

If Durrell's aestheticism seems, in the abstract, redundant—Alexandria is *already*, or should be, according to Orientalist discourse, a sensorium—Durrell's Alexandria is not the Orient, or not entirely so, at any rate, as we will soon see. And we can better understand how Alexandria functions by going back to Jameson. In Conrad, he asserts, the sea is "the privileged place of the strategy of containment." Strategies of containment can be understood as intellectual or formal frames that ideology or narrative constructs to suppress contradiction and maintain the appearance of totality. In *Lord Jim,* the sea functions as both

> a strategy of containment and a place of real business: it is a border and a decorative limit, but it is also a highway, out of the world and in it at once, the repression of work—on the order of the classic English novel of the country-house weekend, in which human relations can be presented in all their ideal formal purity precisely because concrete content is relegated to the rest of the week—as well as the absent work-place itself.[58]

With its dual sense of absence and presence (the absence of work and the presence of the absent workplace), the sea mediates between "here" and "elsewhere." Durrell's Alexandria is another such place. What is repressed, however, is not so much the world of production as the deforming mediocrities of bourgeois life itself, the world of production *and* reproduction, and as Kaja Silverman might argue, the tenuous nature of the dominant fiction (paradoxically, the very edifice upon which bourgeois culture rests). Affording the *Quartet's* expatriate hero, Darley, a range of subject positions unavailable to him in England, Alexandria functions as a space of infinite possibility—and mastery. This, as Said has argued, is what distinguishes the colonial novel from the domestic one. Hence, we see Darley enacting his role as lover of not only the Alexandrian siren Justine, but also the fragile and generous dancer and sometime prostitute Melissa, and the—also beautiful—talented painter Clea. We see him embraced by Nessim, the "prince" of Alexandria and heir to an immense fortune. We watch as he is inducted into "the great game," Alexandria-style, and trades literary barbs with his spiritual sibling, the renowned author Ludwig Pursewarden. It is a world, to borrow Said's phrase, that "holds nothing back" from its Western protagonist. Alexandria is the space where he can be dirt-poor and yet fulfill his dream or destiny or perform the work of the self without attending to the social and economic limitations—and the degradations and insecurities—of the "real" world.

If, in addition, Alexandria functions as the "country-house" retreat where human relations "can be presented in all their formal purity" (Durrell called *The Alexandria Quartet* "an investigation of modern love"), it is itself the domain of exclusions, repressions, and projections, the domain against which the "sovereign self of Europe" has come to define itself.[59] The *Quartet's* Darley would be the embodiment of such a self. More importantly, Alexandria is an imperial space; so, far from being a signifier of "elsewhere," it is itself part of the earthly booty upon which the edifice of capitalism was constructed and is maintained. Yet Durrell's Alexandria is a strangely hybrid space that resists its location in Africa even as that location is itself the condition of the novel's possibility. At once the repudiation and antithesis of Orientalism, Alexandria *is* Europe in Africa. Indeed, Durrell draws his sustenance from its very European-ness, shunning the more patently "Other" realm to which Bowles, for one, was drawn. More to the point, however, it provides a mirror image of the neurotic, self-obsessed community of English hotel dwellers that Durrell depicts in his earlier novel *The Black Book.* And because of this—because of Alexandria's identity with, as opposed to difference from, home—the idea of sensorium, at first so paradoxical, becomes more readily understood.

At the same time, the sensorium represents a way to distinguish Alexandria from the West. Jameson's sensorium not only is the place of sensation, but also is associated with the "archaic," which includes, along with the senses, "certain types of thinking," devalued forms of knowledge: gnosticism, alchemy, and hermeticism, for example, which figure prominently in the *Quartet.*[60] We might include sexual knowledge as well, eroticism being yet another fugitive from rationalization, as Jane Bennett, citing Max Weber, points out.[61] Such "waste products" of capitalist rationalization resemble that which Foucault has characterized as "subjugated knowledges; or "a whole set of knowledges that have been disqualified as inadequate to their task or insufficiently elaborated: naive knowledges, located low down on the hierarchy, beneath the required level of cognition or scientificity" whose reemergence he sees as enabling the act of criticism itself.[62] To the extent, then, that *The Alexandria Quartet* constitutes a spiritual as well as an aesthetic project, Alexandria might represent, through its ruins and its history, its "porosity," a locus of potentially counterhegemonic energies. For the Frankfurt school—and for Lawrence, as we will see— porosity was associated with premodern forms of production and social relations; for Durrell, on the other hand, the association is enabling from the perspective of suprahuman forms of knowledge acquisition. While Durrell does position himself in opposition to Judeo-Christian metaphysics, such subjugated knowledges also serve to shore up his own totalizing aesthetic system. Even here, Durrell's sensorium works to repress the voice of alterity and to reinforce the artist's own subjectivity. For obvious reasons, the archaic discourses he privileges—gnosticism, hermeticism, alchemy —all share affinities and are continuous with the imperial modes of thought that dominate his conceptual theme.[63] He is the supreme knower, the supreme interpreter, the artist-god. As for eroticism, we have seen the extent to which its errant forces have been domesticated.

Alexandria is then both a structural and stylistic matrix for Durrell's ethics of expatriation. At the same time, however, ideology, aesthetic production, and politics come together in the character of Pursewarden, the hinge between the aesthetic and the political, the private and the public, the artist and the civil servant. It is no coincidence, therefore, that it is Pursewarden's suicide (the cause of which remains, however, undecidable) that precipitates the *Quartet*'s denouement: the thwarting of the Coptic plot and the entry of Egypt into its own historical narrative, dispersing most of the major European characters. A notable exception is, of course, the transvestite merchant seaman and local "bimbashi," Scobie, who is beaten to death by a sailor and enshrined as a local saint in the back streets of Alexandria where he resided, the only Western character to have become integrated into the local life of the "popular" quarters. To the extent that Pursewarden's plot may be read as a fictional refraction of Durrell's Cypriot experience, his legacy to Darley is the sure knowledge that art and politics are a fatal mix, and that Alexandria, far from representing "elsewhere," is a strategic hub, an imperial disaster in the making. It is only when Darley leaves Alexandria, then, that the magic words "Once upon a time" may be uttered.

If the Alexandrian artist par excellence, Constantine Cavafy, or "the old poet," as he is called, haunts the pages of Durrell's text, there is the sense that his great poem, "The City," which is cited early on, provides a blueprint for the claustrophobia and anguish of the *Quartet*'s central characters which, the text argues, are really effects of Alexandria itself. The characters are "lived by," rather than living in, the city. The poem is itself an eloquent argument *against* expatriation. Here is "Darley's" own translation, which is included among the "Consequential Data" following the conclusion of *Justine*:

> You tell yourself: I'll be gone
> To some other land, some other sea,
> To a city lovelier far than this
> Could ever have been or hoped to be—

Where every step now tightens the noose:
A heart in a body buried and out of use:
How long, how long must I be here
Confined among these dreary purlieus
Of the common mind? Wherever now I look
Black ruins of my life rise into view.
So many years have I been here
Spending and squandering, and nothing gained.
There's no new land, my friend, no
New sea; for the city will follow you,
In the same streets you'll wander endlessly,
The same mental suburbs slip from youth to age,
In the same house go white at last—
The city is a cage,
No other places, always this
Your earthly landfall, and no ship exists
To take you from yourself. Ah! don't you see
Just as you've ruined your life in this
One plot of ground you're ruined its worth
Everywhere now—over the whole earth?

As the home of the homeless—"Armenian, Greek, Amharic, Moroccan Arabic; Jews from Asia Minor, Pontus, Georgia: mothers born in Geek settlements on the Black Sea; communities cut down like the branches of trees, lacking a parent body, dreaming of Eden"— Durrell's Alexandria is the place of last resort (*Justine*, 62). If the expatriate dream resides in the existence of new lands, lovelier cities, the possibility of making or remaking oneself, Cavafy tells us to forget about it. And yet the *Quartet* is authored by the one who leaves, the one who exists in Alexandria by virtue of his flight from somewhere else, the one whose "ascesis," moreover, consists in negotiating the labyrinth of "Alexandrian" eroticism, whose insular sterility Cavafy's poem evokes.

Death and eros pervade *The Alexandria Quartet*, lending its eroticism just such a quality: that of an ascesis rather than a release. Its lovers, depicted as exemplars of a dying city, perform their rites in an erotic domain that Bataille would hardly recognize. Though *The Alexandria Quartet* is fairly steeped in sexual variety, and the character around which the narrative is wrapped, Justine, is represented to be a nymphomaniac, eroticism provides no relief from the tyranny of the self. Durrell's lovers are mental captives of one another, caught in the play of mirrors and the airless chambers of philosophy, discourse, and paradox. The *Quartet*'s eroticism may be anguished but it is seldom dangerous. If eroticism for Bataille means "assenting to life to the point of death," there is the sense that in *The Alexandria Quartet*, it means assenting to death to the point where life has been emptied of all capacity to reproduce itself. Eroticism is the ascesis of self-knowledge, and yet, as creatures of landscape, its lovers are such that self-knowledge is perpetually denied them. It is their fate not to know themselves, caught as they are in the double bind of history and landscape. All except Darley, that is, who emerges from "the City" heart-whole and intact. No one else is that lucky; everyone else is sacrificed, or maimed, in the parturition that is the artist's birth. Indeed, if Justine is "somebody who might well destroy herself in an excess of wrong-headed courage and forfeit the happiness which she, in common with all the rest of us, desired and lived only to achieve," Darley must be seen as the survivor (*Justine*, 73). If he has, in a sense, been chewed up and swallowed by expatriate experience, he has, nonetheless, been regurgitated.

More than any of the other expatriate narratives we will examine, *The Alexandria Quartet* approaches the contours of romance. It is restorative, or as Leo Bersani might say, redemptive, insofar as it places its faith in the corrective powers of art. It is, therefore, on the side of Good, where, as in Bataille, the good is aligned with survival and against intensity. "Humanity," he writes, "pursues two goals—one, the negative, is to preserve life (to avoid death), and the other, the positive, is to increase the intensity of life."[64] Despite its "scandalous"nature, its invocation of de Sade, its dandling of nymphomania, transvestism, "inversion," incest, and the sexual allure of deformity, the *Quartet* finds itself on the far side of those excesses that, in Bataille, strive toward the extreme limit of the possible. That intensity is one we will see in other expatriate narratives; it is one which requires its protagonists to pursue such intensity blindly and heroically. The Good, to the contrary, "limits the instinct which induces us to seek a value, whereas liberty towards Evil gives access to the excessive forms of value. . . . The very principle of value wants us to go 'as far as possible.' "[65] In other expatriate narratives, eroticism has, before all else, called its subjects to the brink, opening out into something unbearably foreign, something that coincides with the alterity of expatriate experience itself. Eroticism for Durrell is an exercise of the intellect, a means of comprehending and reducing the whole of existence to interiority. Quite simply, there is no outside. There may be anguish, there may be wisdom, but there is no putting oneself into question. That is where Durrell, as a writer of expatriate experience, parts company with Lawrence and Bowles. If their expatriate narratives bear witness to the need for some kind of outsideness, for Durrell the idea of an outside represents, on the contrary, something around which he can wrap himself.

It's important to note, finally, that *The Alexandria Quartet* begins with a double displacement. We first meet Darley on a remote Greek island, Durrell's utopian vision of economic expatriate existence, where he has come to heal himself from the failed love affair with Justine and to commit the experience to textual form. He is thus displaced not only from "home," wherever that particular metropolitan space may be located, but from Alexandria as well. The end of the *Quartet* finds Darley back on that island at the conclusion of the war, where he is helping to build a relay station that will also mark the island's entry into the modern world. He is, in other words, helping to destroy his own aesthetic birthing ground. The economic expatriate, it must be remembered, defines himself by his lack of moral responsibility for his adopted home, *despite* being fully cognizant of the consequences of his acts. Darley writes to Clea:

> We have imported money, and with it are slowly altering the economy of the place, displacing labour at inflated prices, creating all sorts of new needs of which the lucky inhabitants were not conscious before. Needs which in the last analysis will destroy the tightly woven fabric of this feudal village with its tense blood-relationships, its feuds and archaic festivals. Its wholeness will dissolve under these alien pressures. . . . We are picking it apart like idle boys, unaware of the damage we inflict. It seems inescapable the death we bring to the old order without wishing it. . . . In ten years it will be an unrecognizable jumble of warehouses, dance-halls and brothels for merchant sailors. (*Clea*, 265–66)

And so Durrell/Darley, his "stock as an artist" on the rise, abandons the imaginative geographies of the periphery, the one having become too politically resistant to his imperial poetics, the other falling victim to imperial designs of a different nature. Darley sets his sights on southern Europe. Durrell, cured forever of his "islomania" by the Cypress experience, completed the *Quartet* in the south of France, where he lived for the rest of his rather long life. But that is another narrative . . .

3

Italy's Best Gift:
D. H. Lawrence in the Mediterranean

Of D. H. Lawrence, Aldous Huxley writes,

> It was, I think, the sense of being cut off that sent Lawrence on his
> restless wanderings round the earth. His travels were at once a flight
> and a search: a search for some society with which he could establish
> contact, for a world where the times were not personal and conscious
> knowing had not yet perverted living; a search and at the same time a
> flight from the miseries and evils of the society into which he had
> been born, and for which, in spite of his artist's detachment, he
> could not help feeling profoundly responsible.[1]

For all these reasons, Lawrence is an important spiritual ancestor
of both Lawrence Durrell and Paul Bowles. He is the earliest, but
he is by no means the least self-reflective, and in his attempt to illuminate some more profound dimension of human experience he
is more deeply philosophical than either of the others and more
prophetical. Lawrence's intuitive grasp of the ineffable—though
not insensate—areas of being that are inimical to reason flows
from a quality Huxley characterizes as an intense awareness "of the
mystery of the world. . . . Lawrence could never forget, as most of
us almost continuously forget, the dark presence of the otherness
that lies beyond the boundaries of man's conscious mind."[2] On the
other hand, "the dark presence" of otherness seems inseparable,
at times, from the alterity of the periphery, the material space of
the racial, ethnic, or cultural Other that so attracted and sometimes repelled him. Italy provided him a landscape and a culture
that straddled the antique and the modern, a vortex of conflicting
energies and temporal juxtapositions in which to experiment. In
his "Italian" novels, *Aaron's Rod, The Lost Girl,* and *Mr. Noon,* the
search for the good life leads the protagonists away from home to
a place that is at once the familiar South of the Romantic imagination, whose plenitude is full of promise and grace, and the site
of impossible self-alienation and impoverishment. A plural and

ambiguously constructed ethics of expatriation emerges from a reading of these texts that belies any uncomplicated set of assumptions regarding expatriate privilege and self-fashioning.

Nietzsche provides us with two figures that more fully attest to the rigors of Lawrence's expatriate ethos: the tightrope walker of *Thus Spoke Zarathustra*, who makes danger his vocation, "who [does] not know how to live, except by going under" (127), and the "philosophers of the future." Of the latter he writes:

> By the name with which I ventured to christen them, I expressly emphasized their experimentation and their delight in experimentation. Did I do this because, as critics in body and soul, they will love to make use of experimentation in a new, perhaps wider, perhaps more dangerous sense? In their passion for new insight, must they go farther in bold and painful experiments than the emasculate and morbid taste of a democratic century can approve? . . . In fact, among themselves they will admit to a certain pleasure in saying "no," in dissecting, and in a certain circumspect cruelty which knows how to handle the knife surely and delicately, even when the heart is bleeding.[3]

Their self-inflicted "dissections" and "cruelties," practices of self-transformation that are performed on the far side of human sociality and community, represent an ethics of becoming at odds with other-directed forms of ethical practice and bourgeois complacencies. Their refrain, "We must go away, out there, where *you* today are least at home!" evokes this space of risk and reward, its metaphorical distance from home, and the essential difference between the one who leaves and the one who stays home (136, Nietzsche's emphasis). "Today," Nietzsche writes,

> when in Europe the herd-animal alone is honored and alone doles out the honors, when "equality of rights" could all too easily turn into equality of wrong-doings—by which I mean the joint war on everything rare, strange, privileged, . . . today the concept of greatness must embrace the spirit who is distinguished, who wants to be himself, who can be different, who can stand alone, and who must live by his own resources. (137)

Indeed, as Nietzsche writes, such a philosopher "reveals something of his own ideal when he legislates that 'The greatest shall be the one most capable of solitude, the most hidden, the most deviative'" (137). As such, he embodies the very refutation of what Charles Taylor calls the "affirmation of ordinary life," modernity's culturally dominant principle of the good life, which privileges the life of production and reproduction, of work and family, over all other life ways, marking a paradigmatic shift from classical Aristotelian ethics.[4] The Nietzschean model of an ethical self-overcoming that is at once a self-squandering positions the subject at the margins of the familiar, the safe, and the companionable. The self's own creative destruction is the very model of modernity's cultural dynamic so brilliantly illuminated by Marshall Berman. Yet this quintessentially modern figure eschews the metropolis and its often unacknowledged contradictions—flux versus stability, innovation versus convention, individualism versus homogeneity—often to find that such contradictions are not left behind in the West.

The space of endeavor, the utopian "place" on the margins is, in the Lawrence we will be looking at here, the fully embodied geographical domain of Italy. Even so, we can see the Italian novels as an exploration of radical forms of experience that owe little to the holistic notions of authenticity and presence that inform modernist cartographies. In *Beyond Good and Evil* Nietzsche writes,

> The past of every form and mode of life, of cultures that formerly clashed—horizontally or vertically—is flowing into our "modern souls" thanks to [the democratic upheaval of castes and races]. Our instincts now can run back in all kinds of directions; we ourselves are a kind of chaos. . . . Through our half-barbarian bodies and desires we have all sorts of secret entry into places that were closed to any distinguished epoch, above all into the labyrinths of unfinished cultures, and of all the half-barbarisms that ever existed on earth. (147–48)

Nietzsche's "going under" represents an embrace of cultural energies that are open-ended, uncontained, and ungrounded. His "half-barbarian bodies and desires" are sentient and alive, open to unimaginable risks: the terrors—and rewards—of the abyss, the freedom of self-invention. Nietzsche's voracious appetite for multiplicity grows out of modernity itself, out of conditions particular to the metropolitan West at a particular historical juncture, and they are forward and backward looking at the same time. Here modernity has transformed the world into a domain of radical simultaneity, heterogeneity, and incompletion. The margins, as a consequence, often retain their productive charge only in proportion to the subject's exteriority to the Other's world, which can be perceived as static and narrowly drawn.

If the act of expatriation represents the subject's repudiation of the bonds of family, society, culture, nation, civilization—which I will refer to collectively as "home"—the desire for expatriation would appear to take root in a fissure wrought by the play, or a finely-tuned consciousness of the play, between fixed social forms and the complexity of lived existence. No doubt such tensions have always existed, but in modernity the disparities between received interpretations, which tend toward stability, and the more open-ended presence of lived existence are severe and unforgiving. Nietzsche's great gift to modernity was to loosen the hold of received interpretations through an affirmation of their contingency. He reveled in the multiplicities, the heterodoxies, that modernity offered to those heroic figures capable of facing the "chaos" joyfully and creatively, and Lawrence seems to tap into the same blend of atavistic and radically future-oriented energies that enable Nietzsche's project of self-overcoming. For Lawrence, the awareness of ontological and cultural contingency is linked to and continuous with the flight from home and the view from elsewhere.

An extended revery here by the eponymous hero of *Mr. Noon* illustrates this tension from across the border of an imaginative geography:

> For the first time he saw England from the outside: tiny she seemed, and *tight*, and *so partial.* Such a little bit among all the vast rest. Whereas till now she had seemed all-in-all in herself. Now he knew it was not so. Her all-in-allness was a *delusion* of her natives. Her marvellous truths and standards and ideals were just local, not universal. They were just a piece of local pattern, in what was really a vast, complicated far-reaching design. . . . And he became *unEnglished.* His tight and exclusive nationality seemed to break down in his heart. He loved the world in its multiplicity, not in its *horrible oneness,* uniformity, homogeneity. He loved the *rich* and free variegation of Europe, the manyness. His old obtuseness, which saw everything alike, in one term, fell from his eyes and from his soul, and he felt *rich.* There were so many, many lands and peoples besides himself and his own land. And all were *magically different,* and it was so nice to be one among many, to feel the *horrible imprisoning oneness* and insularity collapsed, a real *delusion* broken, and to know that the universal ideals and morals were after all only local and temporal. . . . He seemed to feel a new salt running vital in his veins, a new, *free* vibration in all his nerves, like a bird that has got out of a cage, and even out of the room wherein the cage hung. (134–35, my emphasis)

Of course, the suggestion of a "vast, complicated far-reaching design" is hardly compatible with the idea of contingency. If "universal ideals and morals" are merely "local and temporal," however, one's ability to generalize about the whole from one's own privileged position is undercut. Moreover, the spirit of the text, its passion for the magically different, the richness of diversity, and the freedom from received interpretations—conceived here as "delusional"—as against the "horrible imprisoning oneness" of the alleged universal, is one in which contingency, rather than design, would appear to reign. Its mood is one of enchantment, a mood, Bennett writes,

> provoked by a surprise, by an encounter with something that one did not expect. Surprise itself includes both a pleasant, charming feeling and a slightly off-putting sense of having been disrupted or tripped (up). In enchantment, these two are present in just the right measures so as to combine, fortuitously, in a way that engenders an energizing feeling of fullness or plenitude—a momentary return to childhood joie de vivre. Enchantment begins with the step-back immobilization of surprise but ends up with a mobilizing rush as if an electric charge had coursed through space to you. In enchantment, a new circuit of intensities forms between material bodies.[5]

And enchantment is a good beginning for a narrative of expatriation; the mood of enchantment, under the most felicitous circumstances, is an opening out, a predisposition to ethical generosity.

For the Lawrentian expatriate the exhilaration of arrival hurtles the subject out into the Nietzschean flux and away from the invariably "tight and partial" dimensions of home, which are, which must be, arbitrary and disciplinary. *Aaron's Rod* and *The Lost Girl*, like *Mr. Noon*, pay particular attention to the initial voyage out: the moment when England loses pride of place as the embodiment of Truth.

Being *unEnglished* opens up a space of potentialities, a condition of freedom that subordinates the conscious needs and desires of the subject to those of "the deepest self." Lawrence writes:

> Men are not free when they are doing just what they like. The moment you can do just what you like, there is nothing you care about doing. Men are only free when they are doing what the deepest self likes. And there is getting down to the deepest self! It takes some diving. Because the deepest self is way down, and the conscious self is an obstinate monkey. But of one thing we may be sure. If one wants to be free, one has to give up the illusion of doing what one likes, and seek what IT wishes done. But before you can do what IT likes, you must first break the spell of the old mastery, the old IT."[6]

The deepest self of which Lawrence speaks is a figure that joins the language of psychoanalysis to that of Romanticism. The text is fairly explicit in its evocation of the decentered self, the sense that where consciousness resides, the "real"self does not. The deepest self is a sign both of instinctual drives and uncoded desires *and* of authenticity. If consciousness, the "old mastery," is an ideological construct that speaks the language of bourgeois individualism, then perhaps the deepest self is a more fundamental self that is, in the Romantic sense, a more harmonious blend of instinct and culture. If, on the other hand, the old mastery is a more fundamental ordering or coding of the drives and flows, the deepest self will have no such integrity. The singularity of the term and its intentionality are evidence of a persisting ambivalence toward the status of the self in Lawrence's expatriate writings. I will have occasion to distinguish the deepest self with its essentialist trappings from a self that perpetually remakes itself to make the more "postmodern" Lawrence audible. That is a Lawrence for whom every "IT" casts a spell to be overcome, for whom freedom is precisely the condition of perpetual becoming. There is also a deepest self that is not a self at all, but rather an embodiment of drives that are not uncoded, exactly, but partly so. In either case, expatriation is one means of confounding the obstinate monkey, of breaking the spell of the old mastery.

The Lawrentian ethics of expatriation unfold in a conflicting set of idealized narratives and narrativized desires that move Lawrence's protagonists, on the one hand, toward the one true place and the one true way of being and, on the other, toward nomadism and rhizomatic modes of thought and being. The figures of the migrant and the nomad that Deleuze and Guattari use as exemplars will be useful here in adding a spatial dimension to the differing modes of self-constitution that can be thought of, respectively, as self-invention and self-discovery, or in Nietzschean terms, self-overcoming and the will to truth. The migrant is characterized by flight and reterritorialization, while the nomad "can be called the Deterritorialized par excellence . . . precisely because there is no reterritorialization *afterward* as with the migrant, or upon *something else* as with the sedentary."[7] Lawrentian protagonists also experiment with a variety of ethical orientations: an atavistic ethics that seeks value in the primitive; an ethics of "self-exoticism," a term meant to signify "both a mimetic mode of identification with the exotic Other (i.e. 'thou art that') and a differential or negative mode of identification (i.e. 'I am not the Other'—the Other being the 'not-I')";[8] an ethics of eroticism or an eroticized submission that invests certain geographies with a disabling and seductive power; and an ethics of self-dismantling that mimes the "oceanic" merging of subject and universe. These modes of expatriate experience are then sharply interrogated, complicating rather than affirming the solutions they pose to the problem of the self in modernity; failure—or qualified failure—rather than success, tends to characterize the outcome. Fictional and autobiographical explorations of expatriation that begin on a note of wonder, therefore, become more like studies in disenchantment. The ethics of expatriation, relentlessly focused on the self and a dynamic set of relations between self and world, self and other, self and self, are represented through an exploratory, conditional set of operations.

Lawrence's far-flung travels represent both a temporal quest back to a time before consciousness detached itself from the life-world and a spatial exploration of borderlands where the old and the new, the primitive and the modern, bled into one another —places whose incompletion suggested not only a wished-for porosity between subject and object, light and dark, consciousness and chaos, but also a space for invention and metaphoric play that, at its most extreme, is radically isolating and resistant to the pull of "situatedness-in-displacement."[9] The voyage out is a journey undertaken both in the spirit of weightlessness and in the deep desire for connections forged in a different register of social and individual being-in-the-world. In "The Spirit of Place," Lawrence provides some insight into the painful nature of his own Nietzschean struggles. In attempting to read the American classics in terms of the "novelty" of American experience, he characterizes new experiences in terms of displacement and pain. A new experience, he writes, "displaces so many" old ones and "hurts horribly" (11); the "different feeling" invoked by the old American classics, moreover, results from a "shifting over from the old psyche to something new, a displacement. And displacements hurt. . . . It is a cut, too. Cutting away the old emotions and consciousness. Don't ask what is left" (12).

The unspeakable remainder, as I suggested in Chapter Two, is at the heart of expatriate self-making and unmaking, and I will argue here that it bespeaks a gendered form of anxiety concerning the status of the masculine subject. We saw the extent to which fear of masculine insufficiency permeated *The Alexandria Quartet.* Lawrence's *Aaron's Rod* and *The Lost Girl* are no less haunted by such anxieties, and this even, in the case of *The Lost Girl,* where the protagonist is female. Lawrence's narratives differ from Durrell's, however, in their refusal to recuperate a sense of the efficacy of the dominant fiction. Kaja Silverman's argument concerning the vulnerability of the dominant fiction to historical trauma speaks to all these texts equally. War is the paradigmatic case, and for Lawrence, of course, World War I was the great historical trauma. Indeed, it is difficult to overstate that war's impact on an entire generation. In both *Aaron's Rod* and *The Lost Girl,* the war sends characters across imaginative geographies—or prevents them from moving— in ways that are crucial to the narrative design. But war is not the only type of historical trauma. Silverman and Elaine Showalter make reference to another "crisis" in male subjectivity that arose in fin-de-siècle England as a result, in significant part, of the emergence of the New Woman. The figure of the New Woman is important as a marker not only of changing relations between the genders, but also of categorical instability within the genders, for the male no less than the female, throwing gender identity into flux.

What interests Silverman, however, is not merely the expression of anxiety that flows from such crises, but the representation of masculinities that do not "measure up." She argues that "even in the most normative of subjective instances the psyche remains in excess of [the oedipal] complex, and that in other cases desire and identification may actually function as mechanisms for circumventing or even repudiating the dominant fiction."[10] At times of historical trauma, however, the fissure between lived experience and the social ideal allows other masculinities to emerge more readily. Silverman takes as her object of investigation those masculinities that acknowledge and even embrace the "feminine" attributes of castration, alterity, and specularity, precisely those elements that conventional masculinity must deny.[11] *Aaron's Rod* and *The Lost Girl* are also texts that probe masculine identity. The ethics of expatriation they articulate seem to me intimately related to a profound sense of masculine insufficiency, and the expatriate ascesis they reflect is not, as in *The Alexandria Quartet,* a question of validating one's masculine heterosexual identity and authority, but rather of foregrounding the impossibility of doing so. The displacement of male anxiety onto the geography of the premodern further exacerbates the problem by highlighting the "modern" dilemma of gender identification.

The Lost Girl, Aaron's Rod, and the unfinished work *Mr. Noon*
stage a series of departures from England and arrivals in Italy that
coincide with similar departures and arrivals in Lawrence's life,
and their chronologies are closely intertwined as well. In 1913,
when Lawrence began writing *The Lost Girl* (whose title at that time
was *The Insurrection of Miss Houghton*), he had just come through a
particularly tumultuous period in his life. Lawrence's mother,
Lydia, died in December 1910. In 1911, when Lawrence was in his
midtwenties, a bout of pneumonia ended his teaching career at
Davidson Road School in Croydon after a three-year tenure. The
following year he met and began an affair with Frieda Weekley,
then the wife of a professor at the University College of Nottingham.
Shortly thereafter he left England for the first time to visit relatives
in Germany but ended up traveling with Frieda (who had agreed
to forsake her husband and family for him) through the Alps to
Italy, where they settled for a time in Gargnano. There Lawrence
finished *Sons and Lovers* and began *The Lost Girl.* The writing of this
novel was interrupted by the outbreak of World War I. Lawrence
and Frieda spent the war years in England; however, in 1917 they
were expelled from Cornwall by the military authority on suspicion of espionage. It is around this time that he began writing
Aaron's Rod in London. Lawrence returned in 1919 to Italy, where
he finished and substantially revised *The Lost Girl.* The following
year he started *Mr. Noon* but ceased work on that project to continue writing *Aaron's Rod,* which he completed in 1921. He never
finished *Mr. Noon* and, although the first part of the novel was
published—though not until four years after his death—the second and unfinished part of the novel was not published until 1984.
So it is, perhaps, that these novels point to expatriation as a possible solution, with their shared focus on the subject as site of tension between the centripetal, consolidating pressures of nation,
class, and gender and the centrifugal pressures of the subject's
excess—the disruptive surplus of a lived present—which both
exceeds and abhors fixed social forms, *and* whose very production
was riven by the Great War. In the oft-cited words of Yeats, "the
center will not hold." Italy, of course, had a particular hold upon
Lawrence, not only as the mythic South of the Romantic imagination, but also, in these novels in particular, as a means to recover
the organic community.

In what follows I first explore the imaginative geography of Italy
as it functioned for Lawrence and others of his generation. Then,
turning to the novels, I explore the tension between the impulse to

deterritorialize and the desire for the one true place that informs Aaron Sisson's quest in *Aaron's Rod*, and that between expatriate self-making and unmaking that characterizes the rather different trajectory of Alvina Houghton, *The Lost Girl's* female protagonist. Finally, I consider Lawrence's own relationship to Italy through *Twilight in Italy*, a series of travel narratives, and other assorted writings.

Italy

For Lawrence, Italy promised to ameliorate the affective disjunction between the limitations of social form and the lived surplus of experience, which he also sought in alternative forms of community. Lawrence's "communitarian" impulses reflect an important aspect of his ethics of expatriation, and they sit uneasily alongside the contrary desire to "deterritorialize." Rananim, the small utopian community he hoped to establish after the war ended, anticipated new and different social relations among selves whose totality would be realized within an organic community composed of like-minded souls, "a life in which the only riches is integrity of character. So that each one may fulfil *his own nature* and *deep desires* to the utmost, but wherein tho', the ultimate satisfaction and joy is in the completeness of us all as one. Let us be good all together, instead of just in the privacy of our chambers" [my emphasis].[12] Indeed, we might look to the communitarian philosopher Alasdair MacIntyre for some possible explanation of the lack that structured the desire for Rananim. In *After Virtue*, MacIntyre argues that our language of ethics consists of "the fragments of a conceptual scheme, parts which now lack those contexts from which their significance derived" (2). The unitary scheme having broken up, its dislodged fragments spun off in different discursive directions —religion, aesthetics, law, morality—which produced multiple and often contradictory conceptual frameworks. The lost contexts to which MacIntyre refers are neither mythological nor prelapsarian, but rather flow out of premodern social structures:

> In many pre-modern, traditional societies it is through his or her membership in a variety of social groups that the individual identifies himself or herself and is identified by others. I am brother, cousin and grandson, member of this household, that village, this tribe. These are not characteristics that belong to human beings accidentally, to be stripped away, in order to discover 'the real me.' They are part of my substance, defining partially at least and sometimes wholly my

obligations and my duties. Individuals inherit a particular space within an interlocking set of social relationships; lacking that space, they are nobody, or at best a stranger or an outcast. To know oneself as such a social person is however, not to occupy a static and fixed position. It is to find oneself placed at a certain point on a journey with set goals; to move through life is to make progress—or fail to make progress, toward a given end. (33–34)

For MacIntyre, modernity's unencumbered self acquires "sovereignty in its own realm" only to lose its "traditional boundaries provided by a social identity and a view of human life as ordered to a given end" (34). Italy seemed to promise answers to the problem of self-realization, although, as we will see, the Nietzschean or postmodern Lawrence will eschew such "situated" solutions.

Lawrence, of course, was not alone in his embrace of Italy. Nietzsche valued Italy as "a high academy for convalescence in things intellectual as well as sensual" and "a boundless sunniness and sun-transfiguration that floods an autonomous existence which believes in itself."[13] For members of the Frankfurt school, including Walter Benjamin, Theodor Adorno, Ernst Bloch, Siegfried Kracauer, and Alfred Sohm-Rethel, the Italian town of Positano seemed to embody particularly potent possibilities. Positano, writes John Ely, was for Kracauer "a magical enclave of 'hidden powers,' a 'refugium' typical of antique landscapes or the secret, magical places of children's hollows, hangouts, and 'blind spaces,' in 'our metropoles,'" a space in which to "explore the 'constellations' of a hermetic, secret or symbolic, access to nature—that is, a *mimetic* access to it" (Ely's emphasis) where

> "mimesis," though never specifically defined, serves as a counterpoint to instrumental rationality in the literature of critical theory and, in this tradition, implies substantive relational components among things-in-the-world beyond those of "subjects," "effects," or results of instrumental action.[14]

The concept of "porosity," which resonates—though not explicitly —within Lawrence's writings, signified for Ernst Bloch a quality of certain built environments, both spatial and temporal, that allowed an embedded past or history to emerge, however fragmentary, through gaps or holes in the present:

> In contrast to porose [*sic*] Italy, the Northern style has a sorted-out character, where the clear facades and proportionate ratio of the bourgeoisie make their home. Isn't this precisely the contrast with

porosity? It is the division of labor instead of artisanry, the business of details instead of the bazaar, the gesture in itself confined rather than exuberant, the mathematically regimented understanding instead of the sense of movement, the impressed form which the vital itself develops. (196, qtg. Bloch)

The Newtonian-mechanical space of the northern city is conceived of as empty, where "*emptiness* is the characteristic of a world whose ontological presuppositions are mechanical, lifeless" (208, Ely's emphasis), but "hollow" space, in contrast, is associative, vital space and suggests Henri LeFebvre's *lived space* that pulsates in the interstices of an administered landscape. Despite its associative references to premodern structures of being, however, the concept of porosity is more than a signifier of the organic, preindustrial community. Against the administered landscape, "the porosity of the Italian coastal architecture and the ancient or preindustrial city" where "its 'sleeping places' and 'storehouses' are formed out of the same spaces in the cliffs" suggests a kind of revolutionary potential (208). Walter Benjamin states that "building and action interpenetrate in the courtyards, arcades, and stairways. In everything, they preserve the scope to become a theater of new, unforeseen constellations" (208, qtg. Benjamin).

Porosity is also a signifier of cultural mixing, of a polyvocity born of the particular trajectory of classical knowledge that emerges in Renaissance Italy only after a productive detour through Byzantine and Arabic culture. This aspect of porosity brings to mind, as well, the temporal and cultural juxtapositions that Nietzsche, as quoted earlier, invokes when he speaks of the modern spirit: "Our instincts now can run back in all kinds of directions; we ourselves are a kind of chaos." Paradoxically, it is modernity itself that produces porosity, through the accumulated richness of relics, migrations, and histories that body forth in present time. And so in a variety of related ways porosity represents an alternative to the gridded, rationalized spaces of the industrial north that were as abhorrent to Lawrence—if not more so—as to the German radicals who were roughly his contemporaries. Porosity promised a spatial and temporal amelioration of "the present." Lawrence, we might even say, was on a quest for "porous" places, and he was able not only to articulate a purely Lawrentian porosity, one shed of its overtly political and progressive overtones, but also to embody it aesthetically, through his fiction and his travel writing. His quarrel with "the North," like that of his German counterparts, went beyond its disenchanted landscapes to encompass a range of social and cultural relations that were antithetical, in his view, to a life well lived. Unlike the Germans, however, he was not concerned with the emergence of an engaged *socius*. Indeed, if Kracauer's language echoes Nietzsche's "secret entries" and "half-barbarian bodies," it is Nietzsche's spirit of voracious multiplicity, rather than Kracauer's, that informs Lawrence's imaginative geographies. At the same time, Lawrence's writings on Italy reflect his essential ambivalence toward peasant culture, and allusions to darkness, rather than to light, suggest that agrarian realities are at odds with the South of the literary imagination.

If Italy is a topos whose signifying power often exceeds the capacity of its material realities to deliver, the exhilaration of arrival in Italy is also tempered by the visible signs of "progress" that mar the landscape. For the old metaphors are mobile, and the richness of multiplicity, the concrete specificities of the local, the porosity of multitextured and polivocal antique spaces are under the constant threat of absorption into the abhorred universal and the rationalizing processes of modernity. At the conclusion of *Twilight in Italy,* a collection of essays reflecting his first experience of Italy, Lawrence writes with horror of the encroaching spirit of rationalization as modern highways, "new, mechanical, belonging to a machine life," replace the meandering roads of old Italy:

> Down the road of the Ticino valley I felt again my terror of this new world which is coming into being on top of us. One always feels it in a suburb, on the edge of a town, where the land is being broken under the advance of houses. But this is nothing, in England, to the terror one feels on the new Italian roads, where these great blind cubes of dwellings rise stark from the destroyed earth, swarming with a sort of verminous life, really verminous, purely destructive.[15]

One can read the "great blind cubes of dwellings" as spelling the end to porosity and its temporal and spatial possibilities, which might account for the peculiar terror Lawrence associates with such structures inspire in Italy, as opposed to England, where, Lawrence suggests, people had long ago ceased to recoil from the physical transformations and social dislocations wrought by industrialization. And the terror is greatest at the margins, signifying, as they do, the ever-receding borders of premodern space. Lawrence's loathing of inorganic structures is nowhere more apparent than in the following reflection upon modernity inspired by Italy's new roads:

The roads, the railways are built, the mines and quarries are excavated, but the whole organism of life, the social organism, is slowly crumbling and caving in, in a kind of process of dry rot, most terrifying to see. So that it seems as though we should be left, at last, with a great system of roads and railways and industries, and a world of utter chaos seething upon these fabrications: as if we had created a steel frame-work, and the whole body of society were crumbling and rotting in between. It is most terrifying to realise; and I have always felt this terror upon a new Italian high-road: more there than anywhere.[16]

The inanimate infrastructures of industrial society are antithetical to the social organism. And so, by analogy, are the social structures and social relations forged in the transformation from an agrarian-based society to an urban, machine-based one. Indeed, the "world of utter chaos seething upon these fabrications" is evocative of Wordsworth's "huge fermenting mass of human-kind," implicating the entire project of modernity, as embodied in the northern industrial city, in the internal dissolution of the "social organism." The chaos is neither productive, in the spirit of Nietzsche, nor a fund of revolutionary energies, but represents formless matter, an undifferentiated swarm, a rotting mass, the mass production of subjects. It also reflects Lawrence's interest in degeneration and decay that Howard Booth links to theories of degeneration popular in fin-de-siècle England and that led Lawrence to seek renewal outside its borders.

Despite its vulnerability to the contagion of modernity, however, the agrarian culture of Italy did seem to embody for Lawrence, at times, a locus in which to access the lost contexts to which MacIntyre refers—or something very much like them—and an alternative to the instrumental social relations of industrial society and its nearly constitutive ethical contradictions. Yet while Lawrence drew inspiration from these spaces, he could not find solutions to the problem of the self in a medium so antithetical to his quintessentially modern—and Nietzschean—sensibilities. The essays in *Twilight in Italy* already reflect this tension. In "The Spinner and the Monks," for example, he points out: "The Italian people are called 'Children of the Sun.' They might better be called 'Children of the Shadow.' Their souls are dark and nocturnal. If they are to be easy, they must be able to hide, to be hidden in lairs and caves of darkness. Going though these tiny, chaotic backways of the village was like venturing through the labyrinth made by furtive creatures, who watched from another element" (104). Lawrence feels safe only in the "upper world of glowing light" (110). Such imagery is consistent with his own ambivalence concerning the perceived difference between the "Northern" and "Southern" races, the one steeped in sensual blood-consciousness, mind submerged, the other "purely free and abstract."[17] By the same token, the traditional way of life is "an old static conception," remote from "the great flux of life" that modernity represents.[18] As Howard Booth points out, despite Lawrence's attraction to the new and magically different, his actual contacts with difference had the opposite effect: "He recoiled away from the very thing that had so fascinated him."[19]

A further tension emerges between Lawrence's idealized vision of an androcentric social structure, on the one hand, and his disillusionment with what he perceived to be the rude, spiritually "impoverished" reality of peasant culture on the other. The peasant cultures of the Mediterranean were no less "tight" and "partial" for being organic, and they could not accommodate the "nomadic" impulses that draw sustenance from novelty and diversity. And, of course, the organic was always under threat of absorption by the inorganic, the industrial, and the modern. Hence, the novels under consideration here record increasing alienation, disillusionment, and—other than a protofascist vision of a strong leader and his devoted acolyte—a radical absence of organic community ties. They worry obsessively over selves estranged from the world and each other for whom eroticism, the sensual and passional embrace of "blood consciousness" (of which sexual intercourse is the embodiment), or an eroticized submission to the greater soul of some heroic male figure provides the sole measure of a life well lived. It is only as the perpetual outsider that the subject is able to pursue his goal of self-fashioning. Once on the "inside," the subject sinks into the dark, almost mystical, processes of reterritorialization that, like quicksand, subsume its victim, and the project is annulled. Indeed, Lawrence's more atavistic fictional explorations press beyond a dream of organic belonging entirely and articulate a condition of radical self-dissolution or submission. The alternative of "nomadic" purity, however, can become equally tyrannical and threatens agency through enforced movement rather than stasis. Characters, therefore, reach an impasse, an *aporia;* they are unable or unwilling to reterritorialize or to remain deterritorialized because, paradoxically, as Lawrence would write:

"Men are free when they are in a living homeland, not when they are straying or breaking away."[20] Only the unrealized and untested "communitas" of Rananim, a community of "like-minded souls," seems to offer a space of possible reconciliation.

Nevertheless, the condition of expatriation offered Lawrence an enabling sense of displacement that in itself provided a solution-in-process to the problem of the good life by exposing him to the types of communities modernity was slowly destroying. He was able to live and work productively on the outside of Italian culture with a sense of personal freedom, while its close proximity was a source of inspiration, pleasure, and enchantment. Italy's "porosity," moreover, gave Lawrence access to a fund of spiritual/mystical energies and imaginings that helped him articulate why and how his own culture had failed him. What these novels reveal, finally, is that despite the quest for Rananim, Lawrence is very much an heir to the Romantic naysayers whose reckless experiments in self-dismantling and sensual disorderings are as crucial an underpinning to his ethics of expatriation as is the desire for organic connections.

Aaron's Rod

Aaron's Rod, whose very title suggests something of the masculine anxiety with which its protagonist is beset, is a paradigmatic quest narrative set just after World War I. On Christmas Eve its eponymous protagonist walks out on his wife and three small daughters and—except for one stealthy visit to retrieve a few things—never returns. His restless and incomplete journey out of domestic structure takes him first to London and then to Italy, where the novel leaves him, abject and bereft. When asked in the course of the novel why he abandoned his family, he responds: "It happened to me; as birth happened to me once—and death will happen. It was a sort of death too: or a sort of birth. But as undeniable as either. And without any more grounds."[21] He is, like Lawrence himself, an escapee, belonging in his soul amongst those others "who are best at 'leaving,' those who make leaving into something as natural as being born or dying, those who set out in search of inhuman sex—Lawrence, Miller—stake out a far-off territoriality that still forms an anthropomorphic and phallic representation."[22] And just as surely he is prey to the symbolic. On the other hand, Aaron's act has Christian resonance as well. Is it mere coincidence that he leaves his family on Christmas Eve? What Aaron is unable to articulate but the

novel allows us to infer is that the inadequacy or incommensurability of the available social identities to the human material that
Aaron represents leaves him no alternative. He is by class a worker
—a checkweightman in a colliery—but his intellect and musician-
ship (a flautist competent enough to work professionally in London
orchestras) make class identity anomalous. His artistic and emotional needs exceed the fulfillments of bourgeois domesticity, the
life of production and reproduction that modernity has embraced
as its cultural dominant. His erotic needs, we might also infer,
exceed the satisfactions of heterosexual relations. Because these
available identities—mineworker, father, husband—do not exhaust
Aaron's potential for other and different identities, there is a magical excess to be jealously guarded that might serve as a kind of
raw material out of which redescriptions can be forged. But if
"redescription," Richard Rorty's term for the power of language
"to make new things possible and important", is consistent with
an awareness of contingency and an ethics of diversity, in
Lawrence diversity often runs afoul of the concrete Other, recognition of whom, in intersubjective terms, is problematic.[23]

The novel begins on an ominously racial note. In an alehouse on
the eve of Aaron's departure, there is an extended dialogue among
Aaron, the Jewish proprietress, and an Indian doctor on the subject of Indian self-governance. The tavern is, in effect, an early
incarnation of the global village, a curious stage on which a variety of "Otherings" are played out, interrogated, and confounded
in interesting ways: gentile versus Jew, colonizer versus colonized,
male versus female, worker versus professional. The text lingers
over the landlady's exotic sensuality, aestheticizing rather than car-
icaturing her classic Semitic features—"Her reddish-brown eyes
seemed to burn, and her nose, that had a subtle, beautiful Hebraic
curve, seemed to arch itself"—and then sets up an anomalous contrast between the working-class colliers in the bar who "were the
superior type all, favoured by the landlady, who loved intellectual
discussion," and an Indian, "a little, greenish man—evidently an
oriental" (*AR*, 18). The landlady addresses him as "Doctor," revealing his professional status and, with that, his upper-class origins.
Nevertheless, he speaks "with a little, childish lisp," and "with childish pertinence" (18, 19). The possibility of intersubjective relations
between Aaron and the doctor is deflected by eye contact:

> The little oriental laughed a queer, sniggering laugh. His eyes were very
> bright, dilated, completely black. He was looking into the ice-blue,

pointed eyes of Aaron Sisson. They were both intoxicated—but grimly so. They looked at each other in elemental difference. (24)

The Indian doctor takes his place here as the stranger—the Other within physical but not social reach—in both the text and the pub. The encounter, therefore, despite a condition of mutual intoxication, is in the nature of a mismeeting: the stranger attempting to claim the recognition due subjects in cognitive space. When the doctor asserts the Indian people's right to self-rule, querying: "How can any people be responsible for another race, for a race that is even older than they are, and not at all little children?" he not only repudiates the text's own characterization of himself, but also effectively wields the colonizer's own political discourse defensively. By challenging the boundaries between the ruler and the ruled, the doctor evokes the language of universal equality, a demand that Aaron, in the spirit of Nietzsche, repudiates as a claim upon his sovereignty:

> Aaron Sisson watched the other dark face, with its utterly exposed eyes. He was in a state of semi-intoxicated anger and clairvoyance. He saw in the black, void, glistening eyes of the oriental only the same danger, the same menace which he saw in the landlady. Fair, wise, even benevolent words: always the human good speaking, and always underneath, something hateful, something detestable and murderous. Wise speech, and good intentions—they were invariably maggoty with these secret lustful inclinations to destroy the man in a man. Whenever he heard anyone holding forth: the landlady, this doctor, the spokesman on the pit-bank: or when he read the all-righteous newspapers; his soul curdled with revulsion, as from something foul. (25)

The text's dialogism here marks the point where Aaron, the Nietzschean, parts company with the discourse of liberal democracy. The Indian doctor, the Jewish female, and the spokesman at the miners' meeting are united in their advocacy of a common good seen by Aaron as purely destructive—in the spirit of ressentiment —to the noble, the powerful, and the manly. If Aaron, as heroic though embattled white male, is defined, as here, in opposition to a range of Others marked by race, class, and gender—and they must be perceived as such Others if he is to reject their claim upon him—to what extent will his identity remain tied to inherited languages of Othering? And what implications does this have for the ethics of expatriation? If the pub drinkers together represent a microcosm of diversity within the homeland itself, what does this portend for the voyage out? Aaron's ethical project, we surmise, is not indebted to principles of equality and universal brotherhood, and this puts him at odds with the democratic institutions of home. The barroom encounter is the first step toward expatriation; but that solution will catapult him into an alterity that he is ill equipped to handle.

First, however, Aaron makes his way to London, where he finds work as a professional flautist in the opera orchestra. There he is taken up by a group of mostly middle-class bohemian artists and intellectuals that includes Rawdon Lilly, a character who is very much the image of Lawrence himself ("a little, dark, thin, quick fellow, his wife a fine blonde" [*AR*, 73]). It is Aaron's relationship with Lilly that precipitates the flight from England and mediates between competing or alternative modes of expatriate self-fashioning: migrancy and nomadism. Lilly, like Lawrence, is a professional peregrinator, ever seeking in new surroundings the new within himself. We might say, in fact, that he uses the new to effect redescriptions of himself. The production of a *new* self is as yet quite out of the question for Aaron. He questions the relationship between displacement and self-fashioning. "[W]hat's the good of going to Malta," he asks Lilly. "Shall *you* be any different in yourself, in another place. . . . What's the use of going somewhere else. You won't change yourself." But Lilly tells him that "there are lots of mes [me's]. I'm not only just one proposition. A new place brings out a new thing in a man" (103). "I want to get a new tune out of myself" (106).

In Nietzschean fashion, Lilly counsels Aaron to bracket normative Judeo-Christian values: "Forget the very words religion, and God, and love—" he says, "then have a shot at a new mode. But the very words rivet us down and don't let us move." Aaron is skeptical: "And where should we be if we could?" he asks, to which Lilly responds, "We might begin to be ourselves, anyhow" (291). We can read Lilly's admonition in terms of a kind of Deleuzian anti-oedipalism, a principle of identity formation contrary to what Foucault calls "the old categories of the Negative" that privilege multiplicities and flows over unities and systems.[24] Nevertheless, the desire for perpetual self-overcoming in itself becomes a kind of tyranny. As Lilly explains:

> I am a vagrant really: or a migrant. I must migrate. Do you think a cuckoo in Africa and a cuckoo in Essex is one *and* [Lawrence's emphasis] the same bird?—Anyhow, I know I must oscillate between

north and south, so oscillate I do. . . . I would very much like to try life
in another continent, among another race. I feel Europe is *becoming
like a cage to me.* Europe may be all right in herself. But I find myself
chafing. Another year I shall get out. I shall leave Europe. *I begin to feel
caged.* (*AR*, 290–91, my emphasis)

Indeed, the project is relentless. To Aaron's all-important question
of what it means "to be yourself," Lilly responds, "To me, everything" (291). If to be one's self is to be, at once, *every* thing and the
only thing, however, what does it mean to be Other? Conveniently
sidestepping the substance of Aaron's question, Lilly's punning
evasion nevertheless excludes any principle of subjective relations
between selves. For to the extent that self-artistry is a project bound
up with expatriation, that process implicates the expatriate in a
whole range of social relations with the Other. The primary expatriate conundrum, of which the text is wholly unconscious, is a
simultaneous repudiation and embrace of William Connolly's
assertion that "[t]he world is always richer than the systems
through which we comprehend and organize it.[25] That is to say, the
Lawrentian expatriate loves the world in its diversity and yet finds
the world's "Others" lacking, precisely, in that promised richness.
Lilly, for example, rails against those peoples who "teem by the billion, like the Chinese and Japs and orientals altogether. Only vermin teem by the billion. Higher types breed slower." And by
"higher types," Lilly is not referring here to Europeans, but rather
to the "American races—and the South Sea Islanders—the Mar-
quesans, the Maori blood," of whom he says: "That was the true
blood. It wasn't frightened. All the rest are craven—Europeans,
Asiatics, Africans—everyone at his own individual quick craven
and cringing: only conceited in the mass, the mob. How I hate
them: the mass-bullies, the individual Judases" (*AR*, 97).

Considering Lilly's rejection of values that would reflect toler-
ance and universal brotherhood and his concomitant desire for self-
overcoming, this discourse should not take us completely by surprise. Rorty points out the incommensurability between forms of
self-artistry that privilege radical self-invention, on the one hand,
and the self's obligations to other selves, on the other. Without,
however, sidestepping the reductionist racial discourse with which
Lilly's rhetoric is imbued, we might nevertheless register his exclu-
sion of Europeans from those considered to be "higher types" as an
indication that something other than mere racism is being reflected
here. Terms like "teem," "mass," and "mob," for example, seem to

suggest, with reference to the Europeans at least, the crumbling social edifice referred to in *Twilight in Italy,* or perhaps a certain Nietzschean scorn for the "herd," disgust with bourgeois complacency, Protestant leveling, and the paralyzing impotence of ressentiment. Chris Bongie links exoticism—which is often a constitutive element of expatriate fiction—to individualism. Citing Victor Segalen, a contemporary of Lawrence, he writes: "'Exoticism can only be singular, individualistic. It does not admit plurality.' This plurality that exoticism cannot admit (to) proves synonymous with such ominous abstractions as Society or the State and often has its most vivid figural embodiment in the modern crowd."[26] Lawrence's peculiar racial geographies, by privileging certain decentralized aboriginal cultures, seem to embody a similar critique. Expatriation is one solution to the problem of the masses, liberal society, and the circumscriptions of the modern subject.

Despite his earlier skepticism, Aaron does feel the birthing of a new self within, and Italy proves to be a vital testing ground. Gazing out at the Alps he feels himself

> [o]n the other side of the time barrier. His old sleepy English nature was startled in its sleep. He felt like a man who knows it is time to wake up and who doesn't want to wake up, to face the responsibility of another sort of day. To open his darkest eyes and wake up to a new responsibility. Wake up and enter on the responsibility of a new self in himself. . . . It was so hateful to have to get a new grip on his own bowels, a new hard recklessness into his heart, a new and responsible consciousness into his mind and soul. (*AR*, 151)

The language of sleeping and waking, of resistance and resignation, indicates the push and pull between a past existence that is seen as analogous to sleep— suggesting, perhaps, it is not really an existence at all—and the uncompromising zeal of the Nietzschean experimenter whose "circumspect cruelty . . . knows how to handle the knife surely and delicately, even when the heart is bleeding."[27] Also reflected here is the painful ascesis that Deleuze and Guattari associate with the "negative task"of schizoanalysis, which must be "violent, brutal: defamiliarizing, de-oedipalizing, decastrating; undoing theater, dream, and fantasy; decoding, deterritorializing —a terrible curettage, a malevolent activity."[28] This birthing of a *new* self within Aaron, painful as it is, suggests that Lilly's ambulant lifestyle might, indeed, yield valuable lessons and gives rise to the possibility that a new self is just that which is to be overcome again and again. What might this "new and responsible consciousness" be, if not, in a very real sense, an existential project of self-fashioning?

It may be ironic to us that Aaron should awaken to a new and *responsible* consciousness precisely at the moment of a border experience that places him at the farthest remove from the wife and children whom he had abandoned at the beginning of the novel, but Lawrence is not being ironic. Such a reading would load the term itself with the normative language of care and duty to others, and *particularly* to family and countrymen, that is at issue here. But this new responsibility for what we might now call self-artistry is precisely the locus of Lawrence's ethics of expatriation, and it is not undertaken lightly. Aaron is in the thrall of a calling whose narrative genealogy begins with and is legitimized by Bunyan's *Pilgrim's Progress,* a work that eschews the values of domesticity and production in favor of the solitary quest for spiritual salvation. Aaron, of course, has more earthly concerns, as he attempts to work out the problem of identity and the essential misogyny that seem to underscore the flight from domesticity that forms the core of the narrative. "Woman," here, seems to represent the greatest challenge to the type of masculine self that the narrative strives to articulate. And yet salvation is very much at issue: the two principal crises in the novel from which Aaron must be "redeemed"—Aaron's early illness and the loss of his flute, which occurs at the end—come on the heels of sexual encounters with women. The text is deeply ambiguous concerning heterosexuality, though it does not hold up homosexual relations as any kind of panacea either. The terms of a future relationship between Aaron and Lilly, as we will see, promise to replicate (and then mystify) the same asymmetries in power that structure male-female relations. Only now it is Aaron in the subordinate position; and he is left no recourse but to embrace his lack.

That is where we leave Aaron at the end of the novel; in the beginning, Italy provides a good antidote both to "female domination" and to the Protestant egalitarianism of "the North," where domesticity is inextricably bound up with structures of order and discipline. Indeed, writing from Germany in 1913, Lawrence expresses the same sentiment:

> I *have* suffered the tightness, the *domesticity* of Germany. It is our domesticity which leads to our conformity, which chokes us. The very agricultural landscape here, and the distinct paths, stifles me. The very oxen are dull and featureless, and the folk seem like tables of figures. [Lawrence's emphasis][29]

It is precisely the sense of disconnectedness—an antipathy to communitarian ideals—that seems so exhilarating. To Aaron, "the people seemed little upright brisk figures moving in a certain isolation, like tiny figures on a big stage. And he felt himself moving in the space between. All the northern cosiness gone. He was set down with space around him" (*AR*, 151–52). Strolling through the streets of Novara, he

> surprised himself at his gallant feeling of liberty: a feeling of bravado and almost swaggering carelessness which is Italy's best gift to an Englishman. He had crossed the dividing line, and the values of life, though ostensibly and verbally the same, were dynamically different. (152)

And yet there is a constant awareness of temporal frailty as "the verbal and the ostensible, the accursed mechanical ideal gains day by day over the spontaneous life-dynamic, so that Italy becomes as idea-bound and as automatic as England: just a business proposition" (152).

What excites Aaron from the first is his discovery of the world's plenitude. His wonder at diversity is undimmed even by his awareness of its fragility: "Many worlds, not one world. But alas, the one world triumphing more and more over the many worlds, the big oneness swallowing up the many small diversities in its insatiable gnawing appetite, leaving a dreary sameness throughout the world, that means at last complete sterility" (152). Nevertheless, he is "too new to the strangeness; he had no eye for the horrible sameness that was spreading like a disease over Italy from England and the north" (153). Though he exclaims, "A new world to me. I feel I've come out of myself," he does not readily fashion a new discursive medium (155). Vacillating between the language of revelation (the *world* is new, I am not) and the language of conversion (*I* am a new self), he is confounded by the demand of the Other. The third-class railway carriage in which he is forced to travel—a microcosm of the social space of modernity where neighbor and stranger are randomly juxtaposed—throws social ritual and convention into confusion. Indeed, the abstract Italian and his physical counterpart fail to coalesce for Aaron when he leaves the company of other British expatriates and finds himself a stranger. Both class and culture conspire to poison the intersubjective relations between Aaron and the Italian peasantry—the great inarticulate Other of the novel. While, on the one hand, Aaron is able to admire the loose, unselfconscious demeanor of his fellow passengers, which he contrasts with their English counterparts "all trussed with self-conscious string as tight as capons," on the other, the Englishman in him rises in indignation at the large Italian peasant who has stolen his seat: "There was something insolent and unbearable about the look—and about the *rocky fixity* of the large man, . . . *a solid rock-like* impudence, before which an Englishman quails: a jeering, *immovable* insolence, with a sneer round the nose and solid-seated posterior" (199, 201, my emphasis). The admirable looseness becomes at once rocklike, fixed, and immovable, suggesting that anything that resists the Englishman's superiority, his mobility and dynamism, assumes the nature of a thing, a non-subject, and a limit. Ironically, of course, Aaron's very presence in the third-class compartment is a sign of his own limitations, his own class status—and its anomalousness; he is, literally, without a place.

The text concerns itself with very few meetings—or mismeetings —between the English characters and the Italians other than, of course, the service personnel any traveler in a foreign land might encounter. The one Italian "character" in the novel is an aristocratic marchese who "would have been taken for an Austrian officer, or even a German, had it not been for the peculiar Italian sprightliness and touch of grimace in his mobile countenance" (220). *Aaron's Rod* seems to fix Italian "particularity" at the level of class, remarking, as it does, upon the generic "Northern" character of the marchese. No chance of a mismeeting here. The Italian working man, on the other hand, bears the weight of Italian otherness and authenticity. He is at once the salt of the earth and an intolerable lout. But then, *Aaron's Rod* does not seek answers in the intersubjective relations between self and Other. As we have seen, the narrative's primary interlocutor, Rawdon Lilly, is concerned less with the multiplicity of worlds than with the multiplicity of selves he can produce. Aaron is his disciple.

And yet Italy's homosocial culture, most pungently represented in the peasantry and the land-linked stratum of society, offers an enabling alternative to a generic bourgeoisie: the "Borghesia—the citizens," who are dominated by their wives. The symbol of this great Italian manhood is Michelangelo's David, which gives Aaron "[t]he sense of having arrived—of having reached a perfect centre of the human world" (212). And so Aaron, feeling the eruption of the past into the present, "felt a new self, a new life-urge rising inside himself. Florence seemed to start a new man in him. It was a town of men" (212). Lawrence's description of Italian masculinity evokes a highly charged homoeroticism and an ecstatic Nietzschean abandon:

> The dangerous, subtle, never-dying fearlessness, and the *acrid* unbelief. But men! Men! A town of men, in spite of everything. The one manly quality, undying, *acrid* fearlessness. The eternal challenge of the unquenched human soul. Perhaps too *acrid* and challenging to-day, when there is nothing left to challenge. (213).

The repetition of the word "acrid" suggests carnality and the odor of unwashed male bodies. And this is consistent with the text's imaginative geography, for here in Italy "men had been at their intensest, most naked pitch, here, at the end of the old world and the beginning of the new" (212). But eroticism—of any kind—is dicey and indiscriminate. After sharing a spell "of strange isolation, beyond the bounds of life, as it seemed," with the marchese's wife, who will briefly become his lover, he is rushed by a "rude, brutal little mob of grey-green coarse uniforms that smelt so strong of soldiers" and finds he has been robbed of his portfolio (227, 228). This loss, overdetermined perhaps, points up the fatal conjunction of desire and destruction that eroticism comprehends. But Aaron's attraction to antique Florence, to this "perfect centre" of humanity, also represents a counterpoint to Lilly's vagrancy. Their antithetical desires represent the tension between a reterritorialized and a deterritorialized ethics of expatriation. That is to say, where Aaron delights in reaching what he perceives to be the absolute center, Lilly rejoices in a decentered world wherein "the absolute . . . does not appear at a particular place but becomes a nonlimited locality"; wherein "the coupling of the place and the absolute is achieved not in a centered, oriented globalization or universalization but in an infinite succession of local operations."[30]

The novel's climax occurs when a bomb thrown by political insurgents explodes in the café where Aaron and his friends are sitting. Aaron's flute is destroyed in the blast, and he is dumfounded: "the loss was for him symbolistic. It chimed with something in his soul: the bomb, the smashed flute, the end" (*AR*, 285). The flute itself, of course, is also "symbolistic," for it is not only emblematic of his masculinity, but also a marker of his excess, that fund of identitarian futurity that was to guarantee his autonomy—both literally and figuratively. In its barely camouflaged representation of castration, the text gives full voice to its protagonist's anxieties concerning both masculine authority and sexual identity. The dream of expatriate self-fashioning extinguished, there is only one illumination, one other possible source of the good, and this recalls an earlier London experience when Lilly had miraculously, through a massage of "every speck of [Aaron's] lower body" (96), saved him from a wasting disease (also the result of an erotic encounter with a woman): "With the breaking of the flute, that which was slowly breaking had finally shattered at last. And there was nothing ahead: no plan, no prospect. . . . The only thing he felt was a thread of destiny attaching him to Lilly" (288).

And yet Lilly will be moving on, compelled to pursue the nomadic and polymorphous and to eschew the fixed and essential. Failing to recognize the compulsory nature of his own trajectory—or perhaps because he does—Lilly counsels Aaron to find deliverance through subjection: it is "life submission," "deep, fathomless submission to the heroic soul in a greater man" that, according to Lilly, promises the greatest realization of self. "And whom shall I submit to?" asks Aaron. Lilly, assuming the mask of an exotic religious fetish whose face "was dark and remote-seeming" and "like a Byzantine eikon," responds somewhat coyly, "Your soul will tell you" (299). Lilly's seductive posturing threatens to annul all the worldly multiplicities that have been revealed to Aaron through expatriation and to fix him in a "feminine" or "unmanned" position. And on that note the novel ends. If Lilly is correct, Aaron's project of redescription has failed. Not being the "strong poet" Lilly is, he may be fated to become his acolyte. Lawrence leaves Aaron—and the reader—suspended between competing modes of expatriate self-artistry. In either case, Lawrence tells us, agency is compromised. Having reached the mythic center, Aaron's flute is destroyed; having rejected the idea of organic community, Lilly is fated to wander ceaselessly.

The Lost Girl

For the male expatriate, the flight from home can be a liberating experience, a loosening of the bonds of the "mother" culture. For Lilly, and perhaps Lawrence himself, even the "boundless submission" to a heroic male figure translates as a greater freedom. Aaron Sisson flees a life that was "priced and ticketed," to borrow a phrase from *The Lost Girl*, and despite the fact that expatriation does not erase the lineaments of his class, in a new context he is exotic and attractive precisely for that reason. His personal capital increases.

For Alvina Houghton, the female protagonist of *The Lost Girl*, the trajectory is far more complicated. The novel, in its barest outline, is about an upper-middle-class woman bound for spinsterhood owing to her uncompromising independence, resourcefulness, and self-sufficiency—she is an adept at redescription—who nevertheless falls powerfully under the spell of Ciccio, a rude (in the sense of both unfinished and insolent) but handsome Italian peasant, a player in an itinerant theatrical company. She marries him, and they leave England to settle in a remote and impoverished Italian village. In one sense, the novel seems to take off from the concluding sentiments of *Aaron's Rod*, at once concretizing and parodying the idea of submission to a superior man and solving in this way the problem of "female domination." In another, it represents the failure of the expatriate quest for an organic solution to mechanism and mass society and an acute reflection of Lawrence's own ambivalence toward the living reality of traditional agrarian culture.

Lawrence's use of a female protagonist and a female consciousness to explore expatriate experience calls for some comment, especially insofar as gender—or the construction of gender—figures so prominently in the novel. As I noted earlier, the fin-de-siècle "crisis" in masculine subjectivity was precipitated, to a large degree, by the emergence of the New Woman, single, self-motivated, and independent. Alvina Houghton is a fairly explicit evocation of the New Woman; by contrast, the masculine figures who are her equals in terms of class and social status, including her father, are represented as ineffectual and lacking in virility. Virility is a quality associated with working-class men and dark-skinned foreigners, of whom Ciccio is the quintessence. He is the epitome of everything the bourgeois male is not: inarticulate, uneducated, thoroughly marginal. But he is a sexual magnet, and he is not ineffectual. So, while Alvina dominates her bourgeois counterparts, she willingly submits to Ciccio in nearly every way. Indeed, she derives great pleasure from submission.

Alvina's case is curious. Although she behaves in ways that are consistent with our image, derived from Freud, of the "masochistic" woman, her eventual displacement from the metropolitan center to a premodern or "primitive" domain effectively removes her from the sort of bourgeois patriarchal structures within which her subordination could be "naturalized" to a context in which such subordination appears most *un*natural. She is represented as superior to Ciccio in every way. The effect of this powerful metropolitan/primitive binary is to collapse the bourgeois male and female into a single agent, gendered feminine, while eviscerating her male counterpart, marking a double erasure of the bourgeois male subject. *The Lost Girl* reverses the binary oppositions through which bourgeois sexual identity is represented. Where the masculine principle excludes all that is irrational, sensual, emotional, and carnal, in these texts such qualities are the embodiment of masculinity. We will see a similar dynamic at work in *The Sheltering Sky*, and I have more to say about this later.

Although *The Lost Girl* is a novel of expatriation, Alvina's actual departure from England and domicile in Italy do not occur until the final fifty pages of a book that is nearly four hundred pages long, and this is perhaps because her spiritual or psychological "voyage out" begins nearly at birth. That is to say, the novel stages a number of departures and returns—both geographic and metaphoric—that rehearse the expatriate experience that, paradoxically, brings her "home." On the one hand, expatriation represents the concrete embodiment of her unorthodox sensibilities but, on the other, it "produces" her, finally, as upper-class bourgeois Englishwoman. Put another way, the same pesky "excess" that produced expatriation as a solution to Aaron Sisson's problem of identity moves Alvina into a primal chaos where, if the self is to survive at all as a self, it must shore itself up with the architecture of home. An ethics of expatriation here is animated by an ambivalently constructed atavism: the celebration of instinct over reason, where reason is incommensurate with and cannot contain a kind of passional excess that tears at the psychic fabric out of which "home" is woven. But atavism is dicey, always pushing the risk of dissolution (a risk that, in itself, may be pleasurable) against the subject's desire to be a subject; as if in recognition of this risk, the thinking, reasoning Alvina is always looking over the shoulder of the feeling, arational Alvina. And so atavism threatens at any moment to devolve into play or performance to be terminated at the will of the player. But this, in a sense, is—has always been—the prerogative of the expatriate. Alvina, however, chooses to remain "in character."

The daughter and only child of a fanciful but unsuccessful dabbler in speculative avant garde business ventures, she is born in the mining townlet of Woodhouse (the same fictional town from which Gilbert Noon takes flight) and raised under the shadow of

Manchester House, a vast mausoleum of a building built by her father. Alvina's quirkiness, reflected in "an odd, derisive look at the back of her eyes, a look of old knowledge and deliberate derision" (21), is suggestive of certain inclinations that will radically undermine the traditional narrative of marriage and domesticity that is a counterpoint to the narrative of the novel. If the bildungsroman is the classic form of the bourgeois subject's story of individuation and reinscription into the "womb" of society, then *The Lost Girl*, like Joyce's *Portrait of an Artist as a Young Man*, is the story of its— his or her—disenfranchisement. For the novel stages a series of "internal" expatriations, recording a trajectory of increasing alienation from and disassociation with home—mediated, effectively, through the protagonist's violent attachment to an *in*appropriate suitor. Why?

Beginning with Alvina's father, James Houghton, the bourgeois male appears as effeminate and shallow. Houghton is represented as a dandy, "a tall, thin elegant young man," "genuinely refined," with "a taste for elegant conversation and elegant literature and elegant Christianity," but "withal, of course, a tradesman."[31] Manchester House, by contrast, which he built before his marriage to Alvina's mother, an older woman from whom he had expected (but did not receive) a considerable fortune, is "a vast square building," a "monument," its bedroom "a gloomy Bastille of mahogany" (*LG*, 3). After the birth of Alvina, James Houghton "decamps" to a spare, half-furnished space in another area of the house while his wife languishes in the big, sterile bedroom, developing heart disease "as a result of nervous repressions" (4). A masculine "erection," Manchester House is an apt symbol of a patriarchal function that is both hollow and sterile. Indeed, both James Houghton and Manchester House are dominated by two female figures, Miss Frost, and Miss Pinnegar, who managed the "work girls." Houghton is finally, a weak, ineffectual, and celibate male figure.

Alvina's first romance, which can be seen as a repudiation of her father's "lack," portends the passional excess that will haunt and finally overtake her. Her beau, an Australian, "dark in coloring, with very dark eyes, and a body which seemed to move inside his clothing," straddles the border of acceptability (22). His transformative effect on her was disquieting even to her governess and mentor, Miss Frost:

It was a strange look in a refined, really virgin girl—oddly sinister.
And her voice had a curious bronze-like resonance that acted straight

on the nerves of her hearers; unpleasantly on most English nerves,
but like fire on the different susceptibilities of the young man—the
darkie, as people called him. (23)

The language of light and dark, of fire and ice, sets up the polarities at war in Alvina herself. She is torn by ambivalence. The properly "English" part of her, represented by Miss *Frost* and accessed
in moments of "lucidity" when she saw "clear as daylight," recognized the Australian as a "terrible outsider, an inferior" (24).
But at other times, "she found herself in a night where the little
man loomed large, terribly large, potent and magical, while Miss
Frost had dwindled to nothingness" (23). We have already encountered this juxtaposition in an excerpt from *Mr. Noon*—the
magical and potent quality of what is Other as contrasted with
the sterility and smallness of England—but now alterity is
shrouded in ambivalence. At this stage, England and the higher
emotions win out over "something more primitive still" than
love, but a certain process of "unEnglishing" has been unleashed.
Alvina's disruptive "excess," paradoxically, is proportionate to
her "loss." At once split and doubled, she will remain liminal, a
stranger to herself and to others.

In contrast to the Australian, her next suitor, Albert Witham, is
an exemplar of masculine lack. Despite his working-class background, he has risen to middle-class status after emigrating to
South Africa. Albert is "tall and thin and brittle, with a pale, rather
dry, flattish face, and with curious pale eyes. His impression was
one of uncanny flatness, something like a lemon sole" (63). His lack
of physicality is suggested by his walk, "stiff and erect, with his
head pressed rather back, so that he always seemed to be advancing from the head and shoulders, in a flat kind of advance, hori-
zontal. He did not seem to be walking with his own body" (66).
Despite, then, the phallic nature of his self-presentation, Albert is
clearly misaligned with his own physicality. In fact, wondering
whether he might want to kiss her, Alvina reflects on "the mere
incongruity of such a desire on his part" (69).

Other suitors or quasi-suitors include Mr. May, described
by Miss Pinnegar as "so unmanly! . . . In his dress, in his way, in
everything—so unmanly," and Dr. Mitchell, an older man, "tall,
largely-built, with a good figure," who is also "rather mouthy and
overbearing" (104, 253). Although Mr. May and Alvina become
close, his aversion to female sexuality renders physical intimacy
out of the question. For Alvina's part, "she did not find him at all

physically moving. Physically he was not there: he was oddly an absentee" (113). It becomes clear to Alvina over time, moreover, that Mr. May is more interested in young "navvies" than he is in her. She actually becomes engaged to Dr. Mitchell, whom she initially dislikes: "the great, red-faced bachelor of fifty three, with his bald spot and his stomach as weak as a baby's, and his mouthing imperiousness and his good heart which was as selfish as it could be" (256). Even when Alvina begins to consider him marriageable, however, he appears to her as a "big fish poking its nose above water and making eyes at her" (257). This is not the stuff of virility. And when he courts her and invites her to his home, where he takes pride in showing her about, she finds that his very fine bedroom, with its "old mahogany tall-boys and silver candlesticks on the dressing-table . . . and a hygienic white bed," reminds her of Manchester House "and how dark and horrible it was," and "how she hated it" (263). Although she consents to marry him, being well aware of the bourgeois amenities such a marriage could provide, her desire for Ciccio overwhelms the paltry blessings of a middle-class life, and she reneges.

Not surprisingly, the first part of the narrative worries continuously over her unmarried status, for she becomes more and more estranged from the narrative of courtship and marriage that the novel invokes but eschews in favor of a kind of sublime travesty. Indeed, considering her social status and gender, she chooses to pursue what could be characterized as a relatively nomadic lifestyle. After those failed romantic liaisons, she is saved from a respectable unmarried status by her father's last great venture, Houghton's Pleasure Palace. A movie and vaudeville house, the new enterprise provides a much-needed outlet for Alvina's temperamental peculiarities, and she derives a certain risque satisfaction in her role as pianist for the silent movies. If, as we are told, "[t]here was no hope for Alvina in the ordinary," (84), how does she negotiate the social constraints of modern English life?

Among theater folk she finds an unexpected but attractive rootlessness and lack of structure: "It was so different from Woodhouse, where everything was priced and ticketed. These people were nomads. They didn't care a straw who you were or who you weren't" (118). The "nomadic" here figures, as in *Aaron's Rod*, as an alternative model for self-definition, distinct from both the "priced and ticketed" life of home, where the personal/individual is limited by the contours of social form, and the notion of an

authentic self at the core of the merely social, which is then redeemed through its reconstitution as organic community. Alvina,
moreover, "liked feeling an outsider. At last she seemed to stand
on her own ground" (117). By becoming the stranger at home
through an enabling self-exoticism, she rehearses the ideal of self-
liberation to be lived elsewhere. Hence, by the time an itinerant
group of actors shows up, a "red Indian" act known as the Natcha-
Kee-Tawara Troupe consisting of a madame and four young men,
Alvina is already bored and impatient with normative rules of
social engagement and normative definitions of life goods. Although
Houghton's Pleasure Palace has employed dozens of "acts," surely
it is not coincidental that this troupe, with its atavistic theme, its
exotic routines and primitive costumes, touches a familiar nerve.
She is immediately attracted to Ciccio, the Italian member of the
troupe, and, consistent with the sense of attraction/repulsion that
underlies social relations between Aaron Sisson and the Italian
peasantry in *Aaron's Rod,* there is something off-putting about
him, something almost prehuman about his limited facility with
language.

> And all the time he looked down at Alvina from under his dusky eye-
> lashes, as if watching her sideways, and his mouth had the peculiar,
> stupid, self-conscious, half-jeering smile. Alvina was a little bit
> annoyed. But she felt that a great instinctive good-naturedness
> came out of him, he was self-conscious and constrained, knowing
> she did not follow his language of gesture. For him, it was not yet
> quite natural to express himself in speech. Gesture and grimace
> were instantaneous and spoke worlds of things, if you would but
> accept them. (137–38)

Ciccio's is the charm of a Stanley Kowalski and Alvina, like
Stella, is represented as the victim of a mystical kind of rape that
is at once real and metaphorical. Class status, bourgeois values, the
hegemony of mind over body—the entire tissue of identity is
ripped apart, pierced to the quick by a phallic excess that disrupts
the aesthetic closure of romantic love. More than a simple seduction, Ciccio's embrace signals Alvina's submission to his mysterious potency. This is Bataille's eroticism, "assenting to life to the
point of death":[32]

> So he took her in both arms, powerful, mysterious, horrible in the
> pitch dark. Yet the sense of the unknown beauty of him weighed her
> down like some force. If for one moment she could have escaped from
> that black spell of his beauty she would have been free. . . . But the

> spell was on her, of his darkness and unfathomed handsomeness. And
> he killed her. He simply took her and assassinated her. How she
> suffered no one can tell. Yet all the time, this lustrous dark beauty,
> unbearable. (*LG*, 202)

Eroticism, couched here in the language of the exotic sublime,
resonates powerfully as an interruption of normative romantic
intercourse in which Alvina is so fitfully inscribed and mediates
Alvina's own desire for self-exoticization. Terry Eagleton argues
that the sublime functioned originally as a violent and lawless
counterpoint to the "aesthetic phenomenon of mimesis," the means
by which, through custom and imitation, the hegemony of good
taste and reason installed and maintained itself in eighteenth-
century Britain—a hegemony always potentially undermined,
however, by its own self-referentiality.[33] At once an atavistic throwback to militaristic aristocratic values and a burst of capitalist
adrenaline, the sublime functioned to "prod society out of its
specular smugness" by piercing the stagnating, self-referential veil
of custom. The sublime, in other words, opens a subversive but
contained space for redescriptions. For characters whose languages of self-understanding are imbricated within—even if only
dialectically—the social landscapes and cultural ideologies of home,
the *exotic* sublime can rupture, often violently, the continuities of
the same, producing new kinds of knowledge, experience, and
redemptive energy. Citing Burke, Eagleton notes that the sublime,
"as a kind of terror . . . crushes us into admiring submission; it thus
resembles a coercive rather than a consensual power, engaging our
respect but not, as with beauty, our love"[34]—and we see the oppres-
sive power of the exotic sublime at work in Alvina's utter capitulation to Ciccio's desire. The sublime, as we can see, is the antithesis of enchantment.

And, indeed, Alvina's "love" for Ciccio will always partake of this
ambiguous mix of aesthetic appreciation and acquiescence. She
also, however, uses him to confirm her own ex-centricity, for she is

> *glad* to be an outcast. She clung to Ciccio's dark, despised foreign
> nature. She loved it, she worshipped it, she defied all the other world.
> Dark, he sat beside her, drawn in to himself, overcast by his presumed
> inferiority among these northern industrial people. And she was with
> him on his side, outside the pale of her own people. (*LG*, 215, my
> emphasis)

Her identification with marginality orients her away from reason,
lucidity, and her own "blood ties" toward darkness, foreignness,

and eventually expatriation. In her desire for Ciccio the lineaments of her past identity are submerged in an ecstasy of alterity:

> There comes a moment when fate sweeps us away. Now Alvina felt herself swept—she knew not whither—but into a dusky region where men had dark faces and translucent yellow eyes, where all speech was foreign, and life was not her life. It was as if she had fallen from her own world on to another, darker star, where meanings were all changed. She was alone, and she did not mind being alone. It was what she wanted. In all the passion of her lover she had found a loneliness, beautiful, cool, like a shadow she wrapped round herself and which gave her a sweetness of perfection. It was a moment of stillness and completeness. (387)[35]

And yet, the space of ecstasy is not utopic; it is territorial and geospecific, and eroticism here is a metaphor for expatriation itself. Indeed, it is as if Ciccio's embrace had become Italy and she, Alvina, a wanderer in foreign terrains. And despite his apparent domination of her, it is he who ceases to exist for her as a self; for she is alone and complete. Just as eroticism mimes expatriation here, so it also prefigures the relations between the expatriate self and the native Other. For different reasons, neither lover is capable of recognizing the other as a subject, and this failure of intersubjectivity is, for Alvina, the mark of an ethics of expatriation that celebrates the Other as the self's negation but is curiously obtuse to the Other as subject of his own narrative, an ethics of expatriation that is essentially instrumental even as it seeks release from the instrumentalities of the Same. That is to say, what Alvina values is the solitude and completion she experiences as a result of her union with Ciccio. He completes her, however, in a way that at the same time allows her to extinguish him. Finally, as we will see, it is as a rather impersonal force of nature that he affects her, rather than as a self. Their ties are antithetical to the spiritual requirements of Rananim and instead anticipate the Bowlesian pairings that cast Moroccans as facilitators in the project of self-dismantling, rather than as partners in ethical relation to one another. Eroticism here is clearly *not* about mutuality; it is expressed, rather, in impersonal terms, in terms of domination and submission.

What is more, Alvina's desire for Ciccio, which the highly rational character Mrs. Tuke describes as "atavism," exceeds the socially productive circuits of exchange. Deleuze and Guattari suggest that desire is revolutionary; it runs contrary to the regimes of power and regimentation that seek to appropriate and recode it, and yet "desire does not 'want' revolution, it is revolutionary in its own right, as though involuntarily, by wanting what it wants."[36] And so Alvina, by wanting what "she wants," is propelled toward Ciccio despite her misgivings. Indeed, she struggles against him, unable to acquiesce until, as before, she is overcome by a power so sublime and disabling that she loses all sense of agency. The violence of Ciccio's possession of Alvina is matched only by the religiosity of her submission; indeed, "she felt herself like one of the old sacred prostitutes" (*LG*, 288). And despite the fact that his power operates as a "spell" cast over her, she feels intensely conscious of—and welcomes—her loss of will, which paradoxically is exactly what her will desires.

This headlong fall into the abyss is a trope that will become all too familiar in the work of Paul Bowles. What kind of subject rushes toward its own self-dissolution, where another would sense danger and quickly turn back? What kind of fictional imagination would put such a drama into motion? Judith Butler considers the question in another way, asking "What would it mean for the subject to desire something other than its continued 'social existence'? If such an existence cannot be undone without falling into some kind of death, can existence nevertheless be risked, death courted or pursued, in order to expose and open to transformation the hold of social power on the conditions of life's persistence?"[37] The subject knows not what lies beyond or outside "social existence," only that it cannot even be imagined from within the confines of subjectivity. In her analysis of Bataille's eroticism, MacKendrick writes that bondage and control produce an intensification of "impersonal desire" through which the bounds of the self are overcome. The "subject" frees itself from subjectivity through "another subjection fully sought."[38] Alvina's impersonal desire makes sense in this light. What a peculiar kind of bravery, to walk that tightrope!

Such eroticism is a far cry from the intersubjective love struggle that underlies Gilbert Noon's spiritual rebirth in the semi-auto-biographical *Mr. Noon*, where his lover, Johanna, is seen refusing absolutely to submit to a Bavarian mountaineer precisely because "she would not have love without some sort of spiritual recognition" (317). It may be precisely the problem of Johanna/Frieda that Lawrence seeks to reimagine in *The Lost Girl*. For while desire may be revolutionary, the narrative frees Alvina from a macro or public economy of the "North" only to introduce her into a micro or domestic economy of the "South" that produces its own structural demands. Ciccio is Lawrence's revenge upon the willful woman. The eroticism of *The Lost Girl* is complicated, however, and cannot be reduced to a set of modernist anxieties concerning woman's newly empowered status, although that is clearly a factor. For Alvina does not feel entirely victimized; the violent denial of a normative self is seen as offering its own compensations, although they are unspeakable and incompatible with the values of both courtly and companionate love that underlie and inform modern notions of romance:

> She was under his spell. Only she knew it. She felt extinguished. Ciccio talked to her: but only ordinary things. There was no wonderful intimacy of speech, such as she had always imagined, and always craved for. No. He loved her—but it was in a dark, mesmeric way, which *did not let her be herself.* His love did not stimulate her or excite her. It extinguished her. She had to be the quiescent, obscure woman: she felt as if she were veiled. Her thoughts were dim, in the dim back regions of consciousness—yet, somewhere, she almost exulted. Atavism! . . . Was it atavism, this sinking into extinction under the spell of Ciccio? Was it atavism, this strange, sleep-like submission to his being? Perhaps it was. Perhaps it was. But it was also heavy and sweet and rich. Somewhere, she was content. Somewhere even she was vastly proud of the dark veiled eternal loneliness she felt, under his shadow. (*LG*, 288, my emphasis)

In the novel the lack of companionate intimacy is mystified, in part, by the raw sexuality that is inimical to the polite channels through which it is administered in bourgeois social structures. Nevertheless, while *The Lost Girl* eschews the notion of romantic love in favor of a more intuitive, preconscious love connection, a Bataillian eroticism, we will see that the lack of "spiritual" parity that Johanna insists upon and that is so violently denied to Alvina will emerge as a factor in the way Lawrence represents his own relations with the Italians.

If Alvina's thralldom is to a passion, not a person, and her bondage linked to atavistic fantasies that Italy will allow her to realize, her subjugation becomes concrete and personal once she and Ciccio arrive on the Continent. She becomes a foreign object now, no longer an autonomous Englishwoman; officials "scrutinized her, and asked questions of Ciccio. *Nobody asked her anything—she might have been Ciccio's shadow,"* and her relative invisibility foreshadows something of the self-dismantling she will experience in her new, remotely situated, home (295, my emphasis). Indeed, the journey to Ciccio's native village is itself something of a liminal experience, marking the transition between the rational, lucid, and fungible spaces of the North to the mysterious, shadowy, yet fully embodied spaces of Italy *profonde*. As the landscape becomes more and more savage, more and more remote, Alvina and Ciccio arrive finally in Pescocalascio at day's end and, it seems, at the end of the world itself, a purely Lawrentian "heart of darkness." Alvina finds herself in a "a wild centre of an old, unfinished little mountain town" (304). As in *Aaron's Rod,* the center is dangerous, as opposed to—or as well as—benign. And because the landscape is so fully charged with meaning, the experience of expatriation seems to lose its material grounding until we are brought up short by Alvina's confrontation with the concrete manifestation of raw poverty and a radically different conception of spatial relations. Italy's porous landscape—the unfinished quality of its built environment, the spaces that combine inside and outside, that merge function—are an affront to the Englishwoman's sensibilities. Alvina's response is contradictory. She is both appalled by the barbaric rusticity of her surroundings with their overwhelming sense of dirt and disorder and exhilarated by their alterity, and this sense of doubleness will persist until the end of the novel. Here is no charming, light-infused Impressionist canvas, but the disappointing and alarming encounter with poverty and underdevelopment. What a contrast with Aaron Sisson's joyous arrival in Novara! Lawrence lets us know that not all geographic displacements represent spiritual or existential enhancement. As the text lingers upon the scenery, we are more and more aware of how far Alvina has traveled, as if to hell itself, and how far she is from the "lucidity" of England:

> And so, without any light but that of the stars, the cart went spanking and rattling downhill, down the pale road which wound down the head of the valley to the gulf of darkness below. Down in the darkness into the darkness they rattled, wildly, and without heed, the young driver making strange noises to his dim horse. (305)

If the "gulf of darkness below" calls upon us, as readers, to witness Alvina's descent into the abyss, for her the place "was all wonderful and amazing. . . . To her there was magnificence in the lustrous stars and the steepnesses, magic, rather terrible and grand"

(306). There is also the terror of dislocation as she looks helplessly up at the stars to get her bearing: "Overhead she saw the brilliance of Orion. She felt she was quite, quite lost. She had gone out of the world, over the border, into some place of mystery. She was lost to Woodhouse, to Lancaster, to England—all lost" (306). And we sense intimations of Nietzsche's tightrope walker "who [does] not know how to live, except by going under."[39] The doubleness and contrariety of her response to these wild and startling surroundings is once again apparent. In her journey to the "wild centre" she herself is decentered. For Alvina, getting lost means leaving the world of normative discourse and instrumental reason behind. Getting lost means crossing over into a zone where identity, agency, language, not to mention bourgeois domesticity, are threatened with nullification. Alvina will find her home in a space that seems "wild and desolate." The text is so spare in its simple enumeration of objects in the house that we can almost register from its silences the effect on her:

> Alvina looked at the room. There was a wooden settle in front of the hearth, stretching its back to the room. There was a little table under a square, recessed window, on whose sloping ledge were newspapers, scattered letters, nails and a hammer. On the table were dried beans and two maize cobs. In a corner were shelves, with two chipped enamel plates, and a small table underneath, on which stood a bucket of water with a dipper. Then there was a wooden chest, two little chairs, and a litter of faggots, cane, vine-twigs, bare maize-hubs, oak-twigs filling the corner by the hearth. (*LG*, 310)

The house is ice-cold, and Alvina, "almost stupefied with weariness and the cold, bruising air," climbs into the "icy cold" bed, "dazed with excitement and wonder." The environment itself seems to bear down upon her with the coldness of death, and the repetition of the word "lost" ("She was lost—lost—lost utterly"), like the blows of a hammer or the tolling of a bell, iterates and reiterates Alvina's state of utter desolation and our sense of expatriate disillusionment (313).

It is only in Ciccio's physical presence that she finds warmth, but it is not life giving. Rather it confirms her sense of dissolution; she feels "his power and his warmth invade her and extinguish her. The mad and desperate passion that was in him sent her completely unconscious again, completely unconscious" (313). Gone is the capacity for redescription; gone are the pleasures of nomadic free play. And what is worse, the shock of her new surroundings has a desolating effect not only upon Alvina, but also upon Ciccio and his uncle. Her presence among them seems to introduce a kind of desperation into their hearts, as if they are forced to see themselves through her eyes. Just as Ciccio's narcotic aura bore down upon her in England, so too does the air of Pescocalascio. A negative center of consciousness, Alvina introduces a postlapsarian sense of impoverishment that weighs just as heavily on the natives.

> There is no mistake about it, Alvina was a lost girl. She was cut off from everything she belonged to. Ovid isolated in Thrace might well lament. The soul itself needs its own mysterious nourishment. This nourishment lacking, nothing is well. At Pescocalascio it was the mysterious influence of the mountains and valleys themselves which seemed always to be annihilating the Englishwoman: nay, not only her, but the very natives themselves. Ciccio and Pancrazio clung to her, essentially, as if she saved them also from extinction. It needed all her courage. Truly, she had to support the souls of the two men. At first she did not realise. She was only stunned with the strangeness of it all: startled, half-enraptured with the terrific beauty of the place, half-horrified by its savage annihilation of her. But she was stunned. The days went by. It seems there are places which resist us, which have the power to overthrow our psychic being. It seems as if every country has its potent negative centres, localities which savagely and triumphantly refuse our living culture. And Alvina had struck one of these, here on the edge of the Abruzzi. (314)

And the question arises: was Alvina fated to meet her spiritual demise here or was it, after all, a random outcome of expatriation, the "unfortunate" fall? And "if every country has its potent negative centres," what is the quality of such negativity? For, to be sure, the landscape has its compensations, but they are bound up with elementary forces—to use the words of the rational Mrs. Tuke—forces of the type that quite overwhelm intelligence, forces antithetical to the Englishwoman and the essentially Protestant, rational self at the core of modern individualism. These do not nourish the Christian soul, but rather forge in its place a pagan harshness that is commensurate with the environment and true to the pagan spirit that is alive in the metaphorically "hollow" spaces and "secret entries" of the landscape.

> How unspeakably lovely it was, no one could ever tell, the grand, pagan twilight of the valleys, savage, cold, with a sense of ancient gods who knew the right for human sacrifice. It stole away the soul of Alvina. She felt transfigured in it, clairvoyant in another mystery of life. A savage hardness came in her heart. The gods who had

demanded human sacrifice were quite right, immutably right. The fierce, savage gods who dipped their lips in blood, these were the true gods. The terror, the agony, the nostalgia of the heathen past was a constant torture to her mediumistic soul. She did not know what it was. But it was a kind of neuralgia in the very soul, never to be located in the human body, and yet physical. (315)

The discourse of the sublime transforms the expatriate project into a quasi-divine mission of spiritual self-sacrifice in which the pleasures of self-dismantling are as intense as its terrors. Alvina's transfiguration from subject to one who is subjected reverses the relationship between the self and the site of displacement upon which the expatriate experience—as that which is chosen—is predicated. In a pantheistic world where the rivers speak and snow breathes, "a wild, terrible happiness would take hold of her, beyond despair, but very like despair. No one would ever find her. She had gone beyond the world into the pre-world, she had reopened on the old eternity" (316). These echoes of Lawrence's "mystical materialism" express the luminosity of Alvina's dark moments, where both loss and compensation hang in the grasp of the wholly Other.[40] In going "beyond" she *has* become, in a way, "a sacred prostitute," and we recognize now the significance of the nickname Ciccio has given her: "Allaye," which is a play on several slang words for the female anatomy. Indeed, Alvina is admonished earlier in the novel by Mrs. Tuke (herself in the thrall of a loathsome pregnancy), who asserts that "life is a mass of unintelligent forces to which intelligent human beings are submitted. *Prostituted*" (*LG*, 283, my emphasis).

Despite the sublimity of these porous moments when the antique past rises up into the present, the text is sensitive to practical realities as well. For Alvina, negotiating day to day with the environment is a constant challenge. Eventually, the material crudity of her surroundings and the new webs of interlocution imposed upon her drive her deeper into isolation, shoring up the fragments of her lost world. The bourgeois self, rational and disciplinary, fights back in a flurry of housecleaning and orderliness that seeks to recreate the dwelling in the image of the self—the "English housewife"—and this in contrast with the "hap-hazard, useless way of Italians all day long, getting nothing done" (317). She washed and scrubbed the utensils, the tables and shelves, the settle, the windows; she swept the stone-laid earth of a floor, but to no avail. The place is dirty and ice-cold. Finally she falls ill, and "even in the sunshine the crude comfortlessness and inferior savagery of the place only repelled her" (319). And while Alvina is bound to Pescocalascio by the ties that bind her to Ciccio, she is even more alienated than she was in England, where at least she was mobile. Once again, then, we see the extent of Lawrence's disillusionment with "organic" solutions to the problems of modernity. Once again, we sense his repugnance toward agrarian realities and forms of social intercourse.

For Pescocalascio is not only the enchanted landscape of the sublime, it is also social space. Bauman asserts:

> The 'strangeness' of strangers means precisely our feeling of *being lost*, of not knowing how to act and what to expect, and the resulting unwillingness of engagement. Avoidance of contact is the sole salvation but even a complete avoidance, were it possible, would not save us from a degree of anxiety and uneasiness caused by a situation always pregnant with the danger of false steps and costly blunders. [My emphasis][41]

Alvina is instructed by Ciccio's uncle, for example, *never* to go to the market without either himself or Ciccio. Ironically, social relations in Pescocalascio replicate those of Woodhouse. "Lost, forlorn aborigines," the natives treated her "as if she were a higher being" (*LG*, 316). And there is a failure of recognition on both sides, each locked into an "imaginary," as opposed to a dialogic or intersubjective, conception of the Other that does not permit movement beyond the images of gentlewoman and peasant. Indeed, it is only on the basis of a biological and essentialist commonality with the native women, a shared sense of "the helpless passion for the man, the same remoteness from the world's actuality," that Alvina feels any connection at all with the social life of the village (320). Ciccio and his uncle discourage her even from learning Italian.

Alvina's condition improves when Ciccio and his uncle create a proper "English" space for her with "pots and pans and vegetables and sweet-things and thick, rush matting and two wooden arm-chairs and one old soft armchair" (320), and she becomes pregnant. Rather than more fully integrating her, if not into the community, at least into the dynamic life forces at the center of her new world, pregnancy serves only to underscore the contradictions of her life. This is *not* a narrative of domestic romance. On the one hand, she is finally settled into her own bourgeois space, with "her cups and plates and spoons, her own things," and "a clean room of her own where she could sew and read" (322). She is also productive and learns to spin sheep's wool into thread. If the flow of desire leads out of the enclosure of home, home reasserts itself in the new, spinning order out of chaos. Alvina begins to reterritorialize. On the other hand, certain realizations about Ciccio, whose spatial orientations are essentially porous and premodern, complicate the design:

> Ciccio's home would never be his castle. His castle was the piazza of Pescocalascio. His home was nothing to him but a possession, and a hole to sleep in. He didn't *live* in it. He lived in the open air, and in the community. When the true Italian came out in him, his veriest home was the piazza of Pescocalascio, the little sort of market-place where the roads met in the village, under the castle, and where the men stood in groups and talked, talked, talked. This was where Ciccio belonged: his active mindful self. His active, mindful self was none of hers. She only had his passive self, and his family passion. His masculine mind and intelligence had its home in the little public square of his village. (330)

What frustrates Alvina here is her inability to construct a truly shared domestic space, not Ciccio's denial to her of his thinking self—and this because, finally, "she felt that in matters intellectual he was rather stupid" (331). In fact, the space of the home represents the only link between them, so its devaluation is a real problem.

Despite Alvina's preoccupation with her own domestic space, she has a violent aversion to the interiors of other Italian structures. No doubt Lawrence's own impressions come into play here, as he remarked in a letter to Lady Cynthia Asquith that "the Italians don't consider their houses, like we do, as being their extended persons. In England my house is my outer cuticle, as a snail has a shell. Here it is a hole into which I creep out of the rain and the dark."[42] If the Italian home conjures up images of moles, worms, and other earth dwellers, the interiors of Italian churches inspire a similar sense of disgust. Indeed, so disturbing is their "sense of trashy, repulsive, degraded fetish-worship" that it seems to extend well beyond anti-Catholicism to a generalized horror of the Italians themselves. Alvina feels

> that if she lived in this part of the world at all, she must avoid the *inside* of it. She must never, if she could help it, enter into any interior but her own—neither into house nor church nor even shop or post-office, if she could help it. The moment she went through a door the sense of dark repulsiveness came over her. If she was to save her sanity she must keep to the open air, and avoid any contact with

human interiors. When she thought of the insides of the native people she shuddered with repulsion, as in the great, degraded church of Casa Latina. They were horrible. (*LG*, 333)

Italy's carnality, represented here as, perhaps, a giant maw, stomach, or female sexual organ, is a zone of pollution and potential madness. Part of the problem, this passage suggests, is the confusion between outside and inside that Italy's porosity poses. The outer cuticle that is the Englishman's second skin becomes, in Italy, a medium for contamination rather than a bar to the excesses of disorder, dirt, cold. And there is the sense, as well, that the organic, far from affording relief from alienation and the "priced and ticketed" world, is like a noxious bog, like quicksand, and that being "inside" the organic community is, perhaps, worse than being "home."

For Alvina the church seems to be the locus of these anxieties, epitomizing for her an unwholesome crossing of boundaries between the sacred and the profane. In "The Spinner and the Monks," Lawrence describes the heady brew of bestiality and exoticism that attends his visit to an Italian church:

It was very dark, and *impregnated* with centuries of incense. It affected me like the *lair* of some enormous creature. My senses were *roused*, they *sprang awake* in the *hot, spiced darkness*. My skin was expectant, as if it expected some *contact*, some *embrace*, as if it were aware of the contiguity of the physical world, the physical contact with the darkness and the *heavy, suggestive substance* of the enclosure. It was a *thick fierce darkness* of the senses. But my soul shrank. (105, my emphasis)

Here again we see the North-South binary, now represented in terms of asceticism and carnality. The explicitly sexual nature of Lawrence's language calls forth, as before, genital imagery that is both vaguely repulsive and insistently, alarmingly thrilling. Against the sensual, the visceral, the almost breathless confession of desire, four short words are asserted on behalf of the beleaguered spirit. Where the Puritan North, according to Lawrence, strives for greater and greater abstraction, the Italian church is the abode of the corporeal: "lousy-looking, dressed-up dolls, life size and tinselly, . . . the blood-streaked Jesus on the crucifix; the mouldering, mumbling, filthy peasant women on their knees" (333). How deep is Lawrence's ambivalence toward the materiality, the frank extravagance, of Catholicism's representation of the divine!

Finally, and despite the extreme beauty of the outside world, the sensual overload of sunlight, landscape, and flora leads to the same sense of annihilation for Alvina; there is simply no construct, mental or physical, that can shelter her from the horrors of disintegration. *The Lost Girl* ends on a note of both hope and despair. With the outbreak of the First World War and Ciccio's inscription, Ciccio and Alvina console themselves with the hope for a new life in America upon Ciccio's return. America, we may infer, represents the promise of a dialectical movement forward motivated by the gradual obsolescence of the old way of life. As a young dandy passing through Pescocalascio tells Alvina: "[T]his country is a country for old men . . . You won't stop here. Nobody young can stop here" (334). In a way, the outbreak of the First World War functions to mask the essential failure of this experiment in expatriation. At the same time, America represents a deferral of expatriate resolution. On the one hand, Alvina cannot be integrated into Pescocalascio; on the other, she cannot return "home." She is, literally, without a path, unless that path leads, literally, to the New World. For Alvina does—or did, at any rate—possess a Nietzschean spirit, perpetually recreating herself, inventing her own values; but she can do this only in space that is quintessentially modern. On the far side of social reality where the Nietzschean hero builds his future, she is disabled by the pastness of traditional culture that, paradoxically, is not the locus of productive barbarian energies (these have been emptied out and now erupt in the metropolis). She is divided against herself, desiring both creation and decreation, and seems to lose her way, not so much in the Abruzzi as in the labyrinth of modern anxieties, fears, and desires that attend sexuality, gender, and bourgeois domesticity.

It is appropriate, in a way, that Alvina retains the pejorative nickname given to her by the Tawaras, despite its seeming transmutation into a term of endearment, and despite the fact that the narrative voice of the text continues to refer to her as Alvina. It reflects, perhaps, Alvina's doubleness and the text's uneasiness with the underlying suggestion that Alvina's loss is really her gain, that the ravishing of a more or less middle-aged woman by a young and churlish—but darkly exotic—"foreigner" should somehow be compensation for the sublimation of her will (*The Plumed Serpent* rehearses a similar narrative). Alvina appears to take for granted her intellectual superiority to Ciccio, a reflection, no doubt, of her self-understanding as a Western subject of modernity. Hence, her improbable union with an "inferior" figure who is then contractually invested with legal and symbolic power over her is, in some sense, parodic. Ciccio is a phallic creature whose *symbolic,* as opposed to legal, authority holds no sway over her. In the novel it is Alvina who is conceptually oriented and rational and thus more in alignment with a "modern," as opposed to a "premodern," patriarchal ideal. Indeed, Ciccio is characterized as "stupid" throughout the text. Though rich in physical and sexual power, he is characterized by traits aligned with femininity. The marginality of the "savage" Other, his "feminine" qualities of unreason, sensuality, and emotionality, makes him an inapt representative of the phallus, the Name-of-the-Father.

The Lost Girl is a narrative journey at once into a character's own "heart of darkness" and into the fully embodied landscape of rural Italy. If Alvina, a quintessentially modern subject, contains the darkness of the "premodern" within her, so, too, is Italy Western Europe's own spiritual bog. Industrial England is valued for its lucidity, while the sun-drenched South of the Romantic imagination is the abode of darkness, reversing conventional antimodern tropes. For Lawrence, the "idiocy of rural life," as Engels and Marx have characterized it, represents an inadequate response to the ills of modernity. The Italian narratives, like modernity itself, cannot resolve their own contradictions. The ethics of expatriation, therefore, are about self-making and self-dismantling at the same time.

It is interesting, I think, to contrast *The Lost Girl* with a very similar contemporary narrative, Nadine Gordimer's *The Pickup,* published in 2001. In that novel, the protagonist, Julie Summers, a thoroughly "modern" (in a late twentieth-century sense) young woman, falls in love with an Arab car mechanic who is an illegal worker in postapartheid South Africa. When he is threatened with deportation, she insists upon leaving the country with him. He marries her, and they return to his small village on the edge of the desert to live with his family. Unlike Lawrence, of course, Gordimer grants spiritual and intellectual parity to the foreigner. He is intelligent and fully cognizant of what he believes to be Julie's latest "adventure." The surprise is that while he is intent upon leaving the underdeveloped world and finally succeeds in getting them passports to America, she decides at the last moment to stay. She is as intent upon leaving home (a generic modern world) as he is; there is no common narrative that can contain them. It's interesting too that while Lawrence invests Alvina with a self-shattering desire for the Other that extends to the physical environment from which he comes, Julie Summers actually becomes a more "authentic" self; she establishes ties, experiences "situatedness in displacement." She does this in the context of a society segregated by gender. She lives primarily in a woman's world, gaining the respect of Abdu's mother and sisters. If *The Pickup* marks a real transformation of the ethical project, it nevertheless extends into the twenty-first century the desire to be elsewhere and otherwise. Like *The Lost Girl*, it reflects a continuing sense of ambivalence concerning marriage and domesticity.

Lawrence and the Italians

In *Twilight in Italy*, Lawrence had occasion to reflect upon the relationship of Italians to America; his reflection is, to some extent, a meditation on the difference between the North and the South and the fate of Italians in the "modern" world. He writes of a young Italian, Giovanni, who having spent many years in America had returned to Italy and started a family. Nevertheless he was planning to return alone to America for some indeterminate period of time. This is not a reasoned decision, but an impulsive one:

> There was a strange, almost frightening destiny upon him, which seemed to take him away, always away from home, from the past, to that great, raw America. He seemed scarcely like a person with individual choice, more like a creature under the influence of fate which was disintegrating the old life and precipitating him, a fragment inconclusive, into the new chaos. [43]

Although this passage suggests something of the terror that is outside the construct called home at the heart of *The Lost Girl*, Giovanni is not, like Alvina, "a subject in process," but "a fragment inconclusive." He is, to be sure, a fellow traveler, "belonging in his final *desire* to our world, the world of consciousness and deliberate action" [my emphasis], but not a sharer in that status, for "he seemed like a prisoner being conveyed from one form of life to another, or like a soul in trajectory, that has not yet found a resting-place."[44] Is this the involuntary trajectory of the modernity's Other, a refugee from the poverty and despair of the spaces progress left behind, whose obsolete way of life has rendered him truly homeless? Is he, thus, the servant or migrant laborer who shares in the dislocation but not the "play" of expatriation, or merely the darkest version of the expatriate narrative in which the subject is transformed into an object of destiny? Lawrence's Italian portraits suggest the former.

Faustino, the young Italian who is the subject of "Il Duro," is even less spiritually endowed than Giovanni. "Il Duro," as Lawrence calls him, resembles Ciccio physically and temperamentally. He has also spent a considerable amount of time in America and so, like Ciccio's, his world has been somewhat enlarged. Although Lawrence feels that Il Duro is attracted to him, "almost loves him" in fact, there no sense of identity between them. Lawrence is a subject in process, while Il Duro is fixed, ahistorical, and "as clear and fine as semi-transparent rock, as a substance in moonlight. He seemed like a crystal that has achieved its final shape and has nothing more to achieve" (176–77). With this we are reminded of the "rocky fixity" of the large peasant encountered by Aaron Sisson in the third-class compartment of an Italian train; here the figure is rendered as something of an aesthetic object, but an object to be sure. Even Il Duro's attraction to the Englishmen is represented as the product of mechanical forces rather than that of a desiring subject:

> [The English *signori*] seemed to exercise a sort of magnetic attraction over him. It was something of the purely physical world, as a magnetised needle swings towards soft iron. He was quite helpless in the relation. Only by mechanical attraction he gravitated into line with us. But there was nothing between us except our complete difference. It was like night and day flowing together. (178)

So while Lawrence speaks the language of eroticism in his evocation of Il Duro, the latter is, nevertheless, not a fellow human being. He is, rather, "a creature in intimate communion with the sensible world," who, "like some strange animal god, doubled on his haunches, before the young vines, and swiftly, vividly, without thought, cut, cut, cut at the young budding shoots" before striding away with a "curious half goat-like movement." Lawrence's meditation on Il Duro's refusal to marry is instructive:

> In the flesh there is connection, but only in the spirit is there a new thing created out of two different antithetic things. In the body I am conjoined with the woman. But in the spirit my conjunction with her creates a third thing, an absolute, a Word, which is neither me nor her, nor of me nor of her, but which is absolute. And Faustino had none of this spirit. (177)

Denying "the spirit" of eroticism to Il Duro, there is no basis for intersubjectivity. The face of the Other offers no clue to the self: "He looked at me steadily, finally. And I could see it was impossible for us to understand each other, or for me to understand him. I could not understand the strange white gleam of his eyes, where it came from" (176).

In what kind of social space does Lawrence encounter Giovanni and Il Duro? There is a sense of care for the concrete Other, but the concrete Other is not a self like Lawrence. In the aesthetic space of the text, the portraits are evocative and sympathetic, and we can say that, far from condemning the Italian peasant to caricature or stock representation, we feel Lawrence struggling to understand the limitations of his own judgment and sensitivity, as well as his own desire. This work of the self reminds of me of William Connolly's relational arts of the self, a type of self-artistry that involves "working on yourself in relation to the cultural differences through which you have acquired definition. Doing so to render yourself more open to responsive engagement with alternative faiths, sensualities, gender practices, ethnicities."[45] In some sense, perhaps *The Lost Girl* is a text that mediates Lawrence's desire for the Other. If his limitations include a certain "classism," it may be because Lawrence, on account of his own class identity, finds himself, like Aaron Sisson, oddly placed. If expatriation provides a way to evade one's class status, Lawrence is not above exploring its anomalies.

Mr. Noon/D. H. Lawrence

For Lawrence, then, the periphery functions as a space to lay claim to female Otherness in the name of the masculine, a space of individuation from the mother(land), a reprieve from the limitations of class, and a place to reimagine gender relations. Italy, as Lawrence asserts in *Aaron's Rod*, is a country of men. In the final portion of the novel fragment that is part 2 of *Mr. Noon*, the protagonists, Gilbert and Johanna, who are thinly disguised fictionalizations of Lawrence and Frieda, arrive at the Austrian-Italian border. They respond in different ways:

> The world had changed. One felt it immediately. The station at Trento was still Austrian—there one was still on Germanic ground. But the moment one was outside, in the piazza with its gaudy flowers, and in the streets of the town, one knew one had passed the mysterious dividing line. . . . That secret, forlorn, suspicious atmosphere that pervades all southern towns the moment one leaves the main street was very evident in Trento. Gilbert and Johanna both felt it for the first time. And Gilbert was thrilled, and Johanna all at once felt homeless, like a waif. (357)

Gilbert's love affair with Johanna achieves a transcendent quality in Italy, but his spiritual and sensual awakening is effected through the violence and tearing of parturition:

There are worlds within worlds within worlds of unknown life and joy inside [man]. But every time, it needs a sort of cataclysm to get out of the old world into the new. It needs a very painful shedding of an old skin. It needs a fight with the matrix of the old era, a bitter struggle to the death with the old, warm, well-known mother of our days. Fight the old, enclosing mother of our days—fight her to the death—and defeat her—and then we shall burst out into a new heaven and a new earth, delicious. But it won't come out of lovey-doveyness. It will come out of sheer, pure, consummated fight, where the soul fights blindly for air, for life, a new space. . . . Death to the old enshrouding body politic, the old womb-idea of our era! (369–70)

And here Lawrence echoes, perhaps most poignantly, the admonition of Nietzsche against complacency:

With your values and world of good and evil you do violence when you value; and this is your hidden love and the splendor and trembling and overflowing of your soul. But a more violent force and a new overcoming grow out of your values and break egg and eggshell.[46]

Mr. Noon leaves its lovers as they are. Lawrence abandoned the novel in 1922. But it is likely that "the glamourous vast multipli-city, all made up of differences, mediaeval, romantic differences [that] seemed to break his soul like a chrysalis into a new life" (134) would lead to eventual disillusionment for Gilbert Noon. In a let-ter written that same year, Lawrence explicitly repudiated his flight to marginal zones:

But I do think, still more now I am out here, that we make a mistake forsaking England and moving out into the periphery of life. After all, Taormina, Ceylon, Africa, America—as far as *we* go, they are only the negation of what we ourselves stand for and are: and we're rather like Jonas running away from the place we belong. That is the conclusion that is forced on me. . . . I really think that the most living clue of life is in us Englishmen in England, and the great mistake we make is in not uniting together in the strength of the real living clue—religious in the most vital sense—uniting together in England and so carrying the vital spark through. Because as far as we are concerned it is in danger of being quenched. I know now it is a shirking of the issue to look to Buddha or the Hindu or to our own working men, for the impulse to carry through.[47]

This paragraph is remarkable for its acuity in getting to the psycho-dynamic heart of Orientalism. Commenting on Lawrence's ambiva-lence concerning the Other, Booth observes that

[t]he racial 'other,' different places and cultures, had been seen as offering so much and yet on contact a strong sense of doubt and

insecurity was registered, an uncertainty that contributed to the force of the racist and imperial statements. The theory of a necessary engagement with what is 'other' and non-European as the means by which dissolution and decay might be reversed, with which Lawrence left Italy in 1922, collapsed as a result of his journeying."[48]

And in spite of the plea for a communitarian solution to the entropy of modern life, Lawrence continued to travel, living as an expatriate in zones of the periphery until his death some eight years later. Critics have remarked upon the wildly contradictory comments made by Lawrence in his travel writing and correspondence, which manifest themselves most of all in a series of binary oppositions—realist and mystic, Christian and pagan, misogynist and feminist, confirmed Englishman and confirmed expatriate[49] —which confront one another in imaginative geographies that oppose north to south, center to periphery. It is ironic that the expression "spirit of place," which he popularized and which would be taken up and expanded by Lawrence Durrell, would be so lacking in generosity toward the expatriate. Lawrence writes:

> Every continent has its own great spirit of place. Every people is polarized in some particular locality which is home, the homeland. Different places on the face of earth have different vital effluence, different vibration, different chemical exhalation, different polarity with different stars: call it what you like, but the spirit of place is a great reality.[50]

But, Lawrence argues, bringing us back again to MacIntyre and the values of communitarianism:

> Men are free when they are in a living homeland, not when they are straying or breaking away. . . . Men are free when they belong to a living, organic, *believing* community [Lawrence's emphasis], active in fulfilling some unfulfilled, perhaps unrealized purpose. Not when they are escaping to some wild west. The most unfree souls go west, and shout of freedom. Men are freest when they are most unconscious of *freedom. The shout is a rattling of chains, always was.* [My emphasis][51]

By this logic, then, the protagonists of *Aaron's Rod* and *The Lost Girl* are, indeed, destined to remain at once homeless and fettered, and this duality reflects itself in their existential liminality. For unEnglished though they are, the personal redemption they seek is one of unfreedom, where freedom must be a collective project. Betwixt and between, they find it difficult to turn the space of the periphery into moral space. If the true abode of freedom is communitarian, the dialogism that would underscore such a vision is inherently lacking. "The Spirit of Place," which was written some-time in 1918, was the first of a series of essays known as *Studies in Classic American Literature*. Although the entire collection had been written before Lawrence ever set foot on the North American con-tinent, he had already made the break from England and had begun to reflect upon culture and geography in terms evocative of roman-tic nationalism. Having been produced during the same period of time as the novels discussed here, "The Spirit of Place" throws into relief the tensions that animate their pages. "I break my heart over England," he writes in 1922 aboard ship from Ceylon to Australia.

> Those natives are *back* of us—in the living sense *lower* than we are. But they're going to swarm over us and suffocate us. We are, have been for five centuries, the growing tip. Now we're going to fall. But you don't catch me going back on my whiteness and Englishness and myself. English in the teeth of all the world, even in the teeth of England. How England deliberately undermines England.[52]

Torn between a heroic loyalty to England, the "growing tip" of the world, and a profound antipathy toward its very progressive-ness, Lawrence finds himself condemned to a living death on the periphery among the "inferior races," where he rattles his chains in an ecstasy of passion and despair. In *Twilight in Italy*, he traces the de-divination of the flesh through the movement from pagan-ism to Christianity and the logos, hoping thereby to elucidate the strengths and weaknesses of his own culture. For Lawrence, the Renaissance marked a great turning point for the South. Whereas the North continued on, in the spirit of the Middle Ages, to dis-tance itself more and more from flesh, Italy rededicated itself to the flesh and the senses. In terms of identity this is, for Lawrence, crucial because it is, paradoxically, in the senses that the true "I" resides: "I can never have another man's senses."[53] In pure abstrac-tion, the abode of the North, there can be no me. And we therefore "envy" the Italian "because he worships the Godhead in the flesh," but at the same time, "we feel superior to him, as if he were a child and we adult" (124). And we are superior, according to Lawrence, for having "gone beyond the phallus in search of the Godhead, the creative origin" where "we found the physical forces and the secrets of science," Finally, however,

> [w]e have exalted Man far above the man who is in each one of us. Our aim is a perfect humanity, a perfect and equable human consciousness, selfless. And we obtain it in the subjection, reduction,

analysis, and destruction of the Self. So on we go, active in science and mechanics, and social reform. But we have exhausted ourselves in the process. . . . But our habit of life, our very constitution, prevents our being quite like the Italian. The phallus will never serve us as a Godhead, because we do not believe in it; no northern race does. (124–25)

And this, it seems to me, leaves Lawrence with no place to go. Expatriation in the periphery holds out the promise of personal liberation, existential risk taking, and a radical immersion in the new from which, it is hoped, a new world will emerge. But the expatriate's new world is the already present world of the native. Italy's alterity—its living antiquity, its hollow spaces—represents a sublime complement to the finely tuned "Northern" consciousness, the self abstracted from its concrete particularity, but redounds upon the subject in the alienating glance of the Italian, who is particular. The Italian is envied but often not respected, produced but often not recognized; he is, finally, the abjected image of the subject himself. Maybe it is only in the dialectical movement of the self between home and the world that a new dwelling place can emerge. As Deleuze and Guattari write: "What matters is to break through the wall, even if one has to become black like John Brown."[54] The expatriate, as these novels show us, breaks through that wall.

And through that little crack one has one's first glimpse, as Gilbert had his first sudden newness of experience and life-comprehension in Riva. Afterwards one loses the crack, and sits just as tight under the painted ceiling. Even one chants the praise of the ideal, the infinite, the spiritual. But one will come to the crack again, and madly fight to get a further glimpse, madly and frenziedly struggle with the dear old infinite. And thus rip just a little wider gap in it, just a little wider: after tearing oneself considerably.[55]

4

The Dark Dream:
Paul Bowles and the Quest for Non-Sense

I wanted experience to lead where it would, not to lead it to some end point given in advance. And I say at once that it leads to no harbor (but to a place of bewilderment, of nonsense).

Georges Bataille

It may be, says W. H. Auden, "that in a not remote future, it will be impossible to distinguish human beings living on one area of the earth's surface from those living on any other." It is comforting to imagine that when that day arrives we may be in a position to have the inhabitants of a nearby planet as our Jumblies. There is always the possibility too, that they may have us as theirs.

Paul Bowles

THE PROFESSOR OF PAUL BOWLES'S "A Distant Episode" is one of the earliest Bowlesian questors to move beyond the discursive limits of narrative; he is an exemplar of the Western man of reason undone by the desire for mastery and surrender in his encounter with alterity. Following him, the reader is brought up short, suspended somewhere in the liminal consciousness of a fading Western subject. Where Lawrentian expatriates in Italy are also undone—the destruction of Aaron's flute; Alvina Houghton's loss of a self anchored by class, culture, and national identity; Gilbert Noon's "unEnglishing"—they generally retain the power to remake themselves. True initiates, they suffer loss in anticipation of reconstitution and reentry into a world of structure. While the fictional imagination from which these characters emerge does not, or cannot, represent what form this might take, it does not abandon hope for some dialectical resolution in a fictional beyond. Perhaps in the wake of World War II, however, as images of Auschwitz and Hiroshima entered the consciousness of modernity, the magnitude of human devastation and the likelihood of nuclear holocaust produced a more extreme, more austere ethics and a more exposed, more vulnerable subject, one deeply attuned to destruction. If an ethics of expatriation for Lawrence is about the achievement of freedom through contingency and redescription whose "charge" is derived, in part, through the sublime encounter with horror and abjection, for Bowles the stakes are higher, the paradoxes of freedom more unforgiving; the horror itself becomes central. And Bowles seems compelled to record this story, his narratives bearing witness over and over to the self's undoing.

Bowles's Professor represents a kind of protagonist for whom there can be no reconstitution, a protagonist whose negation of his own "social existence" can be accomplished only through a concomitant annihilation of self. Paradoxically, though, Bowles is far more open than is Lawrence to active engagement with the Other. Indeed, the fictions return obsessively to the meetings and mis-meetings of Western and non-Western characters. Often, the Other is instrumental to the protagonist's project of self-dismantling, but sometimes the text imaginatively explores the Other's viewpoint in ways that both complicate and interrogate the idealized narratives of expatriation that emerge in counterpoint to narrated events. These are narratives of engagement with the cultural other, polyphonic works, but they are far from being cheerful tales of cultural syncretism. More often than not, as in Bowles's third novel, *The Spider's House*, the encountered Other is already cut adrift in the liminality of his or her own unresolved cultural or historical trajectory. To this Bowlesian Other we might compare Lawrence's "forlorn aborigines," whose unsituatedness parallels the unsituatedness of their Western counterparts. With their principals moving in opposite spatial and temporal directions, such meetings do not produce, for the Western subject, the categorical groundings that inhere in notions of authenticity and primitivism. Far from "reauthenticating" him (or her), the Other-in-process tends to further disperse—and confuse—rather than to consolidate the "subject of modernity."

Like Lawrence, Bowles is interested in exploring the Otherness of the space beyond conscious knowing, the space of the self beyond normative structural bounds. For Bowles, however, that space is wholly incompatible with human endeavor (translated as "project" in Bataille's formulation). It is a site of inchoate horror— of which North African landscapes and native quarters are often the fictional embodiment—rather than vitality (or perhaps the vitality of horror), from which there is no return to structure. If we imagine a Bowlesian ethics of expatriation as a mode of self-exploration (conceived, alternately, as self-constitution or self-dismantling) set in motion by the experience of liminality in the periphery, the fiction, like that of Lawrence, offers a number of different stagings of the project. There are works that organize the expatriate experience around scenes of cruelty, bodily violation, and death, such as "A Distant Episode," *The Sheltering Sky,* and *Let It Come Down.* But there are others, such as "Tea on the Mountain," "Here to Learn," and *The Spider's House,* that explore, however provisionally, the possibility of intersubjective recognition between the expatriate and the native. The one represents an ethics of expatriation that is radically isolating and antihumanist, the other an ethics of constructive engagement with the Other in which their co-presence sparks a productive tension that animates each work of fiction. At the very extremes of form, Bowles the expatriate disappears behind a narrative persona that seems indistinguishable from the Moroccan storytellers whose works he has translated.

The Bowlesian expatriate, like those of Lawrence and Durrell, is in flight from the usual panoply of evils associated with modernity: rationalization, standardization, embourgeoisement, the culture of discipline, Nietzsche's "strict network and hairshirt of duties."[1] Like Durrell's *Alexandria Quartet* and the Italian novels of Lawrence, moreover, Bowles's expatriate fictions focus upon what Kaja Silverman calls "marginal male subjectivities," as manifested in figures "who are not equal to the phallic legacy."[2] Like those other fictions, Bowles's work is responsive to historical trauma. There is the shattering experience of the Second World War and, in its aftermath, cultural upheavals at home. The postwar period in both England and America, like fin-de-siècle England, was marked by trauma and categorical instability in terms of masculine self-definition. On the one hand, the "fiction of a phallic masculinity" could not be sustained in the war's aftermath, and Silverman points to a number of Hollywood films, *The Best Years of Our Lives* and *It's a Wonderful Life* among them, as cultural markers of this collapse.[3] On the other hand, the war had liberated women from the home, giving rise to new narratives of female self-empowerment, including sexual empowerment, and new tensions between the genders. In the fifties, a definition of masculinity tied to domesticity and breadwinning seemed to shore up the dominant fiction. Maturity, in this paradigm of manhood, consisted primarily of settling down in marriage, starting a family, managing a home, having an occupation, and assuming civic and social responsibilities.[4] A man who failed to conform to this mode was either immature or unmanly. At the same, despite contemporary psychological understandings of what it meant to be a "mature" individual, conformity came to be associated with emasculation rather than masculinity. An early reaction against this rigidly defined category was the "grey flannel rebel" for whom "conformity" became the byword for male angst. Joseph Boone, citing Leo Braudy, remarks upon a "new prototype of vulnerable, bodily present, and countercultural masculinity, epitomized in film by James Dean, Montgomery Clift, and Lawrence Harvey, and in writing by Jack Kerouac and John Osborne."[5] His point is that the postwar period was characterized by contradictory constructions of masculinity and femininity. The countercultural male image is one that I would equate with a "marginal" male subjectivity, a subjectivity inadequate to the phallic mandate. The Bowlesian expatriate, I suggest, forms a part of this cultural imaginary. Silverman argues that *The Best Years of Our Lives* "openly links the trauma of war to the death drive," which it defines, she says, in terms similar to her own: "a force within the subject which seeks to reduce it to a psychic nothingness."[6] Bowles's ethics of expatriation circle tirelessly around this theme, but open out into something far more interesting.

D. H. Lawrence's novels of expatriation explore the subject's relationship to his or her identity once the culturally imposed structure is determined to be contingent and variable, and from the play of liminality and contingency in the marginal spaces of modernity, interesting social constructions emerge. But once the subject is thoroughly disimbricated from social forms and structures, from the channels of production and reproduction, from subservience to "project," the resulting immersion in chaos can just as easily point toward the horror of Kurtz in the metaphoric heart of darkness, and this is where Bowles's characters are led. In the fifties, Bowles's work was considered emblematic of the existential turn in fiction: the spectacle of man's confrontation with the absurd; his stubborn, even heroic, attempts to act; the heroism of his abjection—in short, modern man's incarnation as antihero. Writing in 1961, Ihab Hassan describes figures like Bowles's Professor as

> heroes in flight from civilization. They are seekers of something they cannot name—the failure of life, the graciousness of surrender, the

meaning of identity—who frequently become victims when they suddenly immerse themselves in a primitive culture which deprives them of the few sanctions Western society still provides. They are drawn to the central, the destructive, element of experience in its most brutal aspect; but they are unequipped to survive the frightful encounter, and their disintegration follows the hypnotic power of inexorable violence. The sinister transformation from pilgrim to prey, from incipient decay to total regression, is unattended by regeneration or self-discovery.[7]

The peculiar kind of fulfillment sought by these characters is, for Hassan, a paradoxical "discovery of self through loss of selfhood, recovery of identity through abnegation of the private will;" in a return to "aboriginal night," they seek freedom in "unconditional surrender."[8] We will see, however, that Bataille, writing several years earlier, characterizes such moments of radical self-dismantling in terms of "sovereignty" rather than surrender.

It is in landscapes of alterity that the Bowlesian protagonist joins cultural dislocation to radical kinds of freedom. Here is Bowles's more ecstatic embrace of that condition, as expressed when he was twenty-one in a letter to the poet Edouard Roditi in 1931:

> can one learn to discard thinking of one's self? it makes happiness sprout from under the armpits of trees, it makes scorpions dance for joy, and cliffs shudder in ecstacy [*sic*]. can one learn to discard one's self? the drums beat all the time. blood knocking at the door, the voice of eros, under the palms, behind the walls, by the fires at night, woven with the singing, mixed in with the pipes that shrill tunes we cannot understand, even as we climb the hill. mixed with the insects that drone. mixed with the rising crisis of our cheeks that lose their scrofulous aspect and become smooth as the plage once more, mixed with the blood beating all night in the hot room, with the fever hovering at the blinds, the ferns scraping, about which we have said so much years ago. will you ever learn the secret? shall i?[9]

To the extent one's goal is to "discard thinking of one's self," certain landscapes seem to invite risk taking. Bowles writes:

> Man is hated in the Sahara . . . one feels it in the sky, in the stories, in the air. It might as well be written in the stars: God Hates Man Pinky is a Rat. But of course, that can be exciting. Where life is prohibited, it becomes a delectable forbidden fruit, and that is the feeling one gets here: each instant is begrudged one by an implacable tyrant.[10]

Like one of those "places which resist us, which have the power to overthrow our psychic being,"[11] the desert is a site of ambivalent desire for Bowles, just as Pescocalascio is for Alvina and Alexandria for Darley. Another such landscape, just as threatening, is that of the native quarter with its serpentine streets and labyrinthine architecture. And, of course, there is Morocco itself, a frontier between Europe and Africa's "heart of darkness." Lying on the westernmost corner of Africa, Morocco, like Egypt, faces Europe to the north across a sea traversed for thousands of years by merchant ships from many continents. Yet the Levantine culture linking the tricontinental shores of the Mediterranean has been profoundly transformed by its contact with the industrial West and the colonial powers. Bowles's Moroccan figures are themselves the hybrid products of colonial occupation. If Lawrence was drawn to Italy as a site of organic return, Bowles seems to be drawn to Morocco both as a means to recuperate some sense of the premodern and as a *social* space. The Moroccan is there at every turn in the road; the native quarter beckons, drawing the Westerner along on the thread of his own desire.

What seems to be at issue is the curious status of those figures drawn to zones of dis-integration, zones where their defining status as individuated souls—as members of community, tribe, nation, and culture—falls away, where the falling away is itself attended by rituals of sexual violation, physical mutilation, and violence. The mismeetings of American expatriates and semi-Westernized Moroccans are dangerous precisely because they occur in the interstices of cultural, religious, and political systems. Scholars as disparate as the anthropologist Mary Douglas and the philosopher Henri LeFebvre have been concerned with the texture and quality of those spaces that, resistant to hegemonies of order and control, subvert the constraints of structure. Blurring boundaries, such spaces also complicate the relationship between the self, already internally divided against itself, and the Other. Bakhtin writes: "To be means to be for another, and through the other for oneself. A person has no sovereign internal territory, he is wholly and always on the boundary; looking inside himself, he looks *into the eyes of an other or with the eyes of another*" [Bakhtin's emphasis].[12] Bowles amplifies the risk, making the radical Other the crucible of the self. So it is with the Professor of "A Distant Episode": "Standing there at the edge of the abyss which at each moment looked deeper, with the dark face of the *qaouaji* framed in its moonlit burnous close to his own face, the Professor asked himself exactly what he felt" (42). It is in the face of the Other that the question of the self arises.

The Bowlesian oeuvre also suggests that the committed wanderer achieves a productive self-estrangement that clears the way for creativity. "When you've cut yourself off from the life you've been living," Bowles states in an interview, "and you haven't yet established another life, you're free. . . . If you don't know where you're going, you're even freer. . . . Probably if I hadn't had some contact with what you call 'exotic' places, it wouldn't have occurred to me to write at all."[13] Like Lawrence's Rawdon Lilly, hoping to get a new tune out of himself in a new place, Bowles links expatriation to creativity. And, as we have seen before in the expatriate narratives of Lawrence and Durrell, there is the negation of attachment, the refusal of the claims of home. Bowles writes to Aaron Copland in 1933:

> I hate America because I feel attached to it, and I don't want to feel that way. In Africa for instance, I can sit and feel unlocated; I can look at the landscape and turn the page and look at another, and it means nothing. But here I look at the landscape, and it looks back at me, and I am frightened of it, and I want to get out as fast as possible . . . I think every place in America is haunted.[14]

For Durrell, Greece was *precisely* the place that looks back, the place that delivers one to oneself. Bowles, on the other hand, seems drawn to opacity. He resists feeling located by locating himself in landscapes that provide no clue to the self. Rather than wisdom or self-knowledge, they offer bewilderment.

In what follows, I first discuss aspects of the French and American literary traditions that inform Bowles's work and the intellectual affinities between Bowles and Bataille. The heart of the chapter is an exploration of the ethics of expatriation through a reading of the fiction, "A Distant Episode," *The Sheltering Sky, Let It Come Down,* and *The Spider's House.* "A Distant Episode" introduces the thematic tension between the desire for self-dissolution or radical existential adventure and the desire for the Other that Bowles continues to explore in *The Sheltering Sky* and *Let It Come Down. The Spider's House* depicts the relationship between an American expatriate living in Fez and an illiterate young boy against the backdrop of impending colonial warfare. What I elicit is the extent to which these texts invoke idealized narratives of expatriation only to call them into question and foreground the depth and complexity of social relations in the periphery. In the final section, I examine the ethics of expatriation in relation to certain aspects of Bowles's own biographical narrative.

Literary Roots and Intellectual Affinities

While I suggest the affinity between expatriate narrative and the excesses of the late Romantics, it must also be said that Bowles's work is firmly rooted in the American literary tradition. American fiction's dark side has been amply documented by critics such as Richard Chase and Leslie Fiedler, who point out the discordant strains of intemperate passion, romantic phantasmagoria, and unresolved contradiction with which it is imbued. Chase, for example, notes that "many of the best American novels achieve their very being, their energy and their form, from the perception and acceptance not of unities but of radical disunities."[15] Fiedler, on the other hand, speaks of "a gothic fiction, nonrealistic and negative, sadist and melodramatic—a literature of darkness and the grotesque in a land of light and affirmation."[16] Indeed, his argument—that horror itself is the quintessence of American literature, that its gothic images reflect, among other things, a national imaginary obsessed with peculiarly American concerns: "a world without a significant history or a substantial past; a world which left behind the terror of Europe not for the innocence it dreamed of, but for new and special guilts associated with the rape of nature and the exploitation of dark-skinned people" (xxvi)—is one that construes American gothic in terms of America's own spatial and temporal liminality. Edgar Allen Poe, whose influence on Bowles is fairly incontestible, was a significant literary forebear. Poe's *Narrative of Arthur Gordon Pym of Nantucket* is a prototypical work of American gothic fiction, representing, for Fiedler, "that distinctively American strain of gothic, in which aristocratic villains of the European tale of terror are replaced by skulking primitives, and the natural rather than the sophisticated is felt as a primal threat" (377). Unlike that of authors whose gothic tropes are firmly embedded in the American landscape, however, the darkness of Bowles's vision is often inseparable from the exoticism of North Africa, a desiring and repetitive vision of estrangement, mismeeting, and, in the early fiction, even death.

In Fiedler's view, the frontier was the space for boyish male adventure stories or for refugees from society, a place where mothers do not come and male companionship may be celebrated. The liminal space of the frontier "was the 'ideal boundary' between two cultures, one 'civilized and cultivated,' the other 'wild and lawless'" (171). That kind of liminality finds its way into Bowles's literary imagination as well, and though Morocco may represent a different kind of frontier experience, I would argue that Bowles's fiction is haunted by many of the same concerns and ambiguities that Fiedler's analysis suggests, albeit with a distinctly twentieth-century cast: global domination, the westernization and homogenization of world cultures, the relationship of the Western subject to his colonized or formerly colonized Other. Twentieth-century concerns demand twentieth-century frontiers. For that reason, also, the whole issue of male companionship takes on a distinctly cross-cultural hue. We need to think of it as a complex interweaving of homoeroticism, cultural curiosity, and the power relations inscribed within any attempt at intimacy in the contact zone.

Invariably for Bowles, the skulking primitives of American Gothic become interlocutors rather than the insinuating projections of psychic scars, be they national or individual, partners in a different kind of enterprise. Deranged psychological states are rooted in radical cultural displacement. The ethics of self-exploration, situated in a historical and political context, are interrupted by the ethical demands of the Other. A project invested in radical antihumanistic energies and goals finds itself imbricated in another set of human relations. For Bowlesian dramas, as I suggested, are enacted in liminal spaces that give rise to both possibility and risk, leading inevitably to a fictional space beyond articulation, and tending, as well, to range far afield from the Western narrative tradition, with its attention to interiority and depth, to the orality and immediacy of Moroccan folk culture.

The expatriate narrative is not unlike the male-quest romance, which, in the late Victorian period, often takes the form of imperial romance. In *A World Outside*, Richard Patteson notes the affinities between the fiction of Paul Bowles and imperial romance as deconstructed and reimagined through the transforming lens of Joseph Conrad. Whereas the classic tale of imperial adventure represents the journey out, the domestication and appropriation of alien space, and the triumphal return of the adventurer, in Conrad's hands the project is undermined, its glory rendered ambivalent. Heroes don't overcome and conquer alterity; they are themselves transformed and made homeless in the process. Bowles shares Conrad's concern with the dark soul of Africa and the perhaps darker one of the West. As committed expatriates, both authors lived the doubleness of that condition whereby "home" is divided against itself; both have dwelt, both figuratively and literally, in multiple linguistic space. More importantly, they have both authored texts that can be read productively as allegories of imperialism and allegories of the soul. Horror is the point at which both readings converge; and horror is invariably located in the contact zone: the site where the self and its internal or external Other battle for sovereignty.

Patteson is concerned with the inadequacy of mental constructs to shore up the imperiled ego. He reads the play between interior space and exterior space wrought by the insufficiency of physical dwellings represented in the Bowlesian text as indicative of the frailty of all human constructs to protect the beleaguered subject against the unremitting "outsideness" of the world. While Bowles's characters often yearn to break free from various structures, when they do they often find themselves unable to create an alternate existential space as, for example, Alvina Houghton manages to do in her Pescocalascio farmhouse; they fail to sustain themselves within the most basic structure of all—identity—leaving them at the mercy of alien forces. I would argue as well that the "dwelling house" that is the human body, a mere porous membrane separating inside from outside, is shown to be as vulnerable to violation as consciousness is. No comfort is to be taken in bodily integrity. On the contrary, there is a certain pleasure to be taken in the violation itself, as we will next discover.

Bowles's work also reflects the influence of the late French Romantics, who, taking their inspiration from the Marquis de Sade, develop an entire aesthetics of ugliness, disease, and debauchery, of which the antihero was the embodiment. Their visionary project, which embraced excess and negation, was tied to a transformation of consciousness and a revaluation of an "objective" world rendered stale and too safe for spiritual gamble. For Rimbaud, "the way to vision is the way of the Christian mystic, turned inside out—a discipline that consists in the systematic violation of both the moral sensibilities and the sensory system by means of dissipation, drugs, and perversity."[17] But such debauchery, far from feeding and multiplying desire, reflects a peculiar kind of ascesis, a "harsh discipline for rooting out the fear, shame, and remorse that are the appurtenances of fallen man in his world of evil," whose purpose is "to achieve that identity with the One Spirit which makes man into a godlike new creature who is endowed with the power of creative, or thaumaturgic, vision, and who dwells in a new reality beyond good and evil" (417). If Rimbaud's hubris seems inconsistent with Bowles's calculated restraint, the excesses of violence and mortification common to much of Bowles's fiction are underwritten by a similar kind of ascesis. Abrams quotes Rimbaud: "'What is needed, is to make the soul monstrous. . . . The poet makes himself a *seer* by a long, immense, and calculated *disordering of all his senses*. . . . For he reaches the *unknown!* . . . He reaches the unknown, and even though, made mad, he should end by losing the understanding of his visions, he has at any rate seen them'" (417–18, Rimbaud's emphasis). And we know that Rimbaud spoke powerfully to Bowles for, writing in 1930 to his friend Bruce Morrissette, Bowles deplores the paucity of Rimbaud texts available for purchase. "Une Saison en Enfer," he queries, "have you even seen it? It seems to me his attitude is completely justified, and would be even moreso were he contemporary." Here is Bowles's recapitulation of Rimbaud's "lovely" mythology:

1 Revolt against Art: (I came to prefer ridiculous paintings) Employment of poetry as an incantation potent to destroy the accepted order of things.
2 Accustoming himself to pure hallucination.
3 Saying vale to the world and entering into Hell. At this time he's eighteen or so. He disappears, never writes another word of poetry.[18]

Against such tortures of ecstasy, or ecstasies of torture, the notion of "pleasure," or the pleasure of expatriate hedonism, pales. Indeed, Bataille, as an heir to this project of radical existential adventure, revalues the pleasure principle itself as a form of restraint to which the pathology of excess is the curative, a *denial* of the demand, precisely, to be *useful:*

> The goal of [classical utility] is, theoretically, pleasure—but only in a moderate form since violent pleasure is seen as *pathological.* On the one hand, this material utility is limited to acquisition (in practice, to production) and to the conservation of goods; on the other, it is limited to reproduction and to the conservation of human life (to which is added, it is true, the struggle against pain, whose importance itself suffices to indicate the negative character of the pleasure principle, instituted, in theory as the basis of utility).[19]

We can see the currents of this particular charge in the Bowlesian oeuvre, as characters such as the Professor, Port and Kit Moresby, and Nelson Dyar make their way inexorably toward the Nietzschean abyss.

Indeed, I would argue that Bataille is Bowles's best interlocutor, and not least because he shares with Bowles a highly idiosyncratic antihumanist humanism that revolves around death, violence, sacrifice, and radical forms of communication based upon the rupture of the conscious self. Bataille writes:

> There is horror in being: this horror is repugnant animality, whose presence I discover at the very point where the totality of being takes form. But the horror I experience does not repel me, the disgust I feel does not nauseate me. . . . But I may, on the contrary, *thirst for it;* far from escaping, I may resolutely quench my thirst with this horror that makes me press closer, with this disgust that has become my delight. [Bataille's emphasis][20]

And the totality to which Bataille refers is one "in which man has his share by *losing himself*" [Bataille's emphasis].[21] Bataille's concept of "inner experience" requires nothing less than the abandonment of discourse, of conceptual apparatuses, of all received wisdom. What emerges from this condition of "bewilderment" or "nonsense" is "sovereignty." He asserts that "consciousness of the moment is not truly such, is not sovereign, except in *unknowing*. Only by canceling, or at least neutralizing, every operation of knowledge within ourselves are we in the moment, without fleeing it."[22] The project, then, for Bataille, as for Bowles, becomes one of extreme *liberation*, where freedom is defined as "Life *beyond utility*," where "[t]o know is always to strive, to work; it is always a servile operation, indefinitely resumed, indefinitely repeated" (302, 305). If the Lawrentian and Bowlesian expatriates both seek *intimacy* in Bataille's sense—which is to say "immanence between man and the world, between the subject and the object"[23]—Bowles is far more willing to risk the subject's total dissolution to achieve that end. Indeed, Bataille's theorization of the world of practice and its negation through acts of violence and self-dismantling provides a rich source of insight into Bowles's early work and the ethics of expatriation that inform it.

Bataille's "inner experience" implies an extreme form of communication. That said, communication for Bataille—and for Bowles as well, at times—is not about syncretism or mutual understanding; it is, rather, a radical existential immersion in totality, operating in waves, pulsations, and useless expenditure.

> It is the separation of terror from the realms of knowledge, of feeling, of moral life, which obliges one to *construct* values uniting *on the*

outside the elements of these realms in the forms of authoritative entities, when it was necessary not to look afar; on the contrary, to reenter oneself in order to find there what was missing from the day when one contested the constructions. "Oneself" is not the subject isolating itself from the world, but a place of communication, of fusion of the subject and the object. [Bataille's emphasis][24]

What Bowles seems to be circling around and Bataille articulates is a rejection of structures of "knowledge" that posit a knowing subject over against a knowable object. Interestingly, both Bataille and Bowles call upon a common source in their articulation of this subject-object fusion: the French anthropologist Lucien Lévy-Bruhl, whose work on so-called primitive cultures led Bowles to theorize a mode of being that he called *"participation mystique"* in which "self and other, subject and object, past and present, animate and inanimate are linked in such a way that there are no clear borders between them."[25] Lévy-Bruhl is also cited extensively in Bataille's work on eroticism. In the Bowlesian text, this preoccupation with fusion results in a constant pressure against the subject's containment, which is represented in terms either of the body's physical violation or of a singular desire for an Other, whose role is *both* to facilitate the self's dissolution *and* to offer alternative modes of human communication. Remembering Bakhtin's assertion that, as a dweller in language, the subject is constituted as much by outsideness as by insideness, there is the sense that self is already fissured, already exposed to the chaos of what is Other. Expatriate life in the periphery magnifies this sense of chaos, and because the subject's webs of interlocution are ruptured, experience advances in inarticulable ways through progressive stages of discursive disengagement, until what is left is either Bataille's sovereign moment of experience or "communication."

There are other ways in which Bowles can be read productively through the penumbra of Bataille's assorted writings. The concern with the inexpedient, with risk, and with domains beyond "sense," for example, can be read as a response to the tyranny of what Bataille calls "project," which is associated with discourse and productive action in the world. Strategies for negating the demands of project require degrees of self-dismantling: carelessness, useless expenditure, neglect, risk, danger. The Bowlesian protagonist can be read as a subject in search of Bataille's "extreme limit of the possible": the point "where, despite the unintelligible position which it has for him in being, man, having stripped himself of enticement and fear, advances so far that one cannot conceive of the possibility of going further" (*IE*, 39). Bataille writes that there is

> *an affinity between on the one hand, the absence of worry, generosity, the need to defy death, tumultuous love, sensitive naiveté; on the other hand, the will to become the prey of the unknown. In both cases, the same need for* unlimited *adventure, the same horror for calculation, for project (the withered, prematurely old faces of the "bourgeois" and their cautiousness).* [21, Bataille's emphasis]

Bataille's writings on eroticism, moreover, articulate the "fascination" between sex and death that Bowles, for his own part, explores in narrative form. It is consciousness of death that, according to Bataille, distinguishes human from animal sensuality.

> Continuity is what we are after, but generally only if that continuity which the death of discontinuous beings can alone establish is not the victor in the long run. What we desire is to bring into a world founded on discontinuity all the continuity such a world can sustain. . . . The stirrings within us have their own fearful excesses; the excesses show which way these stirrings would take us. They are simply a sign to remind us constantly that death, the rupture of the discontinuous individualities to which we cleave in terror, stands there before us more real than life itself.[26]

Eroticism, in other words, "opens the way to death. Death opens the way to the denial of our individual lives"; Bataille then asks: "Without doing violence to our inner selves, are we able to bear a negation that carries us to the farthest bounds of possibility?"[27] In Bowles's fiction, such eroticism is pervasive. In the desire of the expatriate for the native, in the desire of the native for the expatriate, there is a constant thrill of danger that straddles the line between life and death, being and nonbeing. Expatriate eroticism, in the style of Bataille, reaches its apogee in *The Sheltering Sky*.

If Bataillian concepts like the extreme limit, communication, and eroticism portend a journey to inner experience that is purely metaphorical, there are ways in which Bowles's Moroccan landscapes speak to that journey in a more literal sense through fiction. Bataille, were he to have encountered the work of Paul Bowles, might have included him among the authors about whom he writes in *Literature and Evil*. Good and evil, he writes, must be reconsidered in light of the opposition between intensity and survival.

> Intensity can be defined as a value (it is the only positive value), survival as Good (it is the general goal of virtue). The notion of intensity cannot be reduced to that of pleasure because, as we have

seen, the quest for intensity leads us into the realm of unease and then to the limits of consciousness. So what I call value differs where Good and pleasure are concerned. . . . The value is situated *beyond Good and Evil*, but in two opposed forms, one connected with the principle of Good, the other with that of Evil. The desire for Good limits the instinct which induces us to seek a value, whereas liberty towards Evil gives access to the excessive forms of value. Yet we cannot conclude from this that authentic value is on the side of Evil. The very principle of value wants us to go 'as far as possible.' In this respect the association with the principle of Good establishes the 'farthest point' from the social body, beyond which constituted society cannot advance, while the association with the principle of Evil establishes the 'farthest point' which individuals or minorities can temporarily reach. Nobody can go any 'farther.' (74)

There is no doubt that many of Bowles's fictions lead us both into "the realm of unease" and then "to the limits of consciousness," or at least to the limits of consciousness of their protagonists. The principle of value that wants us to go "as far as possible" aligns itself with "Evil" when it leaves the path of "constituted society" and moves beyond the community of understanding that is created and maintained through webs of interlocution that both produce and define "normative" experience. The Bowlesean ethics of expatriation, careless of survival, seem to derive from this instinct toward Evil, toward extreme forms of liberty that culminate in the bewilderment of the extreme limit.

"A Distant Episode"

Nearly all Bowlesian fictions, as Patteson notes, tend to be characterized by a "voyage out," or boundary crossing, into an exotic and disorienting landscape, often represented as the native section of town or a desert-type wilderness, and a narrative chain of events set in motion by the inevitable encounter between the expatriate and the native, which leads to an epiphany of violence or cultural confusion. "A Distant Episode," one of Bowles's earliest short stories, is paradigmatic. A professor arrives in an unnamed Moroccan town prepared to do research in Magrebhi dialects. He inadvertently offends the owner of a café, who sends him on a fool's errand in search of camel-udder boxes. The professor is then assaulted and kidnapped by a group of Reguibat tribesmen, who brutalize him for their own amusement. Eventually, he escapes.

The story suggests, by granting the Professor a title rather than a proper name, that he will perhaps function as more a cultural symbol than an individual. The very association of his title with official, even sacred, knowledge and his ironic investiture with "maps, sun lotions and medicines" suggest as well the inadequacy of these indicia of mastery to a project thwarted on all sides by arrogance and misjudgment: "Ten years ago he had been in the village for *three days; long enough,* however, to establish a *fairly firm friendship* with a café-keeper, who had written him several times during the first year after his visit, *if never since*" [my emphasis]. He is oblivious to the scorn of the chauffeur, who, on learning that the Professor is making a survey of variations on Maghrebi, advises him menacingly to "keep on going south. . . . You'll find some languages you never heard of before."[28] When he makes his way to the café that his "friend" had owned, he is escorted to a table in the front room but "walked airily ahead into the back room and sat down." Although he addresses the qaouaji, or patron, in Maghrebi, the latter responds in "bad French," both a dismissal and refusal of intersubjective communication. The Professor continues to arouse the ire of the qaouaji, who advises him that Hassan Ramani, the café owner in question, is "deceased." The Professor then gives him an inordinately large tip, "for which he received a grave bow," and asks, "Tell me. . . . Can one still get those little boxes made from camel udders?" The response is hostile:

> The man looked angry. "Sometimes the Reguibat bring in those things. We do not buy them here." Then insolently, in Arabic: "And why a camel-udder box?" "Because I like them," retorted the Professor. And then because he was feeling a little exalted, he added, "I like them so much I want to make a collection of them, and I will pay you ten francs for every one you can get for me." (DE, 40)

The Professor's acquisitiveness and inflated air of self-sufficiency seem to render him incapable of properly orienting himself vis-à-vis the Other. The qaouaji, however, offers to show him where he can obtain the boxes.

Making his fateful way through the native village with his Moroccan guide, the Professor comments ruefully, " 'Everyone knows you.' . . . 'I wish everyone knew me.' " " '*No* one knows you,' " responds the Moroccan (41). A short but horrific time later, the Professor is literally stripped of his tongue by Reguibat tribesmen. He is by turns dehumanized and domesticated (in the sense of a wild beast). He is dressed in a costume that rattles and is forced to dance for his captors. Over time, he loses his mind. Toward the end of his captivity, however, consciousness painfully reemerges. The

Professor can no longer perform for his captors like a dancing bear. When he finds himself at liberty following the arrest of his new owner, he breaks out of his confinement in a rage. Still in his costume of jangling tin can lids, he heads out of the village. Taking him for a holy maniac, a French soldier takes a potshot at him but misses. The Professor trots out into the growing chill of evening, and the story comes to a close. In a tragicomic sense, then, the Professor is Bataille's sovereign man who "escapes death, in that he lives in the moment. The sovereign man lives and dies like an animal. But he is a man nevertheless," a comparison made more poignant still by Bataille's linking of the sacred with something "that frees itself from the subordination characterizing the world."[29] The world, for Bataille, is invariably the world of discourse in the service of project.

The idealized narrative rehearsed at the beginning of the story—cross-cultural understanding and friendship, the pleasures of "fieldwork," the acquisition of specialized knowledge—is, by the story's end, painfully dismantled. The Professor's maps are as useless as sunscreen against the desert sun, his painstakingly learned Maghrebi just as ineffectual. On the other hand, it seems to be the fact of Ramani's death and his own sense of disappointment that precipitates the Professor's clumsy and ill-fated attempt to engage the qauoaji in conversation. The camel-udder boxes were but a pretext. The story, then, unfolds with a kind of inevitability, despite the Professor's uneasiness and sense of dread that would have turned another kind of protagonist back in his tracks. And this is the point. He is propelled on by a kind of desire incommensurate with the supposed object of his quest. Following "the lines of escape of desire," he is no longer the man of reason, but the schizo of Deleuze and Guattari. He is no longer the follower of maps, but the Nietzschean experimenter who, in all his foolish vanity,

> walks into a labyrinth; he increases a thousandfold the dangers which are inherent in life anyway. And not the smallest of his dangers is that no one can witness how and where he loses his way, falls into solitude, or is torn to pieces by some troglodytic minotaur of conscience. When such a man perishes it happens so far from human understanding that other men have no feeling for it, no fellow feeling. But there is no return for him, not even a return to human compassion![30]

But he is also culturally and historically produced. In this early story, Bowles represents the systematic deracination of the Western protagonist as a kind of payback. At the same time, however, the

narrative unfolding is born out of desire for the Other, remembered (no matter how naively) as a friend, Hassan Ramani, whose
name the Professor recites as a mantra as he ventures down the
abyss in search of his little camel-udder boxes, the voyage out from
which there is no way back in. As the qaouaji reminds the Professor,
"You can't be there and here" (DE, 41).

In "A Distant Episode" speech is rendered wholly ineffectual.
And when, as in this story, language itself is at issue, when webs of
interlocution are frustrated, even torn asunder by cultural, religious, and linguistic difference, the expatriate subject must find
ways to forge ties if he is to negotiate alterity with integrity. In
Bowles's later fictions, some provisional gestures are made in this
direction, and the relations between Western protagonists and
their native interlocutors become more complex and hence more
ambivalent. "A Distant Episode," however, provides a kind of
blueprint for a number of the narratives to come. For Bowles's
antiheroes—the Professor, Kit, and Nelson Dyar—the architecture
of interiority is, finally, demolished. Irrevocably transformed by
the experience of physical and cultural dislocation, they are left
stranded by the text at the extreme limit of experience—and certainly beyond the bounds of knowledge—which may be, finally,
exactly where their desires lead them.

The Sheltering Sky

The Sheltering Sky was Bowles's first novelistic exploration of cultural dislocation. It tells the story of three Americans, Port and Kit
Moresby and their friend Tunner, who come to Algeria with the
intention of visiting remote areas. The novel expands and bifur-
cates the story of the Professor, with Port and Kit pursuing diverse
narratives that reflect elements of "A Distant Episode." Like that
short story, the novel works with the antithetical themes of existential risk taking and desire for meaningful social engagement
with the Other. At the same time, the various expatriate "mythologies"—escape from the world's increasing homogeneity, curiosity
(sexual and otherwise) about "Other" cultures, the sufficiency of
the expatriate's knowledge and technical proficiency to negotiate
linguistic, cultural, and geographic difference—are interrogated
and definitively put to rest.

While Port and Kit are not expatriates per se, travel—or nomadism
—is for them a way of life; within the context of the narrative,
moreover, they are marked as travelers whose departure from

home is deemed permanent and definitive. Port is a prodigious studier of maps:

> he had only to see a map to begin studying it passionately, and then, often as not, he would begin to plan some new, impossible trip which sometimes eventually became a reality. He did not think of himself as a tourist; he was a traveler . . . belonging no more to one place than to the next.[31]

He shares with Rawdon Lilly the project of nomadism but its contours are different. Far from seeking to get "a new tune" out of himself, Port's motivations are more critical in nature. He maintains: "The difference between tourist and traveler is that the former accepts his own civilization without question; not so the traveler, who compares it with the others, and rejects those elements he finds not to his liking" (*SS*, 6). At the same time, the characterization of a desired trip as "impossible" is already a hint that some more radical form of ascesis is to be undertaken.

The plot is relatively straightforward. Kit and Port are physically estranged, and Tunner is attracted to Kit, although she does not return his interest. After a number of misadventures, including a visit by Port to a desert prostitute and Kit's seduction by Tunner, Port and Kit travel alone toward the desert. Port becomes gravely ill with typhus and dies in a remote desert outpost of the French colonial army. Tunner arrives just as Port is about to die. When Kit realizes that he is dead, she takes off by herself into the desert and is picked up by a traveling caravan. She becomes the sexual slave of a young and handsome merchant named Belqassim, who brings her home disguised as a young man so as not to arouse the jealousy of his other wives. When, however, her gender is discovered, Belqassim marries her in order to silence them. During the period of her "captivity," Kit becomes more and more estranged from her former rational state. Although she has been living in a state of pure sensation, the only reality of which is her sexual relationship with Belqassim, she realizes that she is being drugged. She manages to escape with her money only to find herself robbed and taken advantage of in a strange African city. It is clear that she has "lost her mind." She is finally discovered by the authorities and returned to Oran, where Tunner has been frantically awaiting some news of her discovery. When she realizes that Tunner is there waiting for her, she slips away from her attendant and disappears in a bus filled with native dockworkers.

What begins, therefore, as a mere "phase" in the nomadic existence of Port and Kit—in which, it is hoped, they will both enjoy
the pleasures of exotic travel and recover lost intimacy—ends by
giving the protagonists what they, perhaps, desire even more: *experience.* That is to say, "a voyage to the end of the possible of man"
(Bataille, *IE,* 7). To be an expatriate in this narrative is to *get lost.* At
the same time, however, the very fact of being in the space of the
Other produces other ethical questions. The inexorable path to
dissolution is interrupted by human interactions between protagonists and "natives" which suggest that expatriation is a social condition, as well as a solitary existential adventure. The intriguing
meetings and mismeetings of these figures reveal an ethics of expatriation concerned with engagement and the exploration of social
and discursive forms that are unfamiliar and attractive. So one can
get lost, *and* one can get lost in the space of the Other. The desert
is the novel's privileged site, and it is one rich in all manner of
diverse and contrasting associations: Christian asceticism, nomadic
decenteredness, exoticist mythologies, to name a few.

In her discussion of the American Western, Jane Tompkins
offers an analysis of the desert's significance and appeal that can
help us understand Bowles's rather *different* project. For Tompkins:
"The appeal of the [American] desert lies partly in its promise of
pain, an invitation that is irresistible . . . because it awakens a
desire for spiritual prowess, some unearthly glory earned through
long-continued discipline, self-sacrifice, submission to a supernal
power." The association of the desert with asceticism, an asceticism rooted in physical hardship, isolation, the negation of creature-
ness, prompts us to anticipate spiritual torment and the abnegation of the material in favor of the incorporeal, and yet, argues
Tompkins: "What is imitated is a physical thing, not a spiritual
ideal; a solid state of being, not a process of becoming; a material
entity, not a person; a condition of objecthood, not a form of consciousness. The landscape's final invitation—merger—promises
complete materialization."[32] The desert is, finally, "the landscape
of death" (70). Tompkins's desert is a landscape in which one
achieves transcendence without making the turn inward associated with Christian spirituality. And although it is the staging
ground for a kind of heroic self-constitution, for the assertion of
an identity at odds with the bourgeois ideals associated with
women, religion, culture, and, perhaps most significantly, interiority, the identity to which man may aspire there is a peculiar one:

> To be a man is not only to be monolithic, silent, mysterious,
> impenetrable as a desert butte, it is to *be* the desert butte. By
> becoming a solid object, not only is man relieved of the burden
> of relatedness and responsiveness to others, he is relieved of con-
> sciousness itself, which is to say, primarily consciousness of self. . . .
> Not fissured by self-consciousness, nature is what the hero aspires
> to emulate; perfect being-in-itself. (57, Tompkins's emphasis)

The impulse of Port and Kit Moresby to escape into the landscape seems identical with the wish to acquire the status of object
(which Kit quite succeeds in doing, although not exactly in way
Tompkins has in mind). Instead of pure materiality, however, the
Bowlesian subject is emptied out; in its place there is an outsideness—instead of identity, identity negated; instead of consolida-
tion, dispersal. And it is precisely around issues of identity and
mastery that the Bowlesian text seems to circle tirelessly. The naive
American abroad in the colonial world, equipped though he may
be with all the accouterments of modern travel, cannot assert the
cowboy's simple self-sufficiency. So where Tompkins's cowboy
assumes the fullness and solidity of a boulder, the Moresbys are,
in a sense, scattered. Indeed, one of the central tensions throughout Bowles's early fiction revolves around the difference between
"mastery," in the conventional sense, and Bataille's concept of
"sovereignty," attained, paradoxically, precisely in the moment of
self-squandering. Unlike Tompkins's thinglike cowboy, Port and
Kit Moresby are released from "thingness"; their escape from consciousness is manifested in moments of excess rather than in the
assertion of prowess; nature is continuous with totality rather than,
in Tompkins's formulation, the perfect being-in-itself of a rock.

Bataille, on the other hand, associates the desert with community, and following Nietzsche's injunction "Be that ocean," he
writes: "*Better than the image of* Dionysus philosophos, *the being lost
of this ocean and this bare requirement: "Be that ocean," designate experience and the extreme limit to which it leads.*" But

> [t]he so simple commandment: "Be that ocean," linked to the extreme limit,
> at the same time makes of man a multitude, a desert. It is an expression
> which resumes and makes precise the sense of a community. I know how to
> respond to the desire of Nietzsche speaking of a community having no object
> other than that of experience (but designating this community, I speak of a
> "desert"). (IE, 27, Bataille's emphasis)

It makes sense that the kind of "experience" sought by Port and Kit
Moresby, whose essential condition is one of extreme alienation,

is one that, in however unseemly a manner, provides an amelioration of that condition. This is the case, at least, if we read the text through a Bataillian lens. The way out of alienation is not realized in the terms of a premodern North Africa, however, but in a more collective, Dionysian mode. Bataille's conjunction of desert and community does not point to the idea of "organic return," but rather invokes a domain of postdiscursivity that is internally marked by the "devastation" of modernity, a devastation that is contained within the Bowlesean protagonist:

> *In order to provide the distance of present-day man from the "desert," of the man with the thousand cacophonic idiocies (almost scientific, ideology, blissful joking, progress, touching sentimentality, belief in machines, in big words and, to conclude, discordance and total ignorance of the unknown), I will say of the "desert" that it is the most complete abandonment of the concerns of the "present-day man," being the continuation of the "ancient man," which the enactment of festivals regulated. He is not a return to the past; he has undergone the corruption of the "present-day man" and nothing has more place within him than the devastation which it leaves— it gives to the "desert" its "desert-like" truth; the memory of Plato; of Christianity and above all—the most hideous—the memory of modern ideas, extend behind him like fields of ashes. But between the unknown and him has been silenced the chirping of ideas, and it is through this that he is similar to "ancient man": of the universe he is no longer the rational (alleged) master, but the dream. (28, Bataille's emphasis)*

The hybrid spaces of colonial North Africa are emblematic of such desolation that is internal to "present-day man." If the Moresbys are driven to lose themselves in the "purity" of the desert, the domain where the chirping of ideas is silenced, it is because "nothing has more place" within them than reason's devastating trajectory. The desert is, finally, "the site (the condition) which was necessary for a clear and interminable death" (49).

The Sheltering Sky begins with Port awakening from sleep, a state characterized as "non-being."

> If he had not the energy to ascertain his position in time and space, he also lacked the desire. He was somewhere, he had come back through vast regions from nowhere; there was the certitude of an infinite sadness at the core of his consciousness, but the sadness was reassuring, because it alone was familiar. (3)

Port's melancholic disorientation foreshadows his return to the "vast regions of nowhere," where not only infinite sadness but consciousness itself will be expunged. Poised as he is between sleeping and waking, between continuity and discontinuity, his anguish anticipates the kind of quest that, for Bataille, is linked to the "extreme limit of the possible." Soon, however, the materiality of North Africa counterposes itself to Port's incipient despair. Unlike the Moroccan hinterland depicted in "A Distant Episode" or the Casbah of Orientalist lore, the port city of Oran is hybrid space. The few Arabs present in the café sport worn European clothes. Across the street a radio is blasting opera. The local movie theater is showing a film in Arabic called *Fiancée for Rent*. Port's narrated monologue recalls the ship's landing: "Their little freighter had spewed them out from its comfortable maw the day before onto the hot docks, sweating and scowling with anxiety, where for a long time *no one had paid them the slightest attention*" (6–7, my emphasis). Rendered momentarily invisible, Port would have preferred to get right back on the ship and travel on to Istanbul, but pride (it was his idea to travel to Africa) prevents him from doing so. Then, too, like the Professor, he is reckless, a self-squanderer.

Port's adventure takes shape as he and Kit make their way southward toward the desert. Like Lawrence, Bowles explores his protagonists' existential dilemmas through their engagement with landscape. Cycling along the crest of a desert ridge, for example, Port and Kit abandon their bikes to climb to the rocky summit. "[F]acing the vastness below" and "the proximity to infinite things," Port is at his happiest (99). Later he remarks to Kit that "the sky here's very strange. I often have the sensation when I look at it that it's a solid thing up there, protecting us from what's behind" (100). When Kit asks him what *is* behind, he responds, "Nothing, I suppose. Just darkness. Absolute night" (101). But what is this "absolute night"? And is it really protection that Port is seeking? For surely, the infinite vastness below which he finds so thrilling is but the mirror image of absolute night. Bataille's fragmentary narrative, *Inner Experience*, articulates that which the novel, in its simple and direct discursive style, can but suggest in its anguished restraint:

> Infinite surpassing in oblivion, ecstasy, indifference . . . I see—that which discourse never manages to attain. I am *open*, yawing gap, to the unintelligible sky and everything in me rushes forth, is reconciled in a final irreconciliation. Rupture of all "possible," violent kiss, abduction, loss in the entire absence of all "possible," in opaque and dead night which is nonetheless light—no less unknowable, no less blinding than the depth of the heart. (*IE*, 59)

Bataille's abyss is a space of contradiction and reconciliation beyond discourse. And Port is seen as relentlessly drawn to and approaching this space of inner experience that is at once an opening to totality. The cruel ecstasies of the extreme limit are produced in the rupture, the tearing, of consciousness, where the subject loses its autonomy in the object:

> Forgetting of everything. Deep descent into the night of existence. . . . To slip over the abyss and in the completed darkness experience the horror of it. To tremble, to despair, in the cold of solitude, in the eternal silence of man (foolish of all sentences, illusory answers for sentences, only the insane silence of night answers). (36)

The journey to inner experience is, for Port, mediated by the alluring possibilities of expatriate dislocation. The utter absence of tourist amenities, for example, only increases his excitement, makes him feel "that he was pioneering" (*SS*, 108). Like the Professor, he knows he is courting danger, since travel bulletins "strongly advised" tourists "not to undertake land trips" into the interior portions of French Africa. But if Port

> had not been journeying into regions he did not know, he would have found it insufferable. The idea that at each successive moment he was deeper into the Sahara than he had been the moment before, that he was leaving behind all familiar things, this constant consideration kept him in a state of pleasurable agitation. (109)

In his rush toward danger, he might, in the words of Nietzsche, declaim: "Like a rider on a forward-charging horse, we drop our reins when infinity lies before us . . . . We are in the midst of *our* bliss only when we are most—*in danger*" [Nietzsche's emphasis].[33] I am, of course, arguing that *The Sheltering Sky* speaks through its silences, silences to which philosophers like Bataille and Nietzsche, as fellow journeymen in the domains beyond calculation and instrumental reason, are qualified to speak.

Port's anguish, its association with death, manifests itself, predictably enough, through a feeling of cold, "a deep interior cold." It is the coldness of Alvina's arrival in Pescocalascio, the coldness of death and existential terror and, more literally, the chill of typhus. And it coincides with the loss of Port's passport—a not-so-subtle hint of what is at stake here. He is anxious to get to a town called El Ga'a in the Sahara, a place about which he had been able ascertain very little; people he asked knew merely it was "a large city—always it was spoken of with a certain respect—that it was far away, that the climate was warmer." He realizes, as well, "that it rather suited his fancy to be going off with no proof of his identify to a hidden desert town about which no one could tell him anything" (*SS*, 174). As he gazes out his hotel window, the inner "corruption of the 'present-day man'" seems to prevent him from attaining that sense of continuity with life that is promised by the desert landscape; only through the dissolution of consciousness itself can the natural elements be restored to their own immediacy:

> The landscape was there, and more than ever he felt he could not reach it. The rocks and the sky were everywhere, ready to absolve him, but as always he carried the obstacle within him. He would have said that as he looked at them, the rocks and the sky ceased being themselves, that in the act of passing into his consciousness, they became impure. (173)

So deeply compromised is the cognitive apparatus of the Western subject that the structure of perceptual knowledge itself imparts the impurity (instrumentality) of its own ends to the most elemental objects of cognition. The quest for absolution is annulled by the obstacle of self, shored up with discourse. How deep is the investment here in the project of unknowing! The loss of Port's passport represents the first shedding of the self's apparatus. Once that formidable document is gone, the other aspects of identity are sure to follow. Released, finally, by fever, Port's consciousness can no longer be contained by language.

> Words were much more alive and more difficult to handle, now; so much so that Kit did not seem to understand them when he used them. They slipped into his head like the wind blowing into a room, and extinguished the frail flame of an idea forming there in the dark. Less and less he used them in his thinking. (231)

In the hallucinatory madness of his near-death state, he sees his stomach impaled by a speeding car. In the marriage of blood and excrement, a truly Bataillian moment, he dies, alone in a remote colonial outpost. Bataille's fragmentary prose, encapsulating salient moments in Bowles's text, illuminates the self's trajectory, expanding in the totality that escapes the structure and meaning of language, and succumbing to death, which becomes nearly interchangeable with life:

> In the ideally dark void, there is chaos—to the point of revealing the absence of chaos (there everything is desert, cold, in closed night, while at the same time being of a painful brilliance, inducing fever);

life opens itself up to death, the *self* grows until it reaches the pure imperative. (*IE*, 72)

We can, perhaps, better understand Port's motivations in the light of Bataille's concept of sovereignty, a position of absolute freedom from the injunction to be useful. No longer a tool in the world of practice, no longer a subject whose encounter with death is deferred through project, the sovereign affirms his anguish through useless expenditure, opens himself to the abyss. He is cousin to the Nietzschean experimenter, cousin to the schizo-revolutionary. Port's anger at the immigration authorities at Oran who had refused to let him leave a blank after the word "profession" on his entry papers suggests his affinity with this radical "negativity." Although Kit had volunteered the fact that he was a writer, he had been "infuriated by their stubbornness in insisting upon his having a label, an *état-civil*." We are told that since the death of his father, "he no longer worked at anything, because it was not necessary," but Kit always wanted him to write again, to continue "working" (*SS*, 206). Even when he considered the possibility of writing, something prevented him: "as long as he was living his life, he could not write about it" (207). Indeed, writing, "striving," being productive, would preclude "living"—conceived as being "in the moment." With the invocation of the father, too, we are reminded of oedipal constraints, the dominant fiction, and the "old categories of the Negative" that the schizorevolutionary of Deleuze and Guattari seeks to bypass. The schizo's escape, Port's escape, Bataille's escape to inner experience, form aspects of an ascesis given over to the quest for unmediated experience, useless expenditure, uncoded desire. In *The Accursed Share*, Bataille writes: "I no longer anticipated the moment when I would be rewarded for my effort, *when I would know at last,* but rather the moment *when I would no longer know, when my initial anticipation would dissolve into* NOTHING" [Bataille's emphasis].[34] Port's narrative, I would argue, invokes the same set of principles.

It must also be said that *The Sheltering Sky*, like *Aaron's Rod* and *The Lost Girl*, is marked by characterizations of bourgeois masculinity that reflect a failure of the dominant fiction. Port is an escapee from conformity who is, in every way but one, the antithesis of the "mature," hence fully "masculine," male figure, while Tunner's masculinity is defined by his vacuous good looks. Port does not sleep with his wife but seeks paid-for sex with native prostitutes, while Tunner needs a suitcase full of champagne to effect the seduction of Kit. Despite the "marginality" of Port's masculine status—reflected variously as the inability or refusal to claim his share in the dominant fiction, his victimization at the hands of a prowling native while he is out strolling alone at night, his dream of a castrationlike wounding—he is, nevertheless, an unconventionally heroic figure, living, it seems, at the margins of existential safety. Tunner, on the other hand, who is "astonishingly handsome . . . in his late Paramount way," is the typical American (*SS*, 7). Unlike the Moresbys, who are perpetual travelers, Tunner is aligned with America. When Kit chides him about being a "real American" —and this because "one thing [he] can't stand is filth"—he responds, "You're damned right" (113). If he is as earnest in his attempt to bring his friends home as he is in his effort to seduce Kit, he is, finally, represented as ineffectual and shallow: "Usually there was very little expression of any sort to be found on his smooth face, but the features were formed in such a manner that in repose they suggested a general bland contentment" (7). Kit thinks of him variously as a "bore" or a "dolt." Tunner, we are told, "was an essentially simple individual irresistibly attracted by whatever remained just beyond his intellectual grasp" (62). A hanger-on, he is the figure from whom Kit is in constant flight, an ambivalent symbol of home, honorable and corrupt, earnest and disingenuous, caring but ineffectual, manly in a showy but callow way.

Not surprisingly, then, Kit's story can be read as a response to this "absent" masculinity. It is through eroticism that Kit comes to squander herself, dashing herself to pieces on the shoals of eros. While she has, in the early part of the narrative, been a somewhat reluctant traveler, after Port's death she embarks her upon her own journey, and we need here to attend to the way gender operates in the construction of Kit's narrative, as it recapitulates the peculiar trajectory of *The Lost Girl*'s Alvina, who, against all reason, subordinates herself to a powerfully erotic Other. That Belqassim is indispensable to her project of self-dismantling becomes clear when, confronting the reality of Port's death, Kit contemplates the pleasure of abdicating all responsibility:

> What a delight, not to be responsible—not to have to decide anything of what was to happen! To know, even if there was no hope, that no action one might take or fail to take could change the outcome in the slightest degree—that it was impossible to be at fault in any way, and thus impossible to feel regret, or, above all, guilt. (241)

At once the realization of Kit's greatest fear (the capitulation to some fearful destiny) and her greatest desire (to live without fear in the moment), it is precisely such hope that forms the basis of her narrative. In lieu of responsibility, then, Kit surrenders to the moment, to the desire to be "in" experience. And so, upon Port's death, she steals away in the night. When she comes upon a pool and suddenly craves immersion, she feels "a strange intensity being born within her."

> Life was suddenly there, she was in it, not looking through the window at it. That dignity that came from feeling a part of its power and grandeur, that was a familiar sensation, but it was years ago that she had last known it. . . . As she immersed herself completely, the thought came to her: "I shall never be hysterical again." That kind of tension, that degree of caring about herself, she felt she would never attain them any more in her life. (258)

Here the self is reborn as a nonself; Kit is delivered from the burdens of selfhood and even from the symbolic order of language into a new sensual form of existence. She loses her watch, thus freeing herself from the tyranny of time, eats voraciously, experiences the joy of being. She spends the night under a thick and sheltering bush and resolutely refuses to look back "into the abyss of yesterday and suffer again its grief and remorse" (279). Improbably, then, she hails Belqassim's passing caravan.

Both *The Lost Girl* and *The Sheltering Sky* evince a tension between Western styles of being (coded masculine, as we have seen) and the possibility of being Other. Both Alvina and Kit are torn between "atavism"—and it's important to note that this is a term that both texts use with reference to these characters—and reason. While Alvina has all the attributes of the New Woman, these, of course, may also be thought of as the "burdens of selfhood," and her desire for atavism seems proportional to her status as a quintessential subject of modernity. Kit, on the other hand, is not fully adequate to the task of being a self, although she clearly positions herself as a subject of the modern world. Her "atavistic" reliance upon signs and omens is a way of avoiding the burdens of selfhood, and she is ultimately delivered even of those modernist anxieties that attend her inadequacies. In both cases, the desire to submit to a figure emblematic of the primitive can be related to a desire to escape the demands of modern subjectivity or the burdens of the self. These, I would argue, belong to the domain of the father.

The resistence of Alvina and Kit to modernity extends beyond the burdens of selfhood to the reified quality of modern life. For Alvina, modernity is linked to the "priced and ticketed world" that she comes to abhor in England, as well as the reified social forms to which the plenitude of lived experience must succumb. She is the "odd" woman precisely because there is no social form that can adequately contain her. *The Sheltering Sky*, on the other hand, identifies Kit with the commodities that she carries in her luggage: rows of shoes, evening gowns, bottles of cosmetics and perfumes, which Port refers to as "her pathetic little fortress of Western culture" (166). Even when she abandons her dead husband for the unknown, she makes sure to carefully go through all her luggage and select a number of items to take with her in her overnight bag, her "kit," including her passport and a large amount of money. It's interesting, too, that "Western culture," far from representing a field of philosophical, artistic, and political accomplishment, is here reduced to nothing more than department-store wares. Even so, they are invaluable; she uses the cosmetics to "pay off" Belqassim's wives, who allow her to escape. The money is later stolen from her and she is, finally, object free and "sovereign." Consistent with Georges Bataille's suggestion that the world of practice makes of its subjects "tools" in service of project,[35] these texts represent both the objectified subject—objectified, that is, through association with particularly Western objects or commodities—and the desire of such subjects to free themselves from the world that has objectified them. At the same time, there is ambivalence. Kit is able, briefly, to call out of the depths of her consciousness the sense that something is not right. She needs to send a telegram. Handing a piece of paper with the words "CANNOT GET BACK" to a "blue-eyed man," she realizes with horror that she had "set in motion the mechanism which would destroy her" (320), that the "dark dream would be shattered" (323). This ambivalence is emblematic of the existential conundrum that Bataille's work articulates:

> To live is to exist within limits. Being, therefore, always accords with the limit that defines it. To the extent that it is conscious of itself as existing, being contemplates the idea of not existing with horror.
> In consequence it strives always to maintain the sense of its own existence as an independent essence. However, this existence is incomplete since it separates itself from whatever is other from it. If it is an entirely independent being, it can understand nothing outside of itself. To understand its situation in the world it needs to engage with an other from who it perceives its separation while at the same time

desiring unity with it (this is the importance of communication). Our essence is thus to be incomplete beings. The result is that the limited, discontinuous being, even as it strives to assert its own being and independence, aspires to achieve a state of continuity with what is external to it. This unity is impossible: by achieving its desire of continuity such a being would destroy the very independence which it experiences as its unique and essential personality. But at the same time individual isolation is an imposture. In this sense we always strive towards what will destroy us; our condition is one of loss. We are always living on the edge of an abyss.[36]

And so, it seems, Kit both desires and resists continuity. For if she has been able to effect her liberation from Belqassim with relative ease, the realization that he is now her husband is just as easily dismissed: " 'He's your husband,' she whispered to herself, and stood still a second in horror. Then she almost giggled: it was only part of this ridiculous game she had been playing" (*SS*, 309). The profound psychic disintegration earlier experienced is momentarily made light of; Belqassim becomes an object of mockery.

Interestingly, as in *The Lost Girl*, Kit's narrative reverses the association between men and reason, on the one hand, and women and nature, on the other. Like Ciccio, Belqassim is a creature valued solely for his libido and, more importantly, as a tool for the Western subject's self-undoing. Why do these male-authored texts stage such dramas of female sexual submission, which parody conventional companionate love matches, through the deployment of cultural stereotypes about hot-blooded Latin lovers and bedouin kidnappers? Why are such dramas removed to the marginalized places of the West, where the female Other and the exotic Other confront one another while an absent male subjectivity sits behind the scenes, "paring his fingernails," so to speak? Why is such female submission always incomplete, and why do such female protagonists, who are invariably smarter and more resourceful than their ravishers, rejoice in their thralldom even as they resist it? I do not have all the answers to these questions, but I will suggest that these representations have little to do with misogyny and even less with women. It makes more sense to me that these are figures onto which is projected a marginal masculine subjectivity. How else to explore, in a publicly consumable fashion, the areas of subjectivity excluded by the dominant fiction? How else to account for the ambivalence? In his discussion of *The Alexandria Quartet*, Joseph Boone argues that the Orient becomes a screen onto which its protagonist, Darley, projects his most "forbidden erotic desires" and through this "mechanism of displacement" is able to come into his own as a writer and as a man.[37] I think something similar is going on in these texts, but what is realized, finally, is not the full fruition of masculine privilege, the marriage of the phallus and the penis, but rather its ruination.

At the same time, *The Sheltering Sky*, unlike *The Lost Girl*, is often attentive to alternate possibilities of intersubjective self-fashioning rather than dismantling in the periphery. Ultimately, I would argue, *The Sheltering Sky* is not just about alienation and disintegration; it is also about other ways of relating and other ways of speaking that owe little to notions of intersubjectivity (where the operative word must always be the *subject*). Port and Kit experience, but the novel leaves unexplored, moments of connection that might point outward rather than inward, toward a provisional ethics of expatriation that seeks to approach the path actually chosen by Paul Bowles. Here is the tension between the radically decentering experience of the extreme limit and the desire for connection, engagement, and "situatedness-in-displacement." Although the narrative desire for experience beyond the social spaces that Bauman would characterize as cognitive must be seen as qualitatively different than the desire for *experience* in Bataille's sense of the word, they both result in bewilderment.

So we follow Port, in his first evening wandering, leaving Kit behind at the hotel, ripe for sexual adventure. Here he is made uncomfortable by the gaze of the populace:

> People pushed against him as they passed, stared from doorways and windows, made comments openly to each other about him—whether with sympathy or not he was unable to tell from their faces—and they sometimes ceased to walk merely in order to watch him. (*SS*, 14)

The objectifying gaze of the natives challenges his authority, casts him in a characteristically feminine position. To Port, their faces were masks; he is unable to "read" them. At the same time, however, he is not oblivious to their poverty or to the vast economic gap separating them. He is also disoriented by the town's geography. As the smells grow stronger and the filth more apparent, "this proximity with, as it were, a forbidden element served to elate him" (16). Here is the paradigmatic Bowlesian moment, the wandering protagonist leaving the town limits, intoxicated with danger and the unknown, sniffing "at the fragments of mystery," feeling "an unaccustomed exaltation" (17). Well beyond the last possible suburb, he meets his native interlocutor, who asks, "*Qu'est-ce ti cherches là?*" (And Bowles is careful to render the French as it would be spoken by a native speaker of a certain class.) Port thinks, "Here's where the trouble begins" (18), and so does the encounter, which begins to take the shape of an unwanted sexual advance.

Port responds noncommittally to the Arab in French, but the Arab clearly wants to continue the conversation: "Do you want to take a walk?" "I'll pay you a drink." "What's your name?" "Me," tapping his chest, "Smaïl. So, do we go and drink?" This is the tenor of his dialogue. Port is not forthcoming. The Arab's voice now bears "a truly outraged inflection" (19): "*Qu'est-ce ti fi là? Qu'est-ce ti cherches?*" Port attempts to get away, but the Arab is persistent and follows him. "You didn't wait for me," he said in an aggrieved tone." The Arab attempts to engage him, waving a worn piece of paper insistently: "I was in the Fifth Battalion of Sharpshooters. Look at the paper! Look! You'll see!" (20). Port walks faster, trying to get away, but now things start to look very unfamiliar; he is lost.

> All at once they were in a street which was no more than a passageway. . . . For an instant Port hesitated: this was not the kind of street he wanted to walk in. . . . In that short moment the Arab took charge. He said: "You don't know this street? It's called Rue de la Mer Rouge. . . . There are *cafés arabes* up this way." (21)

Finally, Port consents to join Smaïl for a cup of tea. The café "had a complicated entrance," and as they ascended the stairway "[t]he staccato sound of a hand drum came from above, tapping indolent patterns above a sea of voices" (21). Port was impressed with the place; it seemed so genuine, so Arabic! They converse; Smaïl notices Port's sadness (he had just been thinking of Kit back at the hotel) and offers to introduce him to a girl—not a common whore, but a young dancer recently arrived from her bled, or village, in the desert. Port's interest is aroused; with the promise of sex, rather than a collection of camel-udder boxes, he commits himself to the care of his native interlocutor. At a remote site known simply as "the Turkish fort," down a series of steep steps, Port is introduced into the tent of Marhnia, who after submitting to him tries to rob him. He tries to stop her; she screams. Pursued by her kinsmen, Port narrowly escapes. His wallet is, however, gone, as is Smaïl. The encounter between Port and Smaïl is couched in ambivalence, a classic mismeeting that occurs beyond the social space within which such an encounter could be made sense of. Is Port looking for trouble? Is Smaïl a predator? Is he resentful of Port for rebuffing his preliminary offer of possible friendship? Does Port rebuff him out of fear? These are questions the text allows us to ask but encourages us not to. *The Sheltering Sky* is not about rapprochement.

Later on in the text, Port and Kit share tea in the garden of an Arab shopkeeper whose acquaintance Port has made in the marketplace. Kit afterward complains of the superficial nature of the conversation; the following exchange occurs:

> "I disagree. You don't say a frieze is superficial just because it has only two dimensions."
> "You do if you're accustomed to having conversation that's something more than decoration. I don't think of conversation as a frieze, myself."
> "Oh, nonsense! It's just another way of living they have, a completely different philosophy." (133)

What Port seems to be suggesting here is an aesthetics of communication, a choreography as opposed to an exchange. Western-style modes of dialogue stress the instrumentality of language, its transparency, the interiority behind the screen of language being the essential component. One subject bearing its soul to another. Or, as Patteson points out, language may function as "a medium of cultural penetration" that is nevertheless shown to be wholly inadequate to the task—at least to the extent that it is bound up with a kind of epistemological imperialism. This point is brought home by the slashing of the Professor's tongue. And Patteson remarks that many of Bowles's narratives end in silence—a space beyond normative discourse.[38] Conversation as art, however, would value language differently, stressing not so much the function of language as "meaningful" or "productive" communication, but rather the gilding on a code of social interaction where what matters most might possibly *not* be the speaker's innermost thoughts or utilitarian purpose. Bowles has suggested as much. In a 1974 interview he states that "Moroccans don't make much distinction between objective truth and what we'd call fantasy."

> Statistical truth means nothing to them. No Moroccan will ever tell you what he thinks, or does, or means. He'll tell you some of it and tell you other things that are completely false and then weave them together into a very believable core, which you swallow, and that's what's considered civilized. What's the purpose of telling the truth? It's not interesting, generally. It's more interesting to doctor it up a bit first of all, so it's more decorative and hence more civilized. *And besides, how could anyone be so idiotic as to open himself to the dangers involved in telling the unadorned truth to people?* [My emphasis][39]

If we are uncomfortable with the speaker's reductive approach to Moroccan character and his presumption to "translate" Moroccan practices with regard to truth telling for his Western interlocutor, we might nevertheless grant that Bowles is probably correct in suggesting that once language loses its transparency, speaking the Other's language is not a simple matter of grammar and vocabulary. According to Bowles, communication amongst Moroccans involves "a whole art of pulling the pieces together and trying to get the truth from the other's invention."[40] There is also the emphasis on ritual and community. In a letter to James Leo Herlihy in 1966, Bowles writes that "the formalized life of primitives must be emotionally satisfying, if only because so many of the acts of daily life are performed in the manner of a ritual, and before witnesses."[41] Bowles's articulation of an aestheticized culture in which everyday speech is endowed with the qualities of art turns instrumentality into performance.

Despite Kit's impatience with "aesthetic" modes of conversation, she too experiences the desire for connection and communication, but, as we saw, in a distinctly erotic mode. Eroticism is one way of mediating between the ethics of self-dismantling and the ethics of engagement. As Bataille writes:

> Love expresses a need for sacrifice: each unity must lose itself in some other, which exceeds it. But the happy movements of the flesh have a double orientation. Because going through flesh—going through the point where the unity of a person is torn apart—is necessary if, in losing oneself, one wants to rediscover oneself in the unity of love, it does not follow that the moment of tearing apart is itself devoid of meaning for torn-apart existence. It is difficult to know, in a coupling of beings, how much is passion for another being, how much is erotic frenzy, up to what point the being looks for life and power, and *up to what point it is led to tear itself apart and lose itself.* [My emphasis][42]

When Kit and Port board a bus for El Ga'a, she is attracted to a young Arab who lowers the hood of his burnous and smiles at her. Addressing her in Arabic, he says, *"Hassi Inifel,"* pointing at the earth several times. "Merci," she responds, smiling, although it is doubtful that either she or the reader knows what the words mean (*SS*, 187). Kit's interest is then further aroused: she "could not help noticing how unusually tall he was, what an admirable figure he cut when he stood erect in his flowing white garment. To efface her feeling of guilt at having thought anything at all about him, she felt impelled to bring him to Port's attention" (190). Despite Kit's awareness of Port's worsening state, her outlook, which had been bleak and fearful up until now, improves, and "for the first time she felt a faint thrill of excitement (191). Meanwhile, the young Arab

> spoke just enough French to be undaunted by the patent impossibility of his engaging in an actual conversation with Kit. It appeared that in his eyes a noun alone or a verb uttered with feeling was sufficient, and she seemed to be of the same mind. . . . She listened with complete attention, hypnotized by the extraordinary charm of his face and his voice, and fascinated as well by the strangeness of what he was talking about, the odd way he was saying it. (192)

It seems that Kit is as susceptible as Alvina is to the nonverbal articulations of a young and exotic stranger. When the bus arrives in El Ga'a, the young Arab remains with Kit to help transport Port to the hotel, which is on the other side of town. To Kit, "[h]is face expressed nothing but friendly solicitousness, and she trusted him implicitly," though a short time later, a combination of his aware-ness of her reliance upon him and her perception of "some trace of triumph" in his voice give her pause (193). This ambivalence is never explored, however, as the young man (who remains name-less) is finally tossed aside once his assistance is no longer needed, and he is heard of no more in the novel.

While the interchange foreshadows Kit's eroticized submission later on in the novel, it also functions as a suggestive interruption—but merely an interruption—of the grand narrative of self-dissolu-tion. Here, as in other of Bowles's fictions, the horror of self-loss (a horror that is at the same time sublime and sexy) is always tem-pered by the insistent voice of the Other, whose place in the text can always be read in at least two ways. Whether as facilitator or interlocutor, the Other represents a demand to communicate; the communication, I would argue, in both its ecstatic Dionysian mode ("Be that ocean") and its dialogic one, is an important, if paradox-ical, trope in a body of work characterized in significant part by vio-lence, negativity, and despair. The need for such communication is commensurate with the protagonist's alienation, his existential and *expatriate* alienation. For this reason, Bataille's conception of eroticism, one that attends as carefully to self-loss as it does to self-fulfilment, is a profound marker of expatriate pathos. Eroticism cuts both ways, as do *The Sheltering Sky's* ethics of expatriation. The journey of Port and Kit "to the extreme limit of the possible" is not without its digressions. While their dreams of freedom, adventure, and mastery do not materialize—or, in fact, do materialize but in ways that appear unrecognizable—they are not permitted to indulge their fancies in a social vacuum. The imaginative geography of *The Sheltering Sky* situates the abyss within a social space that demands of its expatriate protagonists that they engage, and they do so with varying degrees of care and attention. It thus remains to other of Bowles's fictions to bring to fruition the suggestive interruption, to fashion the beginnings of a social space in the periphery that mark the space of a humanist ethics of expatriation.

Let It Come Down

While *The Sheltering Sky* represents the space of the Other as a social space for intersubjective exploration only obliquely, *Let It Come Down* more fully examines the relationship between an American expatriate and his Moroccan counterpart. Thematically, the novel covers familiar ground: Western man's desire to escape from the burdens of selfhood, his enigmatic contacts with the native, and his undoing in the unfamiliar geographies of places remote from "civilization." If *The Sheltering Sky*, a far more interesting work, was driven by its characters' excessive yearning to self-destruct, in *Let It Come Down* the protagonist's destructive energies are externalized, if the end result is, arguably, the same. The novel's gratuitous violence, to a great extent overdetermined, puts the issue of expatriate ethics squarely on the table. The act of murder, the culmination perhaps of a radical form of expatriate ascesis, exemplifies the incompatibility between self-overcoming, taken to its extreme, and the positing of any sort of moral space. At the same time, the protagonist's "endangerment," the proximate cause of his murderous act, is commensurate with his vulnerability to the Other, a vulnerability that has shown itself to be benign and even at times pleasurable. If events conspire to turn the young American expatriate, Nelson *Dyar* (the one who kills, but in doing so, effectively dies), into a murderer, there is the sense that violence is, indeed, the only manner of communication that can effectively relieve him of his relentlessly morbid and alienated condition.

Dyar comes to Tangier on the promise of a job by a friend from home. He is befriended by a young Moroccan named Thami Beidaoui who, reluctantly at first, acts as a kind of guide to the native quarter. Dyar is smitten with a young Moroccan prostitute, Hadija, which pits him against an eccentric American lesbian, Eunice Goode, who is her protector. As Dyar's prospective job does not materialize in quite the way he thought it would, he runs short of cash. Eunice Goode manipulates him into accepting an advance from a Russian spy for keeping his ears open. Then, while acting as a courier in his putative employer's money-changing scheme, he gets to the bank too late to deposit the funds. He decides to flee to the Spanish Zone with the money and solicits the help of Thami. They escape by boat to a remote area where Thami's in-laws live. Dyar grows increasingly paranoid concerning Thami's intentions and, in a kif-induced delirium, hammers a nail into Thami's ear, piercing his skull.

Let It Come Down effectively deconstructs expatriate mythology at the same time it foregrounds the idea of communication, both dialogic and collective, in the Bataillian sense. Dyar is a typical Bowles protagonist, anguished and alienated: his "life was a dead weight, so heavy that he would never be able to move it from where it lay."[43] Gnawed at by "the stationariness of existence" (*Let It*, 21), he is impelled one day by the sight of a travel agency to write to an old friend in Tangier who was in the travel business, asking for a job. Just as improbably, his request is rewarded. This being a Bowles novel, however, the stakes are cast in terms of life and death. When he arrives in Tangier, he experiences it as "the danger point. . . . At this moment it was almost as though he did not exist. . . . The old thing was gone beyond recall, the new thing had not yet begun" (19). The old thing was Dyar's life in the States, where he worked as bank teller in a "cage." He believed that "he had done right" in leaving. "All the way across on the ship to Gibraltar, he had told himself that it was the healthy thing to have done, that when he arrived he would be like another person, full of life, delivered from the sense of despair that had weighed on him for so long" (22). Like Lawrence's Aaron Sisson, Dyar equates the crossing of borders with life-giving possibilities. Like Aaron Sisson, the raw material that is his life seems incompatible with the demands of economic and domestic life. He is stung by the need to be productive:

> He tried to imagine how he would feel if, for instance, he had his whole life before him to spend as he pleased, *without the necessity to earn his living*. In that case, he would not have to telephone Wilcox, would not be compelled to exchange one cage for another. *Having made the first break, he would then make the second, and be completely free.* (22, my emphasis)

Tangier, however, is not Italy, and Dyar does not feel any differently having crossed the imaginary (and literal) border. It will only be a matter of time, however, before the second break is made, the break that is definitive and irrevocable, one toward which events catapult him even as he remains deeply naive concerning the quality of freedom.

We get some insight into Dyar's condition when his fortune is read by one of the doyennes of the expatriate community, the Marquesa de Valverde:

> "I see no sign of work. No sign of anything, to be quite honest. I've never seen such an empty hand. It's terrifying." . . . "I mean," she said, "that you have an empty life. No pattern. And nothing in you to give any purpose. Most people can't help following some kind of design. They do it automatically because it's in their nature. It's that that saves them, pulls them up short. They can't help themselves. But you're safe from being saved." (34)

We might wonder about a vision of salvation so deeply in debt to structure and worldly design and the concomitant horror of blank spaces. Being safe from being saved is the point at which, for Bataille, one is truly free. Dyar's empty future is matched by an equally barren interior life: an "anti-ethics." Nevertheless, as he makes inroads into Tangieri social life, he grows uncharacteristically introspective:

> Although he was not given to analyzing his states of mind, since he never had been conscious of possessing any sort of apparatus with which to do so, recently he had felt, like a faint tickling in an inaccessible region of his being, an undefined need to let his mind dwell on himself. There were no formulated thoughts, he did not even daydream, nor did he push matters so far as to ask himself questions like: "What am I doing here?" or "What do I want?" At the same time he was vaguely aware of having arrived at the edge of a new period in his existence, *an unexplored territory of himself through which he was going to have to pass.* . . . He was not moved by the phenomenon; even to himself he felt supremely anonymous, and it is difficult to care very much what is happening inside a person one does not know. At the same time, that which went on outside was remote and had no relationship to him; it might almost as well not have been going on at all. Yet he was not indifferent—indifference is a matter of the emotions, whereas this numbness affected a deeper part of him. (116, my emphasis)

If the unexplored territory of himself corresponds in some sense to the unexplored territory of his new abode, his deep numbness seems to suggest resistance, a surprising lack of curiosity. The necessity of "having to pass through" takes on the quality of an ascesis, the nature of which is enigmatic to Dyar himself. In some fundamental sense, his "interior" self is as remote to him as the outside world. It seems that Dyar, like Port, longs for certain qualities of experience that he cannot articulate. He hopes to find relief from his deep malaise in a new life, but events in Tangier, which have cast him in the unlikely roles of thief, spy, and adulterer, only exacerbate his sense of entrapment. Far from releasing him from subservience, the expatriate community of Tangier has made of him an even greater victim, a tool in the hands of others, thus precipitating a crisis of Bataillian proportions wherein he squanders everything in a paroxysm of violence.

First, however, Dyar explores more conventional means of self-overcoming in the native quarter, where he attempts to retrace his steps to the bar where Hadija works:

> And as he stood there, again he found himself asking the same questions he had asked earlier in the day: "What am I doing here? What's going to happen?" . . . He was trying *to lose himself.* Which meant, he realized, that his great problem right now was *to escape* from his cage, to discover the way out of the fly-trap, to strike the chord inside himself which would liberate those qualities capable of *transforming him* from a victim into a winner. (169, my emphasis)

If liberation is here represented by the infinitely pedestrian term "winning," the effect is, nevertheless, to conflate the winner with the victimizer, a far more dicey transformation. Getting lost in the native quarter, however, is a throwback to more benign expatriate pleasures: "It was rather fun, *being lost* like this; it gave him a strange sensation of security,—the feeling that at his particular instant *no one in the world could possibly find him,*" (168, my emphasis). If, at the same time, however, he desired to "take himself in hand" (a phrase in and of itself suggestive), "between the saying and the doing there was an abyss into which all the knowledge, strength and courage you had could not keep you from plunging" (169–70). I hear, in this line, intimations of Eliot's *Hollow Men,* for the poem's speaker and Dyar share a similar sense of impotence and despair in a world devoid of spiritual energy. Dyar, however, externalizes his anguish; he becomes an actor.

In his resolve to escape from Tangier with the money he has stolen, there is more than a whiff of Nietzschean recklessness:

> There was even a savage pleasure to be had in reflecting that he could do nothing else but go on and see what would happen, and that this

impossibility of finding any other solution was a direct result of his own decision. He sniffed the wet air, and said to himself that at last he was living, that whatever the reason for his doubt a moment ago, the spasm which had shaken him had been only an instant's return of his old state of mind, when he had been anonymous, a victim. He told himself, although not in so many words, that his new and veritable condition was one which permitted him to believe easily in the reality of the things his senses perceived--—to take part in their existences, that is, since belief is participation. And he expected now to lead the procession of his life, as the locomotive heads the train, no longer to be a helpless incidental object somewhere in the middle of the line of events, drawn one way and another. (230)

The escape from Tangier, however, has material as well as metaphoric consequences, one of which is that Dyar has placed himself in Thami's hands. Thami's alterity, the alterity of Morocco itself, first embodied in the nightmarish journey out, becomes threatening precisely to the degree that it provides no guarantee of his own integrity. In Dyar's increasingly disordered consciousness, Thami becomes "the very essence of Oriental deviousness and cunning" (242). What is more, their hideaway cabin is equally insufficient. Its "patchwork door" rattles with the wind. "Silently he cursed it, resolving to make it secure for tomorrow night," and it is with the very tool he obtains for this purpose that he will kill Thami (248). An extraordinary sequence of events, however, precedes the murder.

While Thami is out getting food and provisions from his relations, Dyar flees the cabin and wanders through the alien countryside. Making use of Thami's kif that he had inadvertently left behind, Dyar gets high. His thoughts turn inward, assuming with the influence of the kif a contented but fatalistic aspect. When he comes upon a town, however, his paranoia returns:

> And now as he stood there clutching his briefcase, the people pushing past him on both sides, his mind still muzzy from the kif, he saw with terror that he was hopelessly confused. He had imagined the town would be something else, that somewhere there would be a place he could go into and ask for information; he had counted on the town to help him as a troubled man counts on a friend to give him advice. . . . However, at this moment he was conscious that the props that held up his future were in the act of crumbling. (265–66)

He is hailed by a native in uniform whom he takes to be a policeman. Without hesitation, he forges ahead, ducking into a partly opened door. At the top of the stairs he is welcomed by a man with a friendly face and the sound of drumbeats into a small café crowded with turbaned men, who make room for him on the bench where they are seated. A trance dance is taking place, and a lighted kif-pipe is passed to him. Dyar is uncertain of what he is experiencing, for

> after a day passed largely in the contemplation of that far-off and unlikely place which was the interior of himself, he did not find it difficult now to reject flatly the reality of what he was seeing. He merely sat and watched, content in the conviction that the thing he was looking at was not taking place in the world that really existed. *It was too far beyond the pale of the possible.* (269–70, my emphasis)

This is Bataille country: a realm in which scenes of ritual violation open out into communication, making of its participants a community. The dancer twists spasmodically and then pulls out a knife from within his robes, slashing himself rhythmically with the beat of the drum, and just as rhythmically licking the blood from himself. Dyar is rapt, hardly breathing.

> It could not be said that he watched now, because *in his mind he had moved forward from looking on to a kind of participation.* . . . In a world which had *not yet been muddied by the discovery of thought,* there was this certainty, as solid as a boulder, as real as the beating of his heart, that the man was dancing to purify all who watched. When the dancer threw himself to the floor with a despairing cry, Dyar knew that in reality it was a cry of victory, that spirit had triumphed; the expressions of satisfaction on the faces around him confirmed this. . . . Dyar sat perfectly still, thinking of nothing, savoring the *unaccustomed sensations which had been freed within him.* (270–71, my emphasis)

As John Maier notes, Bowles's rendering of the dancer's "rapture . . . promises more than appears to be realized in Dyar's paranoid fantasies. Maier also suggests that despite the novel's brutal resolution, the trance-dancing scene seems to temper somewhat the overwhelming failure of cross-cultural understanding suggested by the narrative.[44] One could also argue, however, that Dyar's intoxication with Otherness, which is then exacerbated by the *majoun,* a hashish-based confection, offered him by Thami, might be dangerous precisely to the degree that he is susceptible to it. In other words, rather than tempering such failure, the trance dancing precipitates it. Abdul JanMohamed, in his discussion of *A Passage to India,* notes that the very devices—the landscape of India and, in particular, the Marabar Caves, which become the efficient cause of mystical experiences and the major crises in the novel—through which Forster chooses to examine the possibilities of cultural and racial rapprochement (as well as the larger issue of the spiritual and metaphysical meaning of human endeavor that is the central preoccupation of the novel) eventually guarantee their failure. . . . Yet having invested "India" (the land, the caves, and the non-Muslim Indian religions) with this particular metaphysics of identity and difference, Forster recoils from it in mild horror. His subconscious rejection of it is revealed by the chaos and danger that follow each encounter with the all-consuming transcendental identity. . . . Even a momentary transcendence of difference, Forster seems to fear, will lead to uncontrollable chaos.[45]

The metaphysical difference between self and Other that underlies the experience of the Marabar Caves, according to JanMohamed, disallows the possibility of cultural syncretism.

There is another reading, however, that locates the murder of Thami in a domain "beyond good and evil" whose provenance, however, owes more to Bataille than to Nietzsche. Within the context of a philosophy or a sociology that ties together terms like "intimacy," "communication," "violence," "death," and "sacrifice," at once severing them from their imbrication in normative ethical discourse, we can make of this act the culmination of an ascesis that has as its goal the transformation of the human substance itself. The ethics of expatriation that produce murder as their inevitable outcome are not unrelated to the various strategies of self-liberation we have seen elsewhere, but they are more extreme and certainly harder to justify in conventional ethical terms. Dyar, we remember, hopes to realize the ultimate freedom, a freedom antithetical to work and utility. Death is an integral part of that world. In *The Accursed Share* Bataille writes,

Death is a negation brought into operation in the world of practice: the principle of that world is submerged in death like a city in a tidal wave. It is the world of the thing, of the tool, the world of identity in time and of the operation that disposes of future time. It is the world of limits, of laws, and of *prohibition*. It is basically a general subordination of human beings to works that satisfy the demands of a group. But not only does this world run up against unavoidable contradictions, not only is death its unavoidable stumbling block, but the man who has fully satisfied these demands—no sooner has he satisfied them then he calls *actively* for the negation of a servitude that he accepted, but accepted only insofar as it was imposed on him. . . . But beyond this passive negation, active rebellion is easy and is bound to occur in the end: he whom the world of utility tended to reduce to the state of a thing not subject to death, hence not subject to killing, ultimately demands the violation of the prohibition that he had accepted. Then, by killing, he escapes the subordination that he refuses, and he violently rids himself of the aspect of a tool or a thing, which he had assumed only for a time. [Bataille's emphasis][46]

At the same time, however, violence and sacrifice—or the violence of sacrifice— redound upon the individual. Bataille writes:

Paradoxically, intimacy is violence, and it is destruction, because it is not compatible with the positing of the separate individual. If one describes the individual in the operation of sacrifice, he is defined by anguish. But if sacrifice is distressing, the reason is that the individual takes part in it. The individual identifies with the victim in the sudden movement that restores it to immanence (to intimacy).[47]

And there are aspects of Dyar's murder of Thami that call to mind the idea of sacrifice, as that idea takes shape in Bataille's writings.

The principle of sacrifice is destruction, but though it sometimes goes so far as to destroy completely (as in a holocaust), the destruction that sacrifice is intended to bring about is not annihilation. The thing— only the thing—is what sacrifice means to destroy in the victim. Sacrifice destroys an object's real ties of subordination; it draws the victim out of the world of utility and restores it to that of unintelligible caprice. When the offered animal enters the circle in which the priest will immolate it, it passes from the world of things which are closed to man and are *nothing* to him, which he knows from the outside—to the world that is immanent to it, *intimate*, known as the wife is known in sexual consumption. (210)

To sacrifice, then,

is not to kill but to relinquish and to give. . . . What is important is to pass from a lasting order, in which all consumption of resources is subordinated to the need for duration, to the violence of an unconditional consumption; what is important is to leave a world of real things, whose reality derives from a long-term operation and never resides in the moment. . . . Sacrifice is the antitheses of production, which is accomplished with a view to the future; it is consumption that is concerned only with the moment. (213)

What I wish to suggest is that a constellation of ideas emerges in the following passage of the novel—the perception of Thami as a *thing*, the consideration of how that status might be ameliorated, the suggestion that unmediated existence itself, or Bataille's *experience* (in the guise of a rattling door), might dissolve the object's "vast imponderable weight"—which agitates in favor of a more complex reading of the murder:

> Partly he knew that what he saw before him was Thami, Thami's head, trunk, arms, and legs. Partly he knew it was an unidentifiable object lying there, immeasurably heavy with its own meaninglessness, a vast imponderable weight that nothing could lighten. As he stood lost in static contemplation of the thing, the wind pushed the door feebly, making a faint rattling. But *could* nothing lighten it? If the air were let in, the weight might escape of its own accord, into the shadows of the room and the darkness of the light. (*Let It*, 283, Bowles's emphasis)

A key metaphor here is the flapping door of the cabin, which, I would argue, represents not so much Patteson's idea of structural insufficiency as the intimacy of outside and inside that in some way anticipates the drama that will be enacted within. For Dyar, "the loose door was equivalent to an open door. A little piece of wood, a hammer and one nail could arrange everything: the barrier between himself and the world outside would be much more real" (249). The knobless door, in fact, sends out an "ominous message:" "If it opened when he did not want it to open, by itself, all the horror of existence could crowd in upon him" (282). To that degree, then, the door can be said to represent "the *opening out* into an unbearably unfamiliar or foreign condition exterior to the comforts and defenses of consciousness."[48] That is the door to inner experience and the anguish, which sacrifice aims to assuage, of the aporia of being: our essence as "incomplete beings." The result, as we have seen with Kit in *The Sheltering Sky*, is the push and pull between the desire for continuity and the desire to be self, a discontinuous state. "We always," Richardson writes, "strive towards what will destroy us; our condition is one of loss. We are always living on the edge of an abyss."[49]

And if we link the trance dancing to the ritual of sacrifice, and to that definitive moment when "unaccustomed sensations are freed" in Dyar, we can also tie the sacred "act" of the dancer to the excess out of which the murder is produced. Returning again to Bataille:

> The sacred is that prodigious effervescence of life that, for the sake of duration, the order of things holds in check, and that this holding

changes into a breaking-loose, that is, into violence. It constantly threatens to break the dikes, to confront productive activity with the precipitate and contagious movement of a purely glorious consumption. The sacred is exactly comparable to the flame that destroys the wood by consuming it . . . but it is never isolated and, in a world of individuals, it calls for the general negation of individuals as such, . . . the constant problem posed by the impossibility of being human without being a thing and of escaping the limits of things without returning to animal slumber receives the limited solution of the festival.[50]

This conflation of violence and intimacy, then, overflows the bounds of "festival," represented in the novel by that communal rite in which Dyar had participated, exploding in Dyar's act of "glorious consumption."

Finally, of course, the benefits of sacrifice redound upon the sacrificer, not the sacrificed. If the subject is returned to immanent totality through the ritual violation of the object—although in theory there should be a kind of merging of sacrificer and sacrificed in totality—the fact is that one party emerges from the ritual and the other does not. Dyar, then, in negating the servitude represented by the "cage," turns Thami into a tool. The Other is seen as somehow instrumental to the processes of radical self-liberation. But to speak of Thami's murder as sacrifice would require that very inexpendability, for "the precise meaning of sacrifice" is "that one sacrifices *what is useful;* one does not sacrifice luxurious objects" (Bataille's emphasis).[51] Soon after the murder, Dyar is hunted down by the marquesa, who, understanding why he fled Tangier, is prepared to bring him back and make things right. Like Tunner in *The Sheltering Sky,* she is a figure who represents the community of home (even if that is an expatriate community), and like Tunner she must return alone, having witnessed the horror or enigma of sovereignty, its debt to death and brutal disorder. There will be no cushy living and exotic girls in the textual space where Dyar is left suspended; like the Professor and Kit, he is cut adrift and "cannot get back."

Having traced what I perceive to be the narrative "charge" of *Let It Come Down,* its enactment of Dyar's ascesis, I must insist as well upon the novel's thematic counterpoint that points to more conventional notions of communication and, indeed, friendship. Dyar and Thami are also subjects who need and like each other. Indeed, one might argue that Bowles, the expatriate author, pursues an ethics of imaginative identification with the Other, while Dyar is caught within systems of signification that the novel repudiates. Thami and Dyar function to some extent as doubles. John Maier has noted their shared condition of marginality "that makes them outsiders almost everywhere, even in their own communities."[52] A textual precursor to Amar of Bowles's *Spider's House*, Thami has crossed the boundaries of his own deeply Islamic upbringing. His newer friendships, though not profound, have exposed him to the discourse of anticolonialism:

> Two were professors at the Lycée Français, ardent nationalists who never missed an opportunity during a conversation to excoriate the French, and threw about terms like "imperialist domination," "Pan-Islamic culture" and "autonomy." Their violence and resentment against the abuses of an unjust authority struck a sympathetic chord in him; he felt like one of them without really understanding what they were talking about. (*Let It*, 41)

And yet, "he could not think of the mass of Moroccans without contempt. He had no patience with their ignorance and back-wardness; if he damned the Europeans with one breath, he was bound to damn the Moroccans with the next" (44). Paradoxically, Dyar and Thami seem to share a greater affinity with each other than with the members of their own cultural group. Thami, like Lawrence's forlorn Italians, is a Western subject in the making and provides no self-authenticating alterity for the American expatriate.

Their relationship begins on Dyar's first night in Tangier. Encountering Thami in a café for the first time, Dyar regards him "with a certain warmth." Thami agrees to share a drink with him, and "[t]he two men looked at each other. It was the moment when they were ready to feel sympathy for one another, but the tradi-tional formula of distrust made it necessary that a reason be found first" (45–46). While they circle each other distrustfully, there is no hint of the kind of danger encountered by the Professor or Port. In fact, early on there is every indication that Thami is attempting to protect Dyar from the very predators we have seen before in Bowles's fiction. He is even a bit frightened at first that "the Ameri-can was going to ask to be directed to a bordel, and he glanced about nervously to see if anyone he knew was in the café. One rumor he could not have circulating was that he had become a guide; in Tangier there was nothing lower" (45). Already we are worlds apart from *The Sheltering Sky*. Dyar and Thami only meet several times during the course of the novel before they cast their fates together on a flight to the Spanish Zone. As each is forced to negotiate the plight of his own alienation, their narratives converge in the ill-fated voyage out.

Throughout the text, and especially in the passages leading up to the climax, the concrete and culturally conditioned drama of self and Other unfolds, not only in the consciousness of Dyar, but also through the novel's two centers of consciousness, those of Dyar and Thami. They drink together, even take an interest in the same prostitute, and Thami professes genuine affection for the American despite their competition over the girl: " 'You know, Dare—' (Dyar corrected him); '—some night I'll take you to my home and give you a real Moorish dinner. Couscous, bastila, everything. How's that?' 'That would be fine, Thami,' " Dyar responds (166–67). Thami is especially expansive because he has just obtained the money (which he managed to extort from Eunice Goode) to buy a small boat he intends to use in smuggling—which information he shares with Dyar. So it is to him that Dyar turns when he needs to make a getaway. Dyar's "voyage out" of the multiple legal and social entanglements in Tangier, represented by flight to the Spanish Zone, requires not only that he place his trust in Thami but that he negotiate the void beyond Tangier's relatively domesticated space. Dyar's predicament makes him aware of how little he knows Thami:

> His mind turned to wondering what kind of man it was who sat near him on the floor, saying nothing. He had talked with Thami, sat and drunk with him, but during all the moments they had been in one another's company *it never had occurred to him to ask himself what thoughts went on behind those inexpressive features.* (229, my emphasis)

Despite his nervousness, he is able to acknowledge an intelligence and a subjectivity behind the physical features he is unable to "read." As Dyar's characterization of Thami changes from sphinx to "idiotic barbarian" (229), his fear of being "a victim" acted upon by circumstances and manipulated by others increases.

When Dyar wanders through the alien countryside, paranoid and intoxicated with kif, it is to Thami that his thoughts turn:

> How would he feel when he realized his prisoner had escaped, taking with him even Thami's own pipe and mottoui? He wondered if perhaps that might not be considered a supreme injury, an unforgivable act. He had no idea; he knew nothing about this country, save that all its inhabitants behaved like maniacs. Maybe it was not Thami himself of whose reactions he was afraid, he reflected—it

might be only that Thami was part of the place and therefore had everything in the place behind him so to speak. Thami in New York—he almost laughed at the image the idea evoked—he was the sort no one would even take the trouble to look at in the street when he asked for a dime. Here it was another matter. He was a spokesman for the place; like Antaeus, whatever strength he had came out of the earth, and his feet were planted squarely upon it. (263)

Dyar's ambivalent feelings produce conflicting profiles of Thami. For example, Dyar wonders about his own culpability, whether he has committed an "unforgivable act." The very idea of "forgiveness," it seems to me, assumes the existence of a subject that can forgive, a subject whose forgiveness, moreover, might even matter. On the other hand, he reduces an entire nationality to "maniacs" and Thami to their mere "representative."

Standing at the entrance to a small native restaurant, he is alarmed at the sight of "an oversized Berber" who "stood staring at [him] in a manner that the other at first found disconcerting, then disturbing, and finally, because he had begun to ask himself the possible reason for this insolent scrutiny, downright frightening" (263–64). Dyar is convinced that it is one of Thami's henchman, prepared to do his work

with Thami conveniently seated in some respectable home, laughing, drinking tea, strumming on an oud. And this possibility seemed in a way worse, perhaps because he had never been able to see Thami in the role of a brutal torturer, the tacit understanding with his own imagination having been that things would somehow be done with comparative gentleness, painlessly. (264)

Even the Berber, upon reflection, for all his fierceness betrayed no "baseness in the face, nor even any particular cunning—merely a primal, ancient blindness, the ineffable, unfocused melancholy of the great apes as they stare between the cage bars (264). Dyer distinguishes between Thami, with whom he shares by now a certain history and whom he almost grudgingly grants a subjectivity and an aversion to violence, and the Berber, who is thoroughly dehumanized; all natives, it seems, are not alike. As these interior monologues of Dyar are juxtaposed to those of Thami, the narrative reveals the growing disparity between Dyar's perception of Thami and the "real" Thami. According him the "humanity" that Dyar only grudgingly and conditionally grants, the novel embraces to a certain extent those values that the plot appears to eschew. Charged with a powerful and seductive negativity that straddles the sacred and the obscene, the ethics of this expatriate narrative are so radically antihumanist in the traditional sense that they tend to overshadow the metatextual ethics that historicize and relativize difference: an ethics of potential reengagement. But Bowles can be just as withering in his interrogation of the latter.

It would be interesting at this point, I think, to briefly consider the life of Jane Bowles, Paul Bowles's wife, and a significant figure in her own right. They were married in 1938, by which time she was already known as a lesbian. By all accounts, they lived separate and independent erotic lives, though this did not lessen the bond between them. Jane's only published novel, *Two Serious Ladies*, was published in 1943. Several years later she followed Paul to Morocco, where despite the completion of her play *In the Summer House*, which was produced on Broadway, and an important short story, "Camp Cataract," she was unable to complete another novel. Much has been written of her tempestuous relationship with the illiterate market vendor Cherifa, with whom she was obsessed and who seemed at times to dominate her, her many lovers, all women, and her heavy drinking. Jane Bowles suffered a serious stroke in 1957. While she recovered briefly, she was never again able to do any serious writing. She died in 1973 in a clinic in Spain.

One short story, "Everything Is Nice," emerged from Jane's imaginative grasp of the Moroccan experience. The shape of this narrative is very similar to those of *The Sheltering Sky* and *Let It Come Down* in that a "Nazarene" or European wanders through a native town only to be accosted by a "native." In this case, however, both are female. The setting and the Moroccan woman's actions appear intimidating. They meet on the edge of a cliff where the highest street of the town runs. A thick protecting wall separates the street from the drop below. A dog has just slipped on a rock, plunging into the ocean and emitting an "earsplitting" cry. Zodelia, the Moroccan woman, has approached the Nazarene and jabs her basket into her hips to gain her attention. The Nazarine, whose name is Jeanie, has been pretending not to notice her presence. They converse in a relatively benign if enigmatic fashion, and Zodelia invites her to a wedding. They stop for some unappetizing cakes, "dusty and coated with a thin, ugly-colored icing," for which Jeanie pays. Zodelia leads her into an alley and into a doorway. Jeanie asks about the wedding, to which Zodelia replies, "There is no wedding here."[53] They enter a dark room containing mattresses and women sitting on them. An old lady among them is preparing meatballs. The conversation, again, is bizarre, very much in the nature of a mismeeting. The Moroccans, for one thing, can't understand why Jeanie is here and her mother is back in her own country. When the old woman insists that Jeanie eat some of the cakes, she becomes very uncomfortable and backs her way out of the dwelling. Zodelia follows her out and they seem to arrange a tryst for the next day. Zodelia suggests four o'clock, but "it was obvious that she had chosen the first figure that had come into her head."[54] Jeanie returns to the protecting wall, and finds herself filled with some inexplicable longing. There the story ends.

The elements of Bowlesean fiction are there: dread, desire, cultural confusion, the inexplicable uses of language, the abyss itself. What is missing, however, is the lure of the abyss into which Paul Bowles's characters plunge headlong. Jane Bowles provides an ominous enough prelude, and her protagonist becomes frightened, indeed, almost panicked. But she emerges from the social wilderness of that dwelling in full possession of her senses, ready to meet Zodelia again. The story is about mismeeting and about desire, not about radical forms of existential risk taking. There may be a sense of cultural vertigo—the meeting is certainly disorienting—but we do not understand Jeanie to be on the path that Kit set for herself. Is this a gender issue? I believe it is, at least to the extent that the stories of Paul Bowles are driven by anxieties and cultural narratives that are linked, I am persuaded, to issues having to do with the construction of masculinity.

The Spider's House

With *The Spider's House*, written in 1955, Bowles turns to an explicit examination of expatriate life in Fez as it unfolds over a period of several days during a period of growing anticolonialist activism, and he explores it from a number of diverse points of view. We might readily compare this work to Durrell's *Bitter Lemons* in that both texts (written, in fact, within a couple of years of one another) record a Western expatriate narrator's response to colonial uprising, the awakening nationalism of the colonized, and the changing nature of his personal relationships with members of the native population. Of course there are major differences as well. Durrell was himself a colonial and a subject of the colonizing power in whose offices he frequently found work. He was director of information services in Cyprus during the time of the Enosis uprising. His text purports to document real events. Bowles writes from a distinctly American perspective and, as an American and a private individual, he was not associated in any way with the French colonial regime in Morocco. His intention, according to a 1982 preface to the novel, was "to write a novel using as a backdrop the traditional daily life of Fez, because it was a medieval city functioning in the twentieth century," but as a result of rapidly occurring political events, he realized he would have to write "not about the traditional pattern of life in Fez, but about its dissolution." More didactic and outward looking than his earlier novels in terms of its thematic enunciation of political perspectives, *The Spider's House* nevertheless attempts to register the impact of political and social change on a traditional society through the consciousness of an illiterate Moroccan boy, Amar, who is from a poor but respected family of *cherifs*, direct descendants of the Prophet Mohammed. Perhaps even more importantly, however, the text can be read as an ethical practice of the expatriate Paul Bowles in the nature of Connolly's "relational arts of the self." At the same time, *The Spider's House* interrogates expatriate xenophilia as acutely as *Let It Come Down* and other works of Bowles interrogate xenophobia. The ethics of expatriation, therefore, are both textual and meta-textual.

John Stenham, the Western protagonist, is a writer and long-time expatriate resident of Fez. He speaks Arabic, has cultivated the friendship of at least one relatively well-placed Muslim family, and has mastered the "enchanted labyrinth" of the Medina, the native town of Fez (as opposed to the Ville Nouvelle, the colonial town built by the French). For him, the "voyage out," while still disorienting at times, holds few surprises. He is a great champion of traditional society; to him Fez is outside politics and outside time. The idealistic challenge he must face in the novel is the entry of Morocco—and particularly Fez—into modernity. Although he is conscious of history, conscious of the manner in which both he and the world have changed—and not for the better—"the world" does not, or should not, include Fez. Hence in this disenchanted narrative of expatriation, "home" overtakes the expatriate in his refuge. Unlike Lawrence's forlorn Italian landscapes, marred by the signs of modern development, however, Bowles's Fez represents a vibrant political and cultural arena in which the drama of decolonization is enacted.

It is Stenham's relationship with the boy Amar around which the novel turns, although their plots coincide only in the last third of the book. Briefly told, the novel combines two narratives: that of Amar, an illiterate youth who unwittingly becomes the victim of the colonial struggle between Moroccan nationalists and the French authorities, and that of Stenham and his romantic liaison with a fellow American, Polly Burroughs. On the eve of political insurrection, Amar, who has been locked out of the city, finds himself at the café where Stenham and Polly have been taking refreshment. A bomb goes off and Stenham looks to the streetwise boy for some sense of what is going on. Amar, who is now cut off from his family, is briefly taken under the wing of the Americans. Later in the novel, when he is deceived by a group of nationalists with whom he has sought shelter and finds himself in mortal danger, he seeks the protection of Stenham. Just at that moment, Stenham and Polly are heading out for Mèknes, where it so happens Amar's mother and sister have fled. They give him a ride to the outskirts of Fez and turn him loose. Amar is left homeless and friendless, stranded on the road.

Why does Stenham leave the West? A range of disappointments seems to motivate his desire to become an expatriate: spiritual hunger, political disillusionment, and a loss of faith, even, in the ideal of human equality itself because, he believes, "the human heart demanded hierarchies." Before, however, undertaking the voyage out, he journeys inward to his own interior spaces, withdrawing "into a subjectivity which refused existence to any reality or law but its own."[55] This, however, leads to a life of utter meaninglessness. "Like a flame under a glass [the light of meaning] had dwindled, flickered and gone out, and all existence, including his own hermetic structure from which he had observed existence, had become absurd and unreal" (*SH*, 195–96). It is the suffocating "insideness" of his life that precipitates the voyage out. The city of Fez seems to offer the antidote to his spiritual and existential malaise. He envies the traditional Muslim world that, for him, is monolithic in its adherence to the faith and uncomplicated in its attitude toward history. The perceived spiritual plenitude of Islam and its community of practitioners is both "desirable and therapeutic" (217). He also associates Islamic society with a model of subjectivity that eschews depth in favor of a kind of situational immediacy. One thinks of Port and Kit, who are never quite sure of being "in life," and one finds, at the opposite pole of consciousness, a being-in-life that is fresh and immediate, a sovereign *unknowing*, the enigmatic mystery of man at peace with himself, satisfied with his solution of the problem of life; [the Muslims'] complacence came from asking no questions, accepting existence as it arrived to their senses fresh each morning, seeking to understand no more than that which was directly useful for the day's simple living, and trusting implicitly in the ultimate and absolute inevitability of all things, including the behavior of man. (217)

Stenham thinks of the difference between Islam and the West in terms of plot structure. There is the "and then," the essentially unmotivated unfolding of events in the Islamic world, and there is the "because," the idea of cause and effect, in the West. In Morocco

one thing doesn't come from another thing. Nothing is a result of anything. Everything merely *is*, and no questions asked. Even the language they speak is constructed around that. Each fact is separate, and one never depends on the other. Everything's explained by the constant intervention of Allah. And whatever happens had to happen, and was decreed at the beginning of time, and there's no way even of imaging how anything could have been different from what it is. (187)

Stenham's interpretation, in which the "epistemic" is repudiated in favor of the "ontological," is of a piece with his general devaluation of interiority. He blames the Christians, and by that I take him to mean the West generally (although it would be intriguing to think he had in mind the self-confessing, deeply introspective model of Christian subjectivity), for the destruction of this static and unself-reflective way of life, which, in addition to its simplicity, is radically antiutilitarian and antiproductive. That is, in its failure to consider the future as the consummation of productive practice, it is the negation of Bataille's "world of practice."

And consistent with Bataille's notion of sovereignty as a condition of radical *play*, Stenham privileges a time when Fez was "pure," and "there was music and dancing and magic every day in the streets" (187). Now it is "like all the other Moslem countries, just a huge European slum, full of poverty and hatred" (188). While Stenham is attentive to the detritus of imperialism, his overly romantic characterization of what preceded it is redolent of a hackneyed exoticism that is content to circulate the Orientalist imagery of the Casbah. Part of his attraction to Islam is, no doubt, his sense of being excluded. While Islam functions as a kind of spiritual guarantor, Stenham cannot be drawn in. As he wanders through the haunted spaces just outside the walls of the Medina, he is exhilarated by the boundaries that separate, rather than join, inside and outside:

> Yet their beauty existed for him only to the degree that he was conscious of their outsideness, or that he could conjure up the sensation of compactness which the idea of the Medina gave him. It was the knowledge that the swarming city lay below, shut in by its high ramparts, which made wandering over the hills and along the edges of the cliffs so delectable. They are there, of it, he would think, and I am here, of nothing, free. (166)

And we have seen this kind of expatriate weightlessness before, in Lawrence's *Aaron's Rod*. "Italy's best gift to the Englishman" is precisely this combination of proximity and distance that creates in the expatriate the illusion of freedom, of being his own creation.

Despite his avowed xenophilia, however, the novel is as intent upon pointing up his dogmatism as it is critical of the advocates of blind progress or colonialism. For example, the Muslim family with whom he has become intimate was interesting precisely to the degree they conformed to his "Imaginary" view:

> If Si Jaffar and his sons had sold their services to the French, that still did not invalidate their purity in his eyes, so long as they continued to live the way they lived: sitting on the floor, eating with their fingers, cooking and sleeping first in one room, then in another, or in the vast patio with its fountains, or on the roof, leading the existence of nomads inside the beautiful shell which was the house. If he had felt that they were capable of discarding their utter preoccupation with the present, in order to consider the time not yet arrived, he would straightway have lost interest in them and condemned them as corrupt. To please him the Moslems had to tread a narrow path; no deviation was tolerated. (216–17)

Moreover, the passage is not without its own Orientalist overtones: the suggestion that these urban dwellers nevertheless live as nomads within their own home, the characterization of that home as a "beautiful shell," which tends to disparage the quality of its "homeness." It is worth noting here that in his autobiography, Bowles describes the home of a Fassi gentleman, M. Abdessalem Ktiri, where Bowles was a frequent guest, in much the same way. We must credit Bowles, however, for exposing the self-interest at the heart of Stenham's cultural curiosity:

> It would not help the Moslems or the Hindus or anyone else to go ahead, nor, even if it were possible, would it do them any good to stay as they were. It did not really matter whether they worshiped Allah or

carburetors—they were lost in any case. In the end, it was *his own preferences* which concerned him. *He would have liked to prolong the status quo because the decor that went with it suited his personal taste.* (286, my emphasis)

I am reminded here of a similar sentiment expressed by Lawrence Durrell in *Bitter Lemons* when confronted with the Greek Cypriots' national liberation movement.

Even though—or perhaps because—Amar seems to embody Stenham's Muslim ideal, their mismeeting is almost inevitable, and Amar intuits this:

The Nazarene had understood nothing at all; Amar's spirits sank as he perceived the gap that lay between them. If a Nazarene with so much good will and such a knowledge of Arabic was unable to grasp even the basic facts of such a simple state of affairs, then was there any hope that any Nazarene would ever aid any Moslem? And yet a part of his mind kept repeating to him that the man could be counted on, that he could be a true friend and protector if only he would let himself be shown how. (279)

Within minutes, however, "[t]he point of contact was gone; they seemed to be looking in different directions, trying to say separate things, giving different meaning to words" (279). Amar's misguided reliance upon Stenham, in fact, reflects in some way the larger predicament Bowles is concerned to represent. In rendering the transformation of Amar's consciousness as he awakens to the political realities of an anticolonial struggle that pits Muslim against Muslim, as well as Muslim against the French, Bowles attempts to paint an allegorical picture of modernity's disruptions. Indeed, his use of an illiterate youth to represent traditional Morocco reinforces the Romantic (and antimodern) view of traditional culture as the embodiment of prelapsarian innocence. For Amar, education was tantamount to dogma; once his friends had attended school, many of them "had decided what the world looked like, what life was like, and they would never examine either of them again to find out whether they were right or wrong" (17). The decision to forgo school was his own. When he meets his childhood friends, "it seemed to him that they had grown to be like old men, and he did not enjoy being with them, whereas his new friends, who played and fought every minute as though their lives depended upon the outcome of their games and struggles, lived in a way that was understandable to him" (19). Again the Bataillian spirit of revolt against project!

And Amar shares the revulsion toward interiority that many of Bowles's American characters experience. The pleasure of work, for example, frees him from the worrisome nature of thought, the burdens of selfhood: "it was sheer pleasure for him to be completely occupied—the sort of delight he could not know when there was room in his mind for him to remember that he was himself" (37). In a sense, this "deconstruction" of the idea of utility puts *work* in the service of self-liberation. Moreover, we can abstract from this preoccupation with "busy-ness" the sense that expatriation itself functions as a kind of perpetual self-distraction—or attempted self-distraction. When the complications of political insurgency begin to force their way into his consciousness, Amar is no longer able to experience these simple pleasures (nor, for that matter, is Stenham). Instead,

> [h]e felt that he was merely waiting, making the hours pass forcibly by filling them with useless gestures. It was his first indication of what it is like to be truly aware of the passage of time; such awareness can exist only if something is going on in the mind which is not completely a reflection of what is going on immediately outside. (53)

Amar's internal monologues complicate Stenham's Imaginary view of Moroccans. On the one hand, he is a character full of instinctual wisdom—what we would call "street smarts"—and dignity. As such, he embodies all of Stenham's stereotypical ideas about the superiority of native wisdom to Western thought. On the other hand, his curiosity and lively interiority make him stand apart from the undifferentiated community of Islam perceived by Stenham. These qualities are precisely what make him attractive. While Stenham's encounters with the Jaffar family resemble social ritual—an expanded realization of Port and Kit's visit with the merchant—his relationship with Amar promises something more.

In a key episode, Stenham and Polly, accompanied by Amar and his friend Mohammed, leave town for the hills where the festival of Aïd el Kebir will be celebrated. This is not only a convenient way to get out of town, it also provides the expatriates with the opportunity of going "where the natives are," a voyage out while there is still a stage on which to enact that particular drama. While the visit does not prove as perilous as other of Bowles's fictional journeys into the cultural wilderness, Stenham and Polly do consummate their affair there. The festival itself proves to be particularly unsettling for Polly, what "with the shadows and the flames and the great circles of men, hundreds of them, dancing arm in arm, and the orchestras of drums like giant engines pulsing" (313). She reassures herself with the notion that what she is observing is mere spectacle: "That was what she must remember, she told herself, because she felt that the place represented an undefinable but very real danger":

> What she was looking down upon here tonight, the immense theatre full of human beings still unformed and unconscious, bathed in sweat, stamping and shrieking, falling into the dust and writhing and twitching and panting, all belonged unmistakably to the darkness, and therefore it had to be wholly outside her and she outside it. There could be no temporizing or mediation. It was down there, spread out before her, a segment of the original night, and she was up here observing it, actively conscious of who she was, and very intent on remaining that person, determined to let nothing occur that might cause her, even for an instant, to forget her identity. (314)

If Polly's interior monologue reiterates the sense that Stenham had enjoyed, being "above" the Medina and separate and apart from it, the boundary here is infinitely more porous and threatening. Indeed, when she and Stenham cross into that realm to better observe the goings on, she experiences the fearful sensation of being *herself* the Other, the drums

> an unwelcome reminder of the existence of another world, wholly autonomous, with its own necessities and patterns. The message they were beating out, over and over, was for her; it was saying, not precisely that she did not exist, but rather that it did not matter whether she existed or not. . . . It was a sensation that suddenly paralyzed her with dread. (319)

Beset by a sense of both her alterity and superfluousness, she pulls back. She rejects the intimacy of "communication," having no use for a process whereby

> all the members of this particular circle of leaping figures became possessed, took out their souls and threw them onto the pile in the middle (they were doing it, she knew it) so that there was only one undifferentiable writhing mass in there and no one was sure of getting his own back when it was finished. (319–20)

Polly rejects the path to the extreme limit of the possible, that narrative belonging to an earlier, riskier existential project that Bowles now seems eager to relegate to the status of incident rather than theme. He seems far more taken up with destabilizations of a different order that turn upon the concrete relations between self and Other, namely, Stenham's sudden awareness of the presence of "hidden riches" beneath Amar's presumed fungibility. Do these "hidden riches" represent, paradoxically, the very depth and self-reflectiveness that he, Stenham, has come to Morocco to escape? He begins to rethink his position:

> In the beginning the Moroccans had been for him an objective force, unrelieved and monolithic. All of them put together made a *thing*, an element both less and more than human; but any one of them alone existed only in so far as he was an anonymous part or a recognizable symbol of the indivisible and undifferentiable total. They were something almost as basic as the sun or the wind, subject to no moods or impulses started by the mirror of the intellect. They did not know they were there; they merely were there, at one with existence. Nothing could be the result of one individual's desire since one was the equivalent of another. Whatever they were and whatever came about was what they all desired. But now, perhaps as a result of having seen this boy, he found himself beginning to doubt the correctness of his whole theoretical edifice. (335–36)

Indeed, "[i]f there were one Amar, there could be others. Then the Moroccans were not the known quantity he had thought they were" (336). To accept that position, Stenham would have to complicate his own "imaginary" view of the traditional Moroccan that speaks to his own lack as opposed to the cultural specificity of Moroccan society. He had claimed "to have watched them for years." He knew what they were like. When Polly had insisted that he could not know each one individually, he had retorted, "But the whole point is, they're not individuals in the sense you mean" (251). He would have to give up his insistence on absolute alterity and with it, his stake in the continuance of traditional Islamic ways. For if the Moroccans were "much like anyone else," then "very little of value would be lost in the destruction of their present culture, because its design would be worth less than the sum of the individuals who composed it—the same as in any Western country" (336). This is something he will not even allow himself to consider. Moreover, to recognize the Moroccan as an Other, and not a thing, means being open to the Other's demand, means recognizing—or being confirmed in—his own subjectivity. This would undercut the essential tension that is the informing spirit of Bowles's work and that characterizes the project of expatriation itself in its narrative realization. Stenham has no choice but to leave Fez and Amar behind.

One manifestation of this tension is the novel's attempt to validate and explore that which its protagonist emphatically rejects. Stenham has insisted all along on totalizing the Muslim world, making of it an aesthetic and spiritual whole that is at once knowable and yet beyond reach. It marks the place of an aporia. To the extent one is apart from it, one desires it, wants to know it; to the extent one is inside it and knows it, one ceases to be the desiring subject.

> [T]his satisfaction they felt in life was to him the mystery, the dark, precious and unforgivable stain which blotted out comprehension of them, and touched everything they touched, making their simplest action as fascinating as a serpent's eye. *He knew that the attempt to fathom the mystery was an endless task, because the further one advanced into their world, the more conscious one became that it was necessary to change oneself fundamentally in order to know them.* . . . It was a lifetime's work, and one of which he was aware he would *some day suddenly tire.* (217–18, my emphasis)

You can't be here and there. And yet this is precisely what the novel endeavors to do. In the same way, it attempts to render aesthetic space moral by interrogating Stenham's aesthetic relation to Fez in ways that bring to light its moral implications. The aesthetic nature of the cultural object, wherein the "simplest action" becomes "as fascinating as a serpent's eye," renders it vulnerable to the plague of all aesthetic spacings: boredom. It will be only a matter of time before Stenham makes his break with Fez. Bowles, on the other hand, stays on, is known precisely by the fact of his staying on. It is tempting here to juxtapose the biographical. Before doing so, however, we should take another detour through the "feminine" version of the expatriate's story, and one that takes place in Morocco.

Hideous Kinky, written by Esther Freud (the daughter of painter Lucien Freud, and great-granddaughter of Sigmund) and published in 1992, chronicles the nomadic wanderings through Morocco of a counter-cultural mother, referred to as "Mum," and her two young daughters in the mid-Sixties. It is told from the perspective of the younger daughter and is based upon Freud's own memories of her two-year sojourn in Morocco as a child. Like other expatriate novels written by women, it features a kind of seamless—or nearly so—cross-cultural exchange. Freud's Morocco, as compared with that of Paul Bowles, is a site of benign exoticism. Morocco's landscapes do not threaten; the native quarter, in which the characters live, is not disorienting, nor are its inhabitants hostile. The prostitutes who are their neighbors offer to henna the girls' hair and then help themselves to Mum's clothing that she has left out on the line to dry. Mum dresses herself and her children in kaftans from Tangier's bazaar and her children form bonds with beggar girls and local eccentrics. What is more surprising, the fact of Mum's gender is hardly an issue in terms her negotiation of the social space of a highly segregated Islamic society. She takes a Moroccan lover, Bilal, who comes and goes and to whom the narrator becomes quite attached. He brings Mum home to his village and she integrates herself and her children into his extended family (until, that is, Bilal's sister is mercilessly beaten by her father and brothers for going out without a veil during a religious festival). More startling than the cultural anomalies is, perhaps, Mum's rather offhand style of mothering. This takes its toll on the eldest daughter, Bea, though she fully commits herself to the experience of Morocco.

Mum's competence is enviable; she knows how to cook on a makeshift stove with what's available; she can barter her skills as a seamstress for rent; she's a fearless hitchhiker, ripe for adventure and not intimidated by hardship or uncertainty. Hers is a Morocco Bowles would hardly recognize. In Freud's narrative, Morocco is just another locale in which to act out the Sixties moment: meditation, Sufism, "free" love. Wherever Mum goes, she meets figures who, like herself, are adrift in a countercultural imaginary of majoun, vagrancy, and various degrees of disorientation and fecklessness. Freud's expatriate protagonist dwells in a different narrative universe than any we have seen. The serious ethical questions are sidestepped by filtering experience through the consciousness of a five-year-old girl. We don't know what Mum really thinks of Bilal. When the novel ends, Mum and the kids are aboard a train bound for Europe. Bilal has joined them; only at the very last minute is the narrator aware that he will not be returning home with them. He walks backward out of the train car and disappears among the passengers, and I couldn't help being reminded of other natives abandoned on the road once they had served their purpose. *Hideous Kinky* is a lighthearted if touching paean to a childhood made rich and impossibly vivid by the experience of expatriation. Its ethics of expatriation, such as they are, abound in wonder and enchantment. Situatedness in displacement, rather than alienation, forms the basis for its apprehension of difference. Competence rather than self-undoing is the mode of expatriate self-imagining.

Paul Bowles the Expatriate

Bowles's life in Tangier has been the subject of numerous biographies in addition to his own autobiography, *Without Stopping*. With reference to the ethics of expatriation, however, certain facets of his life loom larger than others. I will briefly explore the nature of his own personal relationships with Moroccans, his ethical "self-stylization" within the context of Tangier's notoriously dissolute expatriate scene, and his mentoring of a number of young Moroccan "storytellers," in order to further complicate the already complex ethics of expatriation that his novels articulate. Bowles's relationship with the prototype of Amar is a good place to begin.

When Bowles was in Fez in 1947, he made the acquaintance of a Moroccan youth, Ahmed Yacoubi. The following year, on a return visit with Jane, he was visited by Yacoubi, who began drawing pictures on the hotel stationary. Jane was so impressed with his talent that she prevailed upon Bowles to purchase drawing materials for the boy, then in his late teens. Ahmed continued drawing, and the friendship continued over the next few years. Gradually, the relationship became an intimate one and remained so for a significant period of time. According to Millicent Dillon, Yacoubi was the model for Amar. She describes Bowles and Yacoubi's relationship as "patron to protégé, generous parental figure to indulged younger man."[56] Bowles's "unauthorized" biographer, Christopher Sawyer-Lauçanno, writes that from this summer in Fez [1950] until Yacoubi eventually left Morocco in the mid-1970s, Bowles and Yacoubi would remain friends, mutually teaching and nurturing each other. From Yacoubi, Bowles would learn about the intimate workings of a certain segment of Moroccan society; from Bowles, Yacoubi would develop the ability to know the West and be greatly aided in ultimately making a life there as an artist.[57] And yet Bowles himself makes it clear that such relationships are not at all rooted in the kind of companionate intimacy that attends love relationships in the West. When asked by Dillon to say something about the relationship between a European and a Moroccan in Morocco, he responds: "What was defined was that the foreigner must supply the Moroccan with money. That's all, the amount isn't important, really. As much as the Moroccan can get." And that is the case even if the relationship becomes more intimate. Bowles's exchange with Dillon goes further:

> But you could still feel affection for the other person—deep affection for the other person;

You could, M-m-hm.

But it wouldn't be anything like what is set up in West mores with romantic love—

It wouldn't be like that. No.

So if one enters into that kind of a relationship, idealization isn't a part of it.

Oh, I wouldn't think so. No.

. . .

So one looks at the other person and says, 'This person wants money; that's why they're staying with me.' Is it something like that?

Well, yes.

In other words, you don't say, 'Oh, but still they have to or they ought to love me.'

If you expect them to, you're crazy. A lot of the Europeans do, and then they weep and wail and wring their hands.[58]

Nevertheless, it must be acknowledged that sexual community formed a significant aspect of Bowles's expatriate experience in Tangier. Although he was famously closemouthed on the subject of his sexual experiences, he writes in 1933 to Aaron Copland:

You exaggerate when you claim sex is here [in the United States], for instance. Where in this country can I have 35 or 40 different people a week, and never risk seeing any of them again? Yet in Algeria, it actually was the mean rate. Or do you think that really is not what I want? I think it's what I want, so it must be![59]

Dillon points out that up until 1989, when Bowles made a clear statement concerning his sexual orientation to a French biographer, Robert Briatte, he had refused to say anything publicly regarding the matter, which he quite naturally deemed private. From the perspective of the twenty-first century, it is sometimes hard to imagine the indignities—the terrors—facing an openly gay man, or a man accused of being such: "the disapproval of society, the . . . presence of the police, the possibility of blackmail, all sorts of unpleasant things. So it was best to keep, you know, completely away."[60] In Morocco, of course, things were different.

As recent books on the expatriate community of post–World War II Tangier have documented in great detail, the city was a magnet for adventurers, aesthetes, and thrill seekers of every caste. Michelle Green writes:

In 1947, Tangier was not a place that suggested permanence; its quiet colonial air had been shattered, and a flamboyant boomtown spirit had set in. . . . With much of the Western world shackled by exchange restrictions, high taxes, trade controls and other economic curbs, the 225-square-mile International zone was an island of financial opportunity. . . . Smugglers, counterfeiters, sleight-of-hand bankers, real-estate speculators and even honest entrepreneurs found Tangier to be a postwar promised land rivaled only by Beirut. . . . While it seemed at times that every European in Tangier was caught up in its capitalist fervor, some felt that lucre was the least the city had to offer. A pockmarked past was no liability, and an impressive number of misfits, eccentrics, libertines, black sheep and second sons were able to burrow their way into society. Since few questions were asked of new arrivals, any fugitive could shed his sullied persona and take on the coloration of a solid citizen; spies, war criminals, Nazis, remittance men, disbarred lawyers, unlicenced doctors and defrocked priests had all been reborn in Tangier.[61]

William Burroughs, suggests Iain Finlayson, fixed upon Tangier as a result in part of having read Bowles. He was attracted by his sense of the city as "the last resort of the disinherited, the disillusioned, the degenerate and the depraved. Tangier was the end of the line, the journey towards it a lifetime's nightmare."[62] Marked by excess, from the self-debauchery of Burrough's embrace of drug addiction and rampant sexuality (the desire, for example, "to start at one end of Interzone and screw my way through to the other") to the lavish obscenity of the famed social extravaganzas staged by Betty Hutton and Malcolm Forbes, the expatriate scene appeared to encourage and reward every kind of indulgence.[63] Given these conditions, the transactional nature of personal relations between Moroccans and Europeans makes a great deal of sense, and yet, against this background of license and relative hedonism, Bowles was something of an ascetic. Always circumspect about his personal affairs, his sexual proclivities were never the stuff of narrative, at least overtly. His kif smoking, though a daily routine, never led to dissolution of any discernible nature. He was always courtly, courteous, and impeccably dressed. Like Stenham, perhaps, in *The Spider's House*, "he could not feel at ease with gourmets and hedonists; they were a hostile species" (163).

Foucault, in *The Use of Pleasure*, speaks of a kind of behavioral austerity that linked abstention from physical pleasure "to a form of wisdom that brought [its practictioners] into direct contact with some superior element in human nature and gave them access to the very essence of truth."[64] But such austerity was not linked to social or juridical prohibitions; rather it consisted in certain practices of the self, of certain *"ethical work (travail éthique)* that one performs on oneself, not only in order to bring one's conduct into compliance with a given rule, but to attempt to transform oneself into the ethical subject of one's behavior" (27). Indeed, Foucault's discussion of pagan ethics offers a kind of suggestive medium in which to interrogate Bowles's self-stylization as a romantic but not immoderate subject of rebellion. Foucault's self-moderating ethical subject, whose stylization owes more to aesthetics than to self-knowledge, is a creature of form rather than substance, which is to say that his ethical substance is to be performed rather than found. The resulting "aesthetics of existence" were grounded in "certain formal principles in the use of pleasures, in the way one distributed them, in the limits one observed, in the hierarchy one respected" (89). Paul Bowles, I would suggest, offers us a stylistics rather than a consciousness. For if we look to the novels, we see consciousness everywhere denigrated, repudiated, disemboweled. If we look to autobiography, we find itineraries, meetings with famous people, exotic locales. Bowles's autobiography, *Without Stopping*, was referred to by Burroughs as *Without Telling*, so little did it reveal of Bowles's personal life.

Part of Bowles's "ethical performance" was the cultivation of mentoring relationships among young illiterate Moroccans who were adept at storytelling. These activities began in the early Sixties and intensified during the years of his wife's illness. Bowles recorded their tales in the original Maghrebi, translated them, and procured their publication. The translated works were widely disseminated in the West. While some, if not all, of these liaisons were undoubtedly sexual, they represented as well, both formally and substantively, creative collaborations. Bowles's patronage of the artist Ahmad Yacoubi was an exception, although some of his translated stories were published as well. In 1962, Bowles began to record the stories of Dris Ben Hamid Charhadi a/k/a Larbi Layachi, a watchman in a café at Merkala Beach in Tangier who had also served jail time for selling kif. His stories were published and sold well in several languages. Layachi eventually earned enough money through royalties to marry. Bowles employed him as a "houseboy" until the publication by Gallimard of his autobiographical novel, *A Life Full of Holes*, which detailed a life of poverty, petty crime, prison, and involvement with the gay expatriate community. As Layachi was fearful of official Moroccan reaction to his book, Bowles arranged for him to emigrate to the States. In 1964 he left with William Burroughs and never returned to Morocco.

Bowles's other major protégé was Mohammed Mrabet, a Riffian fisherman and bartender who was inspired by Layachi's example to become a paid author. In the 1960s, Mrabet had replaced Yacoubi as most favored companion after the latter had married, fathered a child, and gradually drifted away from his mentor. (Yacoubi later emigrated to the United States and became associated with the La Mama Theater; he died in New York City in the 1980s.) The collaboration of Bowles and Mrabet was highly productive and continued for more than twenty years. Of Mrabet, Bowles has said that "he's impregnated with the oral tradition of his region. In a story of his it's hard to find the borderline between unconscious memory and sheer invention."[65] In his autobiography, *Look and Move on,* as well as in other works such as *The Lemon* and *Love with a Few Hairs* (which was even adapted as a television play in Britain), Mrabet explores the underside of Tangieri life from the perspective of the poor and disenfranchised who both prey upon and are preyed upon by wealthy and often naive expatriates.

The autobiographical or quasi-autobiographical novels that Bowles has translated represent collaborations that seek to elicit the voice of the native speaking itself. Self-articulation, however, is perhaps not quite an accurate representation of the process by which these stories came into being as literature, for unlike a typical literary translation, there was no original text:

> What Bowles does, in effect, is to "read" an oral "text," interpret it, then reconstruct it in English, bringing into being a written work that is simultaneously a version of an original and an original work in itself. In each case there is a story, authored by the teller, that was recorded on tape, and a piece of literature, written by Bowles, that is the same and yet not the same as the story.[66]

What is produced, therefore, is a "a virtual spider web of intertextuality." These hybrid literary products, then, are only partly works of self-articulation. Absent an original "text" in Maghrebi, their status as "native" literature is compromised. In consequence, Mrabet was commonly held to be a "neo-colonialist collaborator with Bowles" and his work fit only for Western readers.[67] Moreover, as a result of their peculiarly hybrid status, these works are accessible to Moroccan readers only to the extent they are fluent in English or, in some cases, French. To the extent they find an audience, their scandalous—by Islamic standards—subject matter has not enhanced their appeal. On the other hand, absent the collaboration with Bowles, the voices of these storytellers would not be heard at all beyond the immediate circle of their listeners. And, however compromised, they give voice to a class perspective—that of the subaltern—that is rarely heard. But what impact did this collaboration have on the storytellers themselves, aside from financial enrichment? Layachi and Yacoubi ultimately left Morocco. Layachi felt himself obliged to leave as a direct result of his collaboration with Bowles; Yacoubi got in trouble with the Moroccan authorities in 1958 for an alleged sexual indiscretion with the teenage son of some German tourists, although he did not leave Morocco until years later. Mrabet, on the other hand, has prospered, as has Mohammed Choukri, the only one of Bowles's protégés who wrote in classical Arabic.

Bowles's translations from Maghrebi, like his earlier project subsidized by the Rockefeller Foundation which entailed the recording and compilation of Moroccan folk and art music, reflect his concern to record the oral cultural productions of a heterogeneous, largely illiterate, premodern society on the verge of extinction. In that endeavor, Bowles logged more than twenty-five thousand miles in four separate trips through some of the most remote regions of Morocco (and unlike the Professor of "A Distant Episode," succeeded in chronicling many of his adventures in his travel book, *Their Heads Are Green and Their Hands Are Blue*). Ironically, the greatest obstacle to the success of his recording project was the Moroccan government itself, which was not anxious to showcase to the world the "backward" culture of its more provincial citizenry. Although, to a certain extent, much of the music was "performed" rather than arising spontaneously or in the course of ritual, there is the sense that what is being heard is, unlike the project of language translation, the unmediated "production" of the native. Of course, as with any collection or exhibition, such cultural productions risk becoming part objects, mere curiosities, trophies of alterity. And yet is there not some sense that we, who bear so much responsibility for destroying the indigenous cultures of the world, should also do what we can to preserve some record of their existence?

And Bowles himself has not remained untouched by these projects. Richard Patteson has suggested that the collaborative translation process has been singular in its impact upon both his style and insight into Moroccan character. Citing Christopher Miller and Michel de Certeau, Patteson argues that while it may be impossible to speak from the subject position of the native, some approximation is to be hoped for. In other words, a "discourse about the other" might become "a means of constructing a discourse authorized by the other."[68] Bowles, according to Patteson, "in his role as midwife to stories originating in Moroccan minds . . . has come as close as possible to the ontologically impossible point of being both American and Moroccan, both 'here' and 'there,' and his translations mark the ultimate stage in his imaginative assimilation and interpretation of Moroccan culture."[69] We perhaps become perilously close here to the position of John Stenham. Who exactly is it that is doing the authorizing? Is there "*a* Moroccan point of view"? We can appreciate Bowles's accomplishment, I think, and still worry over these questions.

Unhappily for Bowles and the cause of cross-cultural translation, these mentorships have not ended well. In "Symposium on Translation," which appeared in the summer 1997 issue of *The Threepenny Review,* Bowles relates how "the hazards met with in the act of translation are dwarfed by those inherent in publication and consequent remuneration." All three of the Moroccans whose works he has translated "showed continuous lack of trust in my motives each time the question of money arose." Despite the low sales—and consequent lack of royalties—these men continued to make demands upon Bowles for payment. He claims to have been hounded by attorneys and publicly denounced as "a spy for the CIA, a racist, a neo-colonialist, a dangerous criminal who ought not to be allowed to continue living in Morocco, and a robber whose considerable fortune had been amassed by depriving Moroccan writers of their royalties." I leave the last word to Bowles:

> I'm careful not to add that I should have known beforehand that something like this would happen, and that I shall see to it that there will be no repetition of such nonsense because I shall not collaborate again with a Moroccan. Now I am a true racist.

5

Modern Expatriates and Postmodern Expatriate Narratives

Life is different here. We must be equal to the largeness of things.
Don DeLillo, *The Names*

THE ETHICS OF EXPATRIATION that flow out of modernist concerns with discipline and liberation, artifice and interiority, mechanism and organicism, community and alienation, rely to a great extent on a belief in the "unencumbered self," the antecedently situated subject of reason whose freedom to fashion, revise, and pursue his own particular perception of the good is primary. This is the case whether we view the expatriate's story in conventional antimodernist terms or reframe it in terms of self-artistry—be it in the nature of ascesis or radical existential experimentation. Like the metropolitan expatriate, the classic subject of reason is a creature of privilege; "unmarked" by gender, class, race or other (dis)qualifying attributes, he is mobile, well schooled, and affluent enough to indulge his anxieties—anxieties produced, ironically, in the yawning gap across which he looks back upon his "prerational" forebears. Indeed, the "modernist" expatriate who is the subject of this study is very much dead, white, and male. And if to reason he is unambiguously antithetical, it could be said that he nevertheless lives in the shadow of the Enlightenment man. Although D. H. Lawrence, Paul Bowles (only recently deceased), and Lawrence Durrell might have differed in origin, nationality, class, sexual orientation, and political bias, they all came of age in a culture that did not need to confront seriously the claims of the colonized, the non-Western world, internal minorities, feminists, gays, and the like. The *post*modern revision of expatriate narrative is about accountability; it deals self-consciously with the relative positionality of East and West, center and periphery. That is to say, whatever supposed autonomy or intent the self or "subject" embodies, whatever desires or projects it pursues, it remains hostage to the larger national or global networks of power that we now see as enabling, rather than inimical to, those designs. What the postmodern expatriate narrative seems to reveal, in other words, is a fully situated self.

Each of our modernist expatriates, in his own way, experienced expatriation as a private act of renunciation and reward. The periphery was not, in any meaningful sense, the compromised space of colonial domination or capital expansion. The political was left behind in the home country; the liberated subject, now free of the cultural baggage of home, sought in the periphery an arena in which to confront private perils, pursue private amours, recover levels of the self repressed at home. The project was often obsessively self-centered, sometimes, paradoxically, to the point of self-obliteration. At the same time, the idea of place was a powerful trope in the modernist expatriate narrative. For Lawrence, Italy represented at once the exact center of the universe and a raw, pagan landscape full of elemental, prerational forces. An antidote to the industrial geographies of his birthplace, the "priced and ticketed" life in rural England, and, perhaps most importantly, the mechanistic worldviews to which his society seemed dedicated, Italy promised difference: warmth, color, passion, and proximity to, if not community with, preindustrial peasant society. The Italy of Lawrence's expatriate narratives, however, is often rude and disappointing. What is worse, it is often undergoing the very transformations that had rendered "home" so unbearable. Perhaps, then, the quality of expatriate existence depends not upon place, but upon a resistance to place or exposure to many different places. The Lawrentian expatriate tends to be frustrated, conflicted, and not terribly free. He or she is, moreover, wholly ambivalent toward the Italian. Negotiating the social space of the periphery is an unanticipated complication of expatriate life.

The relationship between the Bowlesian expatriate and his Moroccan landscape is far more intimate. The convoluted native quarters and intimidating desert frontiers produce dread and the ideal conditions for radical existential experimentation. If "getting lost" is the desired form of liberation from the demands of work, domesticity, even consciousness, the self-dismantling projects of the Bowlesian expatriate succeed in ways the Lawrentian expatriate can grasp only in isolated moments. On the other hand, for Bowles, the Other's demand for recognition is also more compelling, and his characters' obsessive meetings and mismeetings with their Moroccan counterparts are suggestive not only of desire, but also of the essential parity between subjects fleeing from and advancing toward modernity. Finally, the space of experimentation cannot be separated from the social space of the Other; they intermingle and complicate one another. On his way to the abyss, Bowles "discovers" Morocco, and he remains there.

For Durrell, the idea of place is at once so much more and so much less than it is for either Lawrence or Bowles. Since he's primarily concerned with the imaginative reality of place, rather than what's "out there" in the quotidian world, he takes account of his surroundings in ways that aestheticize, rather than make sense of, perceived alterity. On the other hand, since he often found employment with the British Foreign Office, he was often forced to attend —rather more than he'd like, one senses—to the materiality of the periphery. Not surprisingly, these two "versions" of place sat rather uncomfortably with one another. Durrell's expatriate desires do not make the kind of demands on place that Lawrence's and Bowles's do, nor does place represent the same kind of challenge. Having spent his early childhood in India, Durrell probably found England more radically strange than either Greece or Alexandria. While he shared Lawrence's and Bowles's abhorrence for bourgeois morality and culture, he predicated his rebellion upon a modernist reverence for art and the role of the artist, rather than a disavowal of reason per se. As an aesthete, moreover, he was dedicated to sensual pleasures of all kinds and to the production of an art that was totalizing in its capacity to grasp the truth of life. He needed to find places that were cheap and lovely, although until the success of *The Alexandria Quartet,* he rarely succeeded in sustaining long periods of unemployment. For Durrell, all external phenomena, natives included, were objectified and subjected to aesthetic mastery. The expatriate, then, is a kind of an initiate. The artist, as conquering hero, will return to the West.

With the postmodern turn, however, the periphery "bites back." This is not to say that in much of Bowles's fiction, as well as in *The Alexandria Quartet,* the postcolonial does not resonate powerfully. Indeed, there is no categorical break between the expatriate fictions that I have termed modernist and postmodernist. They reflect, rather, different "structures of feeling." Politics, for example, repudiated by the modernist expatriate, returns to reclaim its truant subject in the postmodern expatriate narrative. As the myth of the autonomous subject gives way to an acknowledgment of the situated self, the expatriate arrives on the scene fully formed by and imbricated in the discourses and sociocultural machinery of home. Dragging about the baggage of national identity, he learns that he can no longer give himself over to the fantasy—or free fall—of liminal experience without being held accountable. And while the postmodern may denote the space of free play, depthlessness, and postnational hybridity in the cosmopolitan West, in the periphery the politics of identity and national autonomy interrupt this narrative, exposing the substructure of political and economic interests that animates "the cultural logic of late capitalism" and the subject of expatriation. In the process, the powerful trope of place is subverted by the idea of positionality. I want to reiterate that no comprehensive treatment of postmodernism itself is offered or intended here. My intent is to track the figure of the expatriate and the contours of expatriate narrative as the preoccupations of modernism give way to other concerns.

In both DeLillo's *The Names* and Ondaatje's *The English Patient*, there is a bifurcation along generational lines between the modernist expatriate narrative and the postmodern one. As the political invades and appropriates the personal, the line is drawn between younger protagonists who return "home" and their older counterparts, spiritual heirs to the modernist expatriate figures whose narratives, in a sense, perish with them in the periphery. It is perhaps no coincidence that the "old men" in these two narratives, Owen Brademas and Count Almásy, are both engaged in the now critically suspect fields of archaeology and cartography. Besides their obvious institutional links, both archaeology and cartography are professional disciplines that "read" the world. And they create powerful "texts" about the shape of the world and its history. It is interesting that while both these professional interpreters of Other places and times renounce their occupational projects, they are denied full absolution for complicity in the crimes of imperial power/knowledge. By giving us protagonists who on the one hand aspire to the "modernist" project of expatriate ascesis, and on the other come powerfully invested in the institutional knowledge-gathering apparatuses of "home," their "situatedness" is made manifest in ways that, of course, the modernist text was far less self-conscious about.

In *The Names*, the expatriate ethos emerges through the juxtaposition not only of the modernist and postmodernist expatriate narrative but through the narratives of its female characters as well. James Axton, the professional risk analyst, is an American expatriate who, to a great degree, represents a departure from his fictional forebears. While his desire to escape feeling responsible may be continuous with theirs, he resists the impulse experienced by those earlier figures to give himself over to the seductions of place, in whatever guise they may appear. Owen Brademas, the archeologist, on the other hand, represents an ascetic strain of expatriate experience whose search for ecstasy, "a displacing, a coming out of stasis. . . . A freedom, an escape from the condition of ideal balance," is tied to the crucible of a chaotic and spiritually dense India (307). A middle path is suggested by the peripheral narrative of Kathryn, Axton's wife, which represents something akin to an ethics of care, a counter-ethics within the context of the novel. To a great extent, it is the masculinist preoccupation with patterns, structures, and systems and concomitant fear of chaos, disorder, and terror that elide the more feminist ethics of care and attention to particularity that strives to articulate itself.

John McClure has pointed out the Orientalist structure of the novel's imaginative geographies: "It is 'like' the old bipolar world of imperial romance: divided West to East into realms of relative security and relative danger, secular reason and religious madness."[1] In this, of course, we see the dialectic between reason and unreason that animates so many expatriate narratives we have examined, and it is fitting that Brademas, the "modernist" expatriate, is drawn to the East. For him, the periphery seems to involve an escape from reason and the sense of words themselves, but unlike, say, a typical Bowlesian expatriate who seeks a way out of discourse in the great "void," he focuses instead upon systems of signification or patterns in the chaos, projects that nevertheless tend to produce an empty frame. But *The Names* also seems to interrogate the Orientalist binary, for its characters' preoccupations with order culminate in the discovery that the cult killings that to a certain degree have obsessed them revolve around order itself: "killing by machine intellect," while the terror of men running in the streets is transmuted into joyful chaos at the Acropolis.

The denouement of the cult's narrative also coincides with another important revelation: Axton's unwitting involvement with the CIA. A postmodern expatriate narrative, therefore, exposes "the dialectic of enlightenment" and the complicity of the "rebel's" private project with the institutional practices of the homeland. It holds its expatriates accountable. In so doing, the imaginative geography of the novel seems to shift its focus from place to positionality. At the same time, the postmodern expatriate narrative, like the modernist version, takes account of the tension between, as McClure states, "secular reason" and its Other. At the center of secular reason's project is the desire to enfold all phenomena into organizing structures. And in *The Names,* various binaries are constructed that are then reversed or deconstructed—systems as against chaos, relations among objects as against objects themselves, abstractions as against particularities, alphabets as against speech acts, inscriptions as against living conversations, reified language as against dialogism—thus challenging the totalizing strategies of the novel's protagonists. On the one hand, the periphery offers its characters an opportunity to escape the responsibilities imposed by reason; on the other, they seek to order the periphery in ways that tend to suggest the abuses with which reason has come to be associated.

Owen Brademas seems to embody this tension. A man "in another world," he likens Europe to "a hard-cover book" and America to "the paperback version."[2] India, on the contrary, "is not a book at all" (*Names,* 23). He is a figure highly suggestive of the modernist expatriate, seeking refuge from the "textualized" West in the Indian subcontinent, a place that seems threatening precisely because of its "atextuality." In his flight from discursive sense, he seems to be swimming against the same currents as his fictional forebears. At the same time, however, he is drawn to the "safety" of Greece, which evokes for him the qualities associated with its antique past: clarity, symmetry, and harmony. Greece is safe, at least in part, because it's *still Europe:* "'No matter now remote you are, how far into the mountains or islands, how deepended you are, *how much you want to disappear,* there is still the element of shared culture, the feeling that we know these people, come from these people" (25–26, my emphasis). Brademas's profession as an archaeologist creates an occupational if not institutional link with now discredited imperialist practices. Indeed, just as Axton's friend Charles Maitland links international business culture to empire—"Opportunity, adventure, sunsets, dusty death" (7)—so Brademas links archaeology to conquest. He tells the story of Rawlinson, an Englishman intent upon decoding the inscriptions on the Behistun rock, who employed a Kurdish boy to copy the figures that were too perilously placed for him to reach by himself. Rawlinson, Brademas points out, and his successor, Norris, were both employees of the East India Company. "Is this," he asks, "the scientific face of imperialism? The humane face?" (80). And I am compelled to think here of Mary Louise Pratt's imperial man of science, in whom is reflected the "utopian image of a European bourgeois subject simultaneously innocent and imperial, asserting a harmless hegemonic vision that installs no apparatus of domination."[3]

But Brademas has come to lose interest in not only the more instrumental-rational aspects of the profession, but also the hermeneutic-dialogic ones:

> At first, years ago, I think it was mainly a question of history and philology. The stones spoke. It was a form of *conversation* with ancient people. It was also riddle-solving to a certain degree. To decipher, to uncover secrets, to trace the geography of language in a sense. In my current infatuation I think I've abandoned scholarship and much of the interest I once had in earlier cultures. (*Names*, 35, my emphasis)

Thinking to opt out of the power/knowledge game, perhaps, he shifts his focus from what the engravings signify to some "mysterious importance in the letters as such, the blocks of characters" (35). Brademas invests the silent stones with sacred meaning. At once a mere ornamental surface and a medium for sacred knowledge that resists signification, the stones become elements in the kind of antirationalist drama one more readily expects to see enacted in the modernist expatriate narrative.

Brademas travels to India to "read" the stones, and with his trek through India, the East asserts itself as a powerful repository of irrational energies. He becomes a "wanderer," afraid to drive, afraid of "[t]he nightmarish force of people in groups, the power of religion—he connected the two. Masses of people suggested worship and delirium, obliteration of control, children trampled" (276). Just as disorienting, perhaps, is the breakdown of Western notions of temporality: "The word for yesterday was the same as the word for tomorrow. Professor Coomeraswamy said that if he asked someone for details of his life, the man might automatically include details from the lives of dead relatives" (279). The whole bewildering landscape and its occupants present a panorama of color and sight redolent of the Orientalist sensorium in which Kipling's Kim makes his home. Even Hindu inscription, "accompanied, as almost everything seemed to be, almost everywhere, by carved images of elephants, horses, dancers, warriors, lovers," is characterized by an excess of signification and reproduces the heterogeneity and polyphony of India (282). The pilgrimage to India, whose explicit purpose is linked to the cult, merges finally with its implicit purpose: the fearful but tempting project of self-disman-tling, "to lose oneself in the mortal crowd, surrendering, giving oneself over to mass awe, to disappearance in others" (285). For Brademas, the desert, epitomized by Mecca, is synonymous with this type of merging, which is both feared and desired with "fear-some driving rapture " (297). Yet Brademas rejects the self-dis-mantling project suggested here and instead hopes for redemption through the recreation of a "Greek" space in "the lost streets" of Lahore where he languishes.

If Brademas frames his quarrel with the West in terms of textu-ality, James Axton's job is to shape raw social and political data concerning "hostile" countries into orderly, consumable form, and he is so seamlessly embedded in the system he serves that he does not even realize his own complicity. Soon, however, his talent for organization evolves into a fascination with a series of apparently random murders. Within the terms of the narrative web that ties both Axton and Brademas to the cult, a tension is developed between the singular and the systemic that goes to the heart, really, of expatriate experience: the ability to "see" particularity. It's inter-esting to note the extent to which the novel's imperial politics mime systems: as Andreas, one of the few Greek characters, tells Axton one night over dinner: "[Y]ou don't see us. . . . The occupiers fail to see the people they control" (237). Indeed, Axton dwells in a Greece that no "modernist" expatriate would have recognized. Not only that, but as McClure writes: "Axton operates in what by now we think of as a postmodern mode, switching countries as quickly as his less privileged contemporaries switch TV chan-nels."[4] Eschewing "the spirit of place" for a postmodern depth-lessness, he is the "company" man, an expatriate only in the sense that he has come abroad to work, to participate in the extended corporation of American capitalism.

Axton had accepted a job in Greece to be nearer his family after the breakup of his marriage. His lack of commitment is spelled out in the "27 Depravities," the list of Kathryn's grievances against him. This is borne out in his attitude toward living abroad:

> I began to think of myself as a perennial tourist. There was something agreeable about this. To be a tourist is to escape accountability. Errors and failings don't cling to you the way they do back home. You're able to drift across continents and languages, suspending the operation of sound thought. Tourism is the march of stupidity. (*Names*, 43)

Indeed, accountability is *precisely* what is at stake here, as Axton will learn by the novel's end. And although the idea of "suspending the operation of sound thought" seems like a revival of the earlier expatriate project, its collapse into tourist "stupidity" puts a new spin on the idea of the irrational. Indeed, Axton's embrace of the tourist's ignominious status marks the distance he has come from the prewar and interwar expatriate traveler studied by critics as diverse as Paul Fussell and Caren Kaplan. Axton assumes a similarly offhand stance toward his adopted homeland, a homeland purely in the technical sense: "Athens was my legal home but I wasn't ready to give up tourism, even here" (44). When asked by a colleague's wife how long he would be staying on, he replies: "Until I begin to feel responsible. New places are a kind of artificial life" (130). For the modernist expatriates, the idea of place tended to be aligned with a more "genuine" kind of life, as opposed to the more "artificial" life back home; however, Axton's stance both resists and parodies that notion. Indeed, by not speaking Greek, Axton resists the idea of "place" and of feeling responsible, and his linguistic shortcomings, as I suggested, are explicitly noted. It's not only that he doesn't know about what's going on in Greece; he's "happy not knowing" (44).

Axton's Greece both references and distances itself from its former literary incarnations. While *The Names* looks back implicitly to the expatriate narratives that precede it, it insists that those narratives have been rendered obsolete by the global marketplace: "Americans used to come to places like this to write and paint and study, to find deeper textures. Now we do business. . . . We were a subculture, business people in transit growing old in planes and airports" (6). In the "postmodern" mode of expatriate existence experienced by Axton's community of international businessmen, the spirit of place that so animated the fictions of writers such as Lawrence, Durrell, and Bowles, grounding narrator and the narrative in densely palpable imaginative geographies, gives way to a spirit of placelessness: the "dead" time of air travel, the generic spaces of airports and planes, the city as hub. That said, the experience of place is still available to Anton's wife and son, Kathryn and Tap, through their affective and dialogic mode of life and relation to the islanders. Indeed, it is DeLillo's Athens and its expatriate community that most pointedly reflect the novel's postmodern sensibility. As Axton explains: "I was a traveler only in the sense that I covered distances. I traveled between places, never in them" (143). For this community of American businessmen, Athens is the "executive refuge." Anchored both geographically and culturally in the West, it functions as safe harbor and gateway to the perilous Near East, where terror and religious fanaticism threaten the sanctity of global capital investment. Axton's relation to Greece, like Greece's relation to the West, is strategic rather than mythopoetic. Where a generation of modernists sought a vital connection to the precapitalist past in the ruins and "unrationalized" spaces of the periphery, in DeLillo's generic world capital

> the sensibility that enables us to see a ruined beauty in these places can't easily be adapted to Athens, where the surface of things is mostly new, where the ruin is differently managed, the demise indistinguishable from the literal building-up and building-out. What happens when a city can't fade longingly toward its end, can't be abandoned piece by piece to its damaged truth, its layered ages of brick and iron? When it contains only the tension and paralysis of the superficial new? (179)

Porosity, once so potent a quality of the built environment, and referenced obliquely in relation to Kathryn and Tap's island abode, is here a harbinger of sterility, an effect of postmodern pastiche.

Mirroring the generic capital in which they reside, the generic business community of which Axton is a part is only superficially grounded. Being abroad is clearly *not* about place. Antithetical to Durrell's aesthetic communities, Axton's crowd consists of dinner companions who are, in large part, "forced by circumstance to get along" (54). Their ties to Athens—as to each other—are superficial, based on instrumentality and expediency. They meet in tavernas or in one another's apartments; and, although they do not often speak of home, their lifestyles are supported by the many perquisites designed to compensate for a life of exile: "The duty-free car, the furlough allowance, the housing allowance, the living allowance, the education allowance, the tax equalization, the foreign assignment premium" linking them to a material base in the United States (193). In this postnational community of toilers in global capital's support system, the denizens of dead time and nonplace take comfort in the routines and checkpoints of air travel:

> air travel reminds us who we are. It's the means by which we recognize ourselves as modern. The process removes us from the world and sets us apart from each other. We wander in the ambient noise, checking one more time for the flight coupon, the boarding pass, the visa. (254)

If identity was once conceived in terms of a self engaged with its own interiority— writing, painting, and studying—now, in more postmodern as opposed to modern fashion (pace Axton), it is a function of difference, of contiguity.

There are, moreover, no grounded expatriates in this community of Western expatriates, no wealthy or bohemian refugees from the monotony of the same who have chosen to cast their fate with the locals. Neither are they conventional romancers. As John McClure suggests: "DeLillo's adventurous Western men are reduced to individual empire-building, obscure archeological or artistic enthusiasms, frivolous pleasures, heartless affairs, and perverse fascinations."[5] The nature of expatriate desire, too, becomes strangely self-referential. In place of the back alleys of the native town where the sexual adventurer of the past might seek his pleasure, *The Names* offers parody: a fumbling and unconvincing encounter between Axton and a bellydancer, Janet Ruffing, who happens to be the very American wife of an American bank officer. And everyone is on the move. This attenuation of "the spirit of place" is further registered by the imaginative geographies that are associated with Axton's "community" of executives who dwell, in a certain sense, in the interstices of places, within channels of commerce and espionage that intersect but are not coincident with the geographies attached to specific place-names.

Making the world safe for capital, the intelligence/business nexus exists to hold the line against terror and chaos, which the novel suggests may be linked not only to physical terrorism but also to language, as evidenced by Brademas's fear of India's atextuality. And there are certain parallels between antiterrorism and textuality as well. In Geoffrey Galt Harpham's discussion of asceticism and textuality, he argues that speech represents "a principle of kinetic disorder which it has always been the goal of philosophy (and writing, and ethics) to order and contain."[6] Citing Ernst Cassirer, Harpham writes that "it is for philosophy, for dialectic, to bring this change to a standstill, to transmute the mobile and uncertain shapes of words into steadfast and constant concepts."[7] Indeed, Axton's own line of work, risk analysis, is somewhat analogous: "material flowed into Athens from various control points around the Mediterranean, the Gulf and the Arabian Sea. It needed structuring, it needed perusal by someone with intellectual range" (*Names*, 48). It needed, in other words, the form of a coherent narrative, a text, a counterpoint to "people running in the streets," an oft-repeated image in the novel. Moreover, as we learn at the end of the novel, Axton's various "good works" (and DeLillo's choice of words here is worth noting for its irony)—"To fill in here, do a review there, restructure some offices, seeing to sagging morale," translating nations into the statistical evidence of more or less risk to capital (143)—merge the productive and coercive faces of global domination.

Part of accountability is the ability to see particularity, and this is something Axton takes away from his final meeting with Brademas, whom he has tracked down in his obscure surroundings. In this "Greek" space that Brademas has constructed to escape the materiality of the object world, Axton comes to enjoy a newly discovered respect for the object. In a bizarre sense, he seems to learn that attention to the object and dialogic relations are linked.

> I judged the amount of time that had to pass before he would be ready to recite the ending, before the stillness would yield. This is what I was learning from the objects in the room and the spaces between them, from the conscious solace he was devising in things. I was learning when to speak, in what manner. (308)

His departure is marked by a sense of vision newly sensitized to the object world. Unlike Brademas, he is willing to embrace both the object and its context, at once a validation and celebration of India's materiality, seen as if for the first time:

> Bare bulbs were arranged on strings over tiers of nuts and spices. I paused every few feet to see what was here, nutmeg and scarlet mace, burlap bags of coriander seeds and chilies, rock salt in crude chunks. I lingered at the tray of dyestuffs and ground spices, heaped in pyramids, colors I'd never seen, brilliances, *worlds*, until finally it was time to go. (309, my emphasis)

Axton feels he'd "been engaged in a contest of some singular and gratifying kind" and "whatever [Brademas] had lost in life-strength, this is what [Axton] had won" (309).

His return to Athens coincides with two apparently related incidents: the discovery that his supposed employment as a risk analyst has been a cover for CIA intelligence gathering, and an attempt on the life of his friend David Keller. We begin to wonder then whether Axton's occasional anxiety about setting limits—cutting down on wine at first, then total abstinence and daily jogging—reflects some unconscious anxiety concerning his own activities, both professional and in terms of his interest in the cult. He runs "to stay interested in [his] body, to stay informed, and to set up clear lines of endeavor, a standard to meet, a limit to stay within." Eschewing the classic running outfits of his compatriots, he "never wore the clothes"; he ran "disguised as an ordinary person, a walker in the woods," thus paralleling his covert if involuntary involvement in CIA activities (323). Axton then comes to believe he was the assassin's intended target. Having had his fill of death, he turns in his resignation and prepares to return home, but not without giving up the "names" of his CIA contacts to the authorities and then taking time to study his Greek and make a pilgrimage to the long-avoided Acropolis, perceived now as wholly human, "a cry for pity." Our "offering" to this secular temple is, he finally asserts, "language."

Indeed, language is a recurring theme throughout the novel. "Why is it we talk so much here?" Axton asks. "Inconceivable, all this conversation, in North America. Talking, listening to others talk. . . . It must be life outdoors. Something in the air" (79). A typical "North American," in some respects, Axton is not an adept at learning languages, although he is, at times, sensitive to the functions of conversation. Small talk with his wife, for example, seems "to yield up the mystery that is part of such things, the nameless way in which we sometimes feel our connections to the physical world" (32). Even the sounds of speech and human interaction on a hot Athenian night seem redolent with a kind of unanticipated richness: "People everywhere are absorbed in conversation. . . . Conversation is life, language is the deepest being. . . . Every conversation is a *shared narrative*, a thing that surges forward, too dense to allow space for the unspoken, the sterile" (52, my emphasis).

Nevertheless, Axton's own ability to share narrative is deeply compromised, and his attraction to the cult, because "[i]t's the only thing I've been right about," points to the parallels between his language games and theirs (300). The cult chose its victims by matching their initials to the initials of place-names. For Axton, the game is slightly less macabre. His inability to pronounce certain Greek place-names has put him in mortal fear of Niko, the friendly concierge in his apartment building, who knows no English and is always anxious for a chat. Niko would always query him as to his comings and goings. And so: "In time I began to lie. I would tell him I was going to a place that had a name I could easily pronounce. What a simple, even elegant device this seemed. Let the nature of the place-name determine the place" (102–3). Such "inauthentic" (I use the term advisedly) conversation must be contrasted with the very different type of transaction between Niko and Axton's son, Tap, whose intercultural socialization has taken place on the Greek island where he has spent the summer with his mother:

> Niko spoke Greek to Tap as he'd never spoken to me, with vigor and warmth, eyes shining. I see my son in the small tumult of the moment. He knows he has to handle this alone and does it conscientiously enough, shaking the man's hand, nodding madly. He is not experienced at hearty rapport, of course, but his effort is meticulous and touching. He knows the man's pleasure is important. He has seen this everywhere on the island and he had listened to his mother. We must be more precise in the details of our responses. This is how we let people know we understand the seriousness and dignity of their feelings. Life is different here. We must be equal to the largeness of things. (89)

Kathryn and Tap provide a rich counterpoint to the systems of signification and abstraction that preoccupy the adult male characters in *The Names*. Here attention to and recognition of the Other is prioritized, and it is effected through dialogism, a dialogism that takes individuality and the visceral register of thinking and judgment seriously. We might also recognize here something of Seyla Benhabib's discussion of an ethics of care that values equity and complementarity over the law and abstract justice. In terms of our relations with the Other,

> each is entitled to expect and to assume from the other forms of behavior through which the other feels recognized and confirmed as a concrete, individual being with specific needs, talents and capacities. . . . The moral categories that accompany such interactions are those of responsibility, bonding and sharing. The corresponding moral feelings are those of love, care and sympathy and solidarity.[8]

Kathryn, who has such important truths to impart to her son, finds the world of things endlessly fascinating. Indeed, such objects seem to exist to teach us important lessons about the boundaries of the self:

> She was digging to find things, to learn. Object themselves. Tools, weapons, coins. Maybe objects are consoling. Old ones in particular, earth-textured, made by other-minded men. Objects are what we aren't, what we can't extend ourselves to be. Do people make things

> to define the boundaries of the self? Objects are the limits we
> desperately need. They show us where we end. (*Names*, 133)

Axton's perceptual energies flow in a different direction. Where
he sees a "coded flight of birds," Kathryn, he is sure, "would know
what kinds of birds they are" (179). Even Tap would rehearse the
names of objects, and Axton "could see him store these names and
the objects they belonged to, for safekeeping." On the other hand,
what Tap learns from both Axton and Brademas is that "'character' in English not only means *someone* in a story but a *mark* or *symbol*" (10, my emphasis). Yet we have seen that even Axton, by the
novel's end, has learned to respect the dignity of objects.

The ethics of care and attention to particularity that Kathryn
practices and teaches to her son seem to carry over to her relationship to place as well. The novel's imaginative geography
rewards Kathryn with an understated yet decidedly textured relationship with the local people; she is firmly grounded on the island
where she works (indeed, as an archaeological assistant, she is literally "in" the ground most of the time) and, provisionally at least,
integrated into the village community. Unlike the generic world
capital Axton's Athens has become, Kathryn's island returns us to
the more fully embodied spaces of the earlier expatriate narratives,
most notably in the Mediterranean. The modernist ethics of expatriation, paradoxically, despite their investments in structures of
domination, seem more capacious, more stubbornly determined
to cross borders, take risks, remain open.

Like Kathryn, Axton's friend Ann Maitland is a devotee of the
particular, and her propensity to take lovers in every new country
in which her husband's job has required them to settle represents
an investment in the purely local that also harkens back to a more
textured expatriate history. These indiscretions are the antithesis
of Axton's pathetic tryst with the American bellydancer in train-
ing whose earnest striving to get all the moves right represents a
kind of refreshing innocence that makes Axton's de facto rape all
the more crude. Not surprisingly, he assesses Ann's behavior in
purely instrumental, "imperial" terms:

> Possibly you want to deepen the experience of a place. A place you
> know you will have to leave some day, most likely not by choice. . . .
> The loss of Kenya, the loss of Cyprus. You want to keep something
> for yourself that isn't a tribal mask or figurine. A private Cyprus, a
> meditation. How does a woman make these places hers as well as her
> husband's when after all it's his job that determines where they go,
> and when they go and when they leave. (161)

Despite the suggestion that there is an equivalence between the accumulation of cultural artifacts and lovers and the embedding of love affairs within the language of conquest and appropriation (this is, after all, Axton's [and DeLillo's?] response to her adultery), there is the sense that deepening the experience of a place might actually have an intersubjective dimension. The messiness of emotion and human imperfection, however, is not allowed to intrude upon the analysis. The question of Ann's pleasure is sidestepped. Axton is more interested in these love affairs as "themes" and "motifs" in her life" (161).

The narratives of Kathryn and Anne are marginal to the novel's trajectory. Kathryn, like her husband, returns to North America, but not without imparting to *The Names* the sense that there might be ways to negotiate the ethics of expatriation that are both wise and generous. That said, however, the novel is far more concerned with the lessons learned by Axton, whose emerging sense of responsibility, his acknowledgment of his own accountability, now requires that he return to the United States. More importantly, by denying Brademas his redemptive moment, the novel at once repudiates the project of self-dismantling and the expatriate preoccupation with freedom that are associated with a modernist ethics of expatriation. Ironically, it is Brademas, the speaker of five languages, who turns from language's intersubjective mode to its mode of signification on the one hand, and the non-sense of tongues on the other, and Axton, for whom basic conversational Greek remains a mystery, who learns the "truth" of language, its orality and expressiveness.

"The largeness of things" demands not only that we attend to particularities but that we measure up, so to speak, that we hold ourselves accountable. This means acknowledging not only one's complicity but also one's "ethical" shortcomings, which are dramatized, it is suggested, through the cult's ability to fascinate: "The murders are so striking in design that we tend to overlook the physical act itself, the repeated pounding and gouging of a claw hammer, the blood mess washing out. We barely consider the victims except as elements in the pattern" (171). What does this tell us about expatriate narrative? The modernist expatriate ethos, fueled by a philosophical investment in the self—as opposed to the subject—seems to have run out of cultural steam. If the self—or subject—is situated, then there are no "private projects" in the periphery. "Considering the victims" means, in a sense, acknowledging oneself as the victimizer. A postmodern expatriate sensibility, then, points the protagonist inevitably toward home. *The Names*, however, seems to gesture toward a middle position somewhere between a modernist ethos of nonaccountability and a postmodern ethos focused only on position. An ethics of care restores the immediacy of place and values the Other in all of his or her particularity, gesturing toward a kind of provisional, nontotalizing universalism. Such an ethics must reach beyond the postmodern to embrace, paradoxically, the desire of the modernist expatriate even as it repudiates the investments that sponsor his project. If such a position is unrealizable within the terms of *The Names*, it is not unimaginable within the contemporary imagination, as *The English Patient* will more poignantly suggest.

If a central ethical problem in *The Names* is the privileging of systems over particularities, scripts over conversations, the lessons learned are, finally, subordinated to questions of positionality. Ondaatje's *The English Patient*, in much the same way, evocatively explores constructions of the Western expatriate subject that privilege fluidity and permeability only to *re*position its characters along national lines. For characters trapped in the networks of global warfare, it is national identity that gives the lie on the one hand to other more cosmopolitan and affective types of affiliations and communities, and on the other to the allegedly private projects or practices that the modernist expatriate was wont to pursue. The former strive to embody an openness to strangers, an ethics of friendship that is interrupted, if not overwritten, by global politics and racism, while the latter are revealed to be unwittingly complicitous with the goals and practices of imperialism

Though written some ten years after *The Names*, a narrative of the historical "present," *The English Patient* returns us to the interwar years. The English patient, Ladislaus de Almásy, is the interwar expatriate whose story was rendered in semiautobiographical terms by Lawrence, Bowles, and Durrell. Now, however, his interpreter is a writer whose trajectory is the obverse of theirs. Born in 1943 in Sri Lanka (then Ceylon), Ondaatje moved to England in 1954 and later emigrated to Canada, where he has lived since 1962. *The English Patient* revisits the problem of the Western subject's desire for liberation from the demands of social form, national identity, and instrumental reason. Refracted, however, through the counter-narrative of Kirpal Singh, or Kip, the sapper, this now familiar narrative is attentive to postcolonial, postmodern concerns. Like *The Names*, *The English Patient* articulates an expatriate ethos that breaks down along generational lines. "Old men," in pursuit of their private desires in the periphery, either languish there or expire in some liminal space, while a younger generation goes back home.

In the space of narrative where the postmodern, postcolonial imagination meets, in the English patient, the "humane face of imperialism" (to quote DeLillo's Owen Brademas), Ondaatje juxtaposes global feeling and feeling global. As Western characters, displaced by desire or by war, come to embrace and valorize the peripheral Other, Western nations wreak havoc on the Other's world. While nationalism deforms its subject, Orientalism deforms the Other; together they make Hiroshima possible. The novel's postmodern sensibility, however, complicates the idea of national identity, opening up different kinds of associational structures. If modernity takes shape through the emergence of the nation-state and the figure of the citizen/subject, postmodernity finds this subject at once localized and dispersed. That is to say, in its attention to the local and the particular on the one hand, and the global and postnational on the other, postmodernism has little use for "the state." At the same time, postmodern expatriate fiction takes account of its protagonists' positionality, their cross-imbrication in the weave of cultural, national, and imperial narratives. *The English Patient* seems to embrace this conflicted or bifurcated sensibility, as does *The Names*. Although Axton negotiates his way professionally within the global circuits of capital and affectively through the particular locales where his family is located, his lack of national commitment does not, finally, absolve him of accountability. *The English Patient* drives this point home even more powerfully.

Resolutely antinationalist and anti-imperialist, *The English Patient* nevertheless reveals the extent to which those values, in themselves, may not be *in*consistent with Western cultural and military domination and Orientalist structures of knowledge and feeling. That is to say, the desire to become "unEnglished," to borrow a phrase from Lawrence, may render the expatriate inattentive to his own participation in the very activities from which he seeks to distance himself. Almásy draws the maps that allow Western troops to invade and despoil—to desecrate—the desert. And it is the expatriate's positionality, not his desire to be repositioned or unpositioned, that matters, finally, in the accounting that is rendered. The countries of the West may be at war, but their citizens perhaps appear indistinguishable from one another to the atomic bomb's Asian victims. Indeed, the bomb itself is the "brainchild" of a particularly Western cosmopolitan intellectual venture. So even as the text valorizes the more "visceral" aspects of relationality, as well as modes of thought and figures that appear to be exterior to the "State," it demonstrates the extent to which those values cannot, or cannot yet, be realized.

We saw, in *Aaron's Rod*, an ethics torn between a desire for "deterritorialization" and a desire for reterritorialization in the one true place. In *The Names*, deterritorialization takes the form of global capital and the "global expansion of Western circuits and systems," the one true place a vestigial wrinkle in postmodernity's cultural psyche.[9] In *The English Patient*, however, these antithetical spatial modes converge in the space of the desert, where Almásy's search for the Good leads him to cast off "the clothing" of his country, his ancestry, his name, and the desire for conquest and appropriation. He is, at this stage, the modernist expatriate whose project demands some "curative" for the problems of the self that are the legacy of the Western subject. Almásy, like DeLillo's Brademas, is a curious figure. Like Brademas, he is drawn away from home to the periphery by occupational demands. Like Brademas, his professional projects allow him to play out his essentially modernist fantasies about liberation. At once the embodiment of Bowlesian asceticism and Durrellean sexual energy, Almásy's passion is as antihumanist as it is wholly human. Already rendered liminal by his status as an Eastern European fluent in a number of languages, he is capable of "passing" as an Englishman and is able to "slip across borders, not to belong to anyone, to any nation."[10]

Almásy, we may posit, is in flight from, among other things, "a fully named world" (*EP*, 21). Not quite analogous to the "textualized" West from which Brademas sought refuge, a fully named world, with its Judeo-Christian resonances that posit namer and named in relations of dominion and subordination, is antithetical to Almásy's expatriate ethos. Where names and naming are associated with domination, ownership, ancestral ties, and stable geographies, Almásy embraces an ethics of anonymity and chooses the desert, a site of radical liberation, as "the one true place." A refugee from the fully named world, he is returned to that world anonymously only to be fully named. The modernist subject, apparently free to lose—or find—himself, gives way to a postmodern subject position whose plotting exposes an inescapable positionality. It is, indeed, one of the ironies of these postmodern expatriate fictions that characters at once so mobile and "nomadic" are at the same time so fully and firmly positioned. Through Ondaatje's narrative we see the refraction of an ethics tenuously constructed through a dialectic of naming and anonymity that, although wholly compromised by the demands of the nation-state and vulnerable to the tentacles of national identity that insinuate themselves insistently into the remotest corners of the earth, nevertheless continue to resonate powerfully in favor of a kind of global feeling. The desert and the community of desert explorers that represent a kind of utopian ideal are always already undermined, Ondaatje insists, by the "deformities" of nationalism. Nevertheless Almásy serves as an exemplar of an expatriate ethos that values affective communities over instrumental collectivities, individuals rather than nation states: "the one voice against all the mountains of power . . . the single unspoiled thing" (269).

Almásy's recounted narrative, interestingly, occupies roughly the same historical time and place as *The Alexandria Quartet*. Durrell, as we have seen, actually spent the war years in Cairo and Alexandria. Like Geoffrey Clifton, in fact, he was a man "embedded in the English machine," both as a colonial and as a "functionaire" in the Foreign Office whose fictional counterparts in *The Alexandria Quartet* represent collectively all that *The English Patient* seems to repudiate so eloquently. Clifton, a marginal character who nevertheless emblematizes and precipitates the novel's crisis, is the hinge between the two texts. Like Durrell's Pursewarden, he is undone by an act of betrayal, but where the *Quartet* worries anxiously over a fanciful Coptic plot that disturbs old friendships and political alliances, *The English Patient* indicts the very system of identities and allegiances upon which such conflicts are based. If it is adultery and not war that destroys Almásy, his end is nevertheless overdetermined by their mutual imbrication. And yet both *The Alexandria Quartet*'s Darley and *The English Patient*'s Almásy reject institutional affiliation and an ethics of duty and service in favor of the personal and the private. But where the *Quartet*'s enunciation, steeped in the imperial design, leaves us in no doubt as to the "proper" alignment of the world, *The English Patient* invites us to contemplate a world without divisions or alignments.

If the *Quartet*'s Darley chooses art over both love and politics, the ethics of expatriation that emerge nevertheless reflect Durrell's "imperial aesthetic"—his mastery of a dialectic between contemporary Alexandria, the decadent issue of an illustrious Greek past and a mongrel present and its spiritually impoverished denizens, the imposition of a "heraldic" truth upon the ramifying, chaotic, and untotalizable "real"—and through these exercises, the cultivation of a self who leaves its indelible mark on the city. Alexandria is a monument to history, layered with the detritus of antiquity, and so the *Quartet*, it seems, strives for its own kind of monumentality. And if Alexandria's ruins provide a blueprint of the present, a key to its modern-day inhabitants, the *Quartet*'s Darley reads history from the top down. That is to say, he is concerned with the kings, the queens, and the empires: the glory of greater Greece in the pre-Islamic city. *The English Patient*'s imaginative geographies are also indebted to the past: to the "lost" histories of desert, as well as the historically dense regions surrounding Florence, Italy. But history in *The English Patient* functions differently. Almásy's guide to the desert landscape is Herodotus, whose goal is to seek out the cul-de-sacs rather than the grand boulevards of history. He is a man who seems to identify himself with the marginal. So Almásy, when he is not in the desert, haunts the back streets of the native quarter that Durrell's Darley shunned: he is, as the text tells us, "[l]ost in another Egypt" (245).

Almásy's desire for the Other, reflected in his proclivity to wander through those quintessentially "native" spaces, renders him a kindred spirit to Bowles the novelist, as well as the Bowlesian expatriate protagonist. As he is wafted along on his boat of sticks by the bedouins, we join him on a Bowlesian-type itinerary full of music, dance, mysticism, and exotic ritual with, however, none of the Bowlesian dread. Indeed, Ondaatje's bedouins are antithetical to Bowles's cultural hybrids that troll the borderlands between the native and modern towns. For if Bowles's Moroccans are seen as agents of death, a particularly Bowlesian kind of deliverance, Almásy's bedouins are surely more benign. They save his life. Almásy's desert is just as pure as Bowles's Port Moresby might have wished it to be. Almásy's desires draw him toward the alternative worlds of the Other. We have seen, however, that DeLillo's Brademas both desires *and* resists the material immediacy of the East. The "atextual" nature of India suggests to him both danger and disorder. If he reads the world in terms of its relative textualities, it is India's unreadability that confounds the senses, making the project of "getting lost" possible. The signifying sublime of

Hindu inscription, the replacement of diachronic modes of temporality with synchronic ones, the impossible diversity of form, color, and sound, converge upon him with alarming immediacy. The vertiginous quality of this Eastern "sensorium" both terrifies and attracts him, and so his paranoia and fear drive him into a correctly proportioned "Greek" space devoid of light and color. But Brademas, one might say, implodes rather than dissolves. In this, his energies seem to flow in a direction different from those of Almásy. So while we leave Brademas expiring in his cell in the "lost streets" of Lahore, Almásy finds himself truly at home only in the desert, precisely because he is, or may be, thereby dispersed. The desert is at the heart of Almásy's modernist ascesis, an ascesis that is at the same time a postmodern dissemination or nomadism.

Ondaatje's desert is the place of the sacred. At once impervious to the technological productions of instrumental reason and rich in associations with Christian asceticism, the not-yet-disenchanted topos of the desert is the site of a possible utopia where "nature, assuaged and at peace, would be free from domination, would cease to be dependent on it and would clear the way for some other mode of being."[11] In a place where "it easy to lose a sense of demarcation" because "nothing was strapped down or permanent, everything drifted," the subject loses its physical integrity as well, so that when Katharine dies she becomes indistinguishable from the acacia trees and cave drawings that surround her (*EP*, 18, 22). DeLillo focuses on this quality of the desert as well, but his associations are more overtly religious and more ideologically invested. For *The English Patient*'s band of explorers, the desert was "[t]he place they had chosen to come to, to be their best selves, to be unconscious of ancestry" (246). Indeed, Almásy affirms, "Everything that ever happened to me that was important happened in the desert" (177).

Ondaatje's desert is also the site of community, a place that makes alternative modes of social relations possible, relations that owe nothing to race, ethnicity, or national origin. "Desert Europeans," Almásy and his comrades spent the greater part of the 1930s mapping the deserts of northern Africa,

> a small clutch of a nation between the wars, mapping and reexploring. We gathered at Dakhla and Kufra as if they were bars or cafes. An oasis society. . . . We knew each other's intimacies, each other's skills and weaknesses. We forgave Bagnold everything for the way he wrote about dunes. (136)

Bagnold, it is later suggested, was associated with British Intelligence, as was Clifton, whose job was "keeping an eye on [Almásy's]
strange group in the Egyptian-Libyan desert. They knew the desert
would someday be a theatre of war" (252). Almásy's perspective of
this world presents a stark contrast to the instrumentalizing gaze
of the British machinery of state; the bedouin, he says, were "the
most beautiful humans I've met in my life. We were German,
English, Hungarian, African—all of us insignificant to them.
Gradually we became nationless. I came to hate nations. We are
deformed by nation-states" (138). In the desert, he avers, these
deformations are smoothed out, rendered invisible. Rendered
invisible, perhaps, but not immaterial, for it is the Western war
among nations, finally, that realigns and redistributes the community of desert explorers along national lines. Almásy is forced
to acknowledge that "suddenly there were 'teams.' The Bermanns,
the Bagnolds, the Slatin Pashas—who had at various times saved
each other's lives—now had split up into camps," and he too is
pressed into service, lending his specialized knowledge to the "bar-
barians" who would "come through the desert with no sense of
what it was" (168, 257). More importantly, perhaps, it is the Western
war that realigns and redistributes the community dwelling at the
Villa San Girolamo along recognizably Orientalist lines.

If the desert is Almásy's "one true place," it functions quite differently in the other expatriate fictions we have examined. We
know that for Bowles the desert seems to embody or reflect a
Bataillian sense of the "extreme limit" and the related project of
self-dismantling. Durrell's desert, on the other hand, is at once the
pastoral abode of his Coptic aristocrats and the limit space of
"greater" Europe, beyond which stretches the dark immensity
of Africa. This bifurcation is reflected in the Hosnani brothers,
Nessim the banker, a Westernized secularist, and his hare-lipped
younger brother, Narouz, identified with the land and the highly
combustible and "irrational" energies represented by religious and
nationalist fervor. The desert is barbarian, bestial, a deformation.
In *The Names*, the desert is, alternately, a place of death, dissolution, and absence. Airborne businessmen experience the desert as
a place of nothingness ("the Empty Quarter") from the safety of
airplanes, while the cult is drawn there to enact its demise. For
Brademas, the desert is synonymous with a kind of ecstatic self-dismantling of which the convergence of the faithful in Mecca appears
emblematic. What desires does Ondaatje's desert answer to?

Almásy is not, or at least not to the extent of his Bowlesian counterpart, in search of the extreme limit. The rigors of desert life do not confound sense but rather instill a kind of wisdom. Moreover, Ondaatje's desert serves as a proving ground where physical hardship, isolation, and disorienting landscapes are all subject to mastery, but Almásy's mastery of the desert is rooted in love and the profoundest respect, and his knowledge of the desert seems not to be predicated upon the relation of subject and object. The desert, empty of the indicia of history, represents an ethics of anonymity, but unlike a more modernist concern with radical existential experimentation such as we would find in Bowles, Almásy's quarrel is with constructions of identity that are overly indebted to drawing boundaries and asserting power. It is not so much a question of getting lost, then— although that is what Almásy, in a very real sense, does—as of de-alienating oneself from the bare elements, forfeiting one's claim to dominion.

> The desert could not be claimed or owned—it was a piece of cloth carried by winds, never held down by stones, and given a hundred shifting names long before Canterbury existed, long before battles and treaties quilted Europe and the East. Its caravans, those strange rambling feasts and cultures, left nothing behind, not an ember. All of us, even those with European homes and children in the distance, wished to remove the clothing of our countries. It was a place of faith. We disappeared into the landscape. Fire and sand. We left the harbours of oasis. The places water came to and touched . . . *Ain, Bir, Wadi, Foggara, Khottara, Shaduf.* I didn't want my name against such beautiful names. Erase the family name! Erase nations! I was taught such things by the desert. (138–39)

The desert, for Ondaatje, might be said to represent a space in which to realize the classic ideal of friendship.

Writing about the "Eu-topia" of friendship, Peter Murphy calls attention to friendship's "third term": the "milieu" or "Great Idea," some "inexhaustible objectivation" under whose penumbra friends assemble. He characterizes this as "the Good":

> Friends are *friends of the Good* as the essential condition of their friendship. Drawn to each other by the rational interest in the Good that they see in one another, each friend draws pleasure from the other's participation in the Good, enjoying the idiosyncracies, the qualities, the shading and nuances of the other's participation. [Murphy's emphasis][12]

Astonishingly, Murphy offers, by way of example, a decidedly imperialist venture: "cartographers with a common desire to chart new regions" (171). Friendship, which he likens to politics, is distinguished by an "equality of difference." That is to say, "[f]riends are often quite different, yet in one important respect they are "equalized" (made the same), namely by their relationship to the "Great Idea" (172). Against the idea of friendship, Murphy cites the "modern bureaucratic state," a quasi-mechanical social form in which "citizens become preoccupied with rule making instead of forging *rapports* modeled on the ties of friendship," a social form that promises equality but obsessively measures inequality (177, Murphy's emphasis). More to the point, "[f]riendship is a gift in the sense of *grace;* it is given by a prime mover—a cause, an idea" (177, my emphasis). The "Great Idea," then, as imperial venture—though it need not signify such—seems an aptly ambiguous metaphor for the penumbra under which the desert explorers gather.

Murphy situates his ethics of friendship in a familiar imaginative geography, that of the Mediterranean: "Friendship," he writes, "is an ethos of the South":

> It is not a trope of the modern world. It fits at best uneasily into a modernity created by Northern Europe—a North whose handmaidens (the Protestant Reformation, the sovereign nation-state, the Industrial Revolution, and the reach of global communications) ushered in an unprecedented social formation. . . . True friendships have been made notoriously difficult by the modern age's suffusion with the values of the Calvinist North—the values of work and of inwardness and privacy. (180–81)

Friendship does not belong "to the placeless or space-less realm of interiority" but rather "needs locales," the public or semi-public gathering places of the café, the piazza, the waterfront (181, 183). What is more, friendship is activity and *movement:* "Peripatesis plus companionship—on the road against the backdrop of the beautiful island or in the cafés of the piazza, mingling together with the ghosts of the past" (184). The porous spaces of the Mediterranean that the members of the Frankfurt school found so conducive to theoretical speculation—and friendship—are enabling not merely because of their revolutionary promise but also as a living abode for a community of friends modeled on premodern, pre-rationalized modes of association. Almásy's desert, then, is at once the Good and the place where the seekers of the Good gather and exchange greetings, information, comradeship. Through the mediation of Herodotus, moreover, it is the place where lost histories emerge, not through ruins, but through the tireless efforts of desert explorers, through textuality. This project, too, however, is wholly dishonored.

The semiotics of space suggested by Deleuze and Guattari help us illuminate the imaginative geographies represented by the desert and how the idea of "place" functions in *The English Patient*. They use textural metaphors, "the smooth and the striated," nomad space and sedentary space, to contrast different modes of occupying the earth and of thinking. The surface that is smooth affords no single totalizing perspective, no central point from which all points radiate; movement from point to point is "rhyzomatic."

> Smooth space is a field without conduits or channels. A field, a heterogeneous smooth space is wedded to a very particular type of multiplicity: nonmetric, acentered, rhyzomatic multiplicities that occupy space without "counting" it and can "be explored only by legwork."[13]

Striated space, on the other hand, is rationalized, reified, space, space meant to be settled. Thus, "sedentary space is striated by walls, enclosures, and roads between enclosures" (381). Moreover,

> even though the nomadic trajectory may follow trails or customary routes, it does not fulfill the function of the sedentary road, which is to *parcel out a closed space to people,* assigning each person a share and regulating the communication between shares. The nomadic trajectory does the opposite; it *distributes people (or animals) in an open space,* one that is indefinite and noncommunicating. (380, Deleuze and Guattari's emphasis)

Sedentary space implies regulation and apportionment; it is associated with the power of the state. Nomad space, on the contrary, is anarchic. Like the porous spaces of the Mediterranean, the desert provides a counterpoint, asserts a resistance to, the machinery of the modern state—indeed, to national identity itself.

If the desert is where one comes to be one's best self, what kind of self is that? One answer, clearly, is that one's best self is a self disencumbered of the "clothing" of country, and so the motif of nakedness is central to the text. The postmodern answer to this essentially "modern" problem of what is genuine and what is merely an outer covering or veneer is, of course, that we are "produced" precisely through these exterior structures or veneers, that we are, in a sense, constituted by, among other cultural formations, the clothing of our countries. This is perhaps what the idea of positionality is about. *The English Patient* also, however, explores particular styles of being that are "nomadic" or decentered rather than "sedentary" or nation-centered. The character Caravaggio asserts: "'Some of the English love Africa. A part of their brain reflects the desert precisely. So they're not foreigners there'" (*EP*, 33). And we may extrapolate from that something of what draws Almásy, the English patient, to this inhospitable terrain. He embodies certain qualities of nomad thought. He is a man that does not "believe in permanence" (230). His adulterous lover, Katharine, tells him, "You slide past everything with your fear and hate of ownership, of owning, of being owned, of being named" (238). So the radical freedom of deterritorialization is linked to ideas not only about ownership, but also about naming.

Naming is thus a central problematic in *The English Patient*. Indeed, it is Almásy's failure to correctly "name" Katharine that precludes her rescue. It is his hatred of names and naming that, in part, dooms their affair, for without the dialectical relationship between identity and difference, there can be no intersubjectivity:

> when one remains within the established field of identity and difference, one readily becomes a bearer of strategies to protect identity through devaluation of the other; but if one transcends the domestic field of identities through which the other is constituted, one loses the identity and standing needed to communicate with those one sought to inform.[14]

Nevertheless, where *The English Patient* associates naming and the power to name with Western styles of knowledge—knowledge by appropriation—and institutional power, Almásy stands for another kind of naming:

> There was a time when mapmakers named the places they travelled through with the names of lovers rather than their own. Someone seen bathing in a desert caravan, holding up muslin with one arm in front of her. Some old Arab poet's woman, whose white-dove shoulders made him describe an oasis with her name. . . . So a man in the desert can slip into a name as if within a discovered well, and in its shadowed coolness be tempted never to leave such containment. (*EP*, 140–41)

For the novel links the desire to impose one's name upon some geographic or scientific discovery with other kinds of brutality. The explorer, Fenelon-Barnes, for example, "wanted the fossil trees he discovered to bear his name. He even wanted a tribe to take his name, and spent a year on the negotiations" (139). The same individual was discovered by Almásy to be keeping a small Arab girl tied up on his bed while traveling with a bedouin caravan. Then, too, Almásy and his group are involved in just the sort of knowledge acquisition that is associated with conquest and global mapping and, as if to drive the point home, it is precisely their specialized knowledge, Almásy's in particular, that is appropriated for wartime use. In fact, the work of another notorious expatriate, Norman Douglas, was similarly appropriated. His travelogue, *Fountains in the Sand*, Paul Fussell tells us, was even more useful to the Allied forces than were the official materials in planning the North African campaign[15]—the military campaign that, ironically, figures so prominently and tragically in *The English Patient*.

As Deleuze and Guattari point out, "the forces at work within space continually striate it," and "in the course of its striation it develops other forces and emits new smooth spaces."[16] The smooth and the striated, we see, are inextricable. Even so, they represent antithetical modes of spatial organization. "Nomad science" and "State science" are parallel formations that represent antithetical modes of knowledge acquisition based upon the same logic: smooth space "is occupied without being counted," while striated space "is counted in order to be occupied" (362). Nomad science is precisely that way of thinking that is free from reliance upon institutional—or "sedentary"—knowledge, where possession, we are accustomed to saying, is nine-tenths of the law. The difference between nomad science and state science is one of "becoming and heterogeneity, as opposed to the stable, the eternal, the identical, the constant," of "following" rather than "reproducing" (361). Whereas "reproducing implies the permanence of a fixed point of *view* that is external to what is reproduced," following requires movement and a kind of immersion:

> One is obliged to follow when one is in search of the 'singularities' of a matter, or rather of a material, and not out to discover a form; when one escapes the force of gravity to enter a field of celerity; when one ceases to contemplate the course of a laminar flow in a determinate direction, to be carried away by a vortical flow; when one engages in a continuous variation of variables, instead of extracting constants from them. (372)

While *The Names* attempts to problematize a too steadfast inclination to the processes of reproduction, in *The English Patient*, following, rather than reproducing, is the preferred modus operandi, and the novel valorizes nomad thought insofar as it represents a counterpoint to the authority of institutions. So much of the poetic energy of *The English Patient* seems to derive from the tension between institutions and individuals, and the novel is full of characters who define themselves against the "authoritative discourses" to which they have been beholden. Their receptiveness to the Other suggests a kind of cosmopolitan ethics at odds with the institutions with which they are associated. As an expatriate, Almásy is paradigmatic; the desert enables him to become "his own invention," or so he would like to believe (*EP*, 246). Indeed, both Almásy and Kip are "nomad" thinkers, but coming out of the periphery, Kip embodies the savvy of the *bricoleur* rather than Almásy's encyclopedic wisdom.

> He had come from a country where mathematics and mechanics were natural traits. Cars were never destroyed. Parts of them were carried across a village and readapted into a sewing machine or water pump. The back seat of a Ford was reupholstered and became a sofa. Most people in his village were more likely to carry a spanner or screwdriver than a pencil. A car's irrelevant parts thus entered a grandfather clock or irrigation pulley or the spinning mechanism of an office chair. . . . What he saw in England was a surfeit of parts that would keep the continent of India going for two hundred years. (188)

Through the doubling of Almásy and Kip, *The English Patient* finds ways to indict the West long before it renders its final accounting. As with the bedouin, for whom "tools and utensils were made from the metal of crashed plains and tanks" (5), a literal beating of swords into ploughshares, the logic of a nonconsumer society is to reabsorb the detritus of industrialization and translate it into productive and benign uses. In a reimagining of the commodity, the colonized and former colonized restore use-value to part objects set adrift by their expulsion from a labor economy. This decentered, nonalienated form of labor, a guerilla industry of sorts, restores dignity to the artisan, privileges the innovator and the mechanic. Indeed, we might contrast such guerilla tactics with the Western model: the beating of plowshares into swords, as suggested in Hanna's annotation of Kipling's *Kim*.

Nevertheless, it is Almásy and not Kip who, "reposed in his bed like a king" (14), presides over the alternative community—consisting of Almásy; Hana, his nurse; Kip; and Caravaggio, the spy hunter, who is an old friend of Hana's father—that evolves at the

Villa Girolamo, a space that, like the desert, offers utopian possibilities. The villa, however, located in the hills of Tuscany, the heart of Renaissance Italy, is quite unlike the desert. Situated in the "striated" space of a modern state, it is saturated with history, religion, art, philosophy—and semiotic density as well. At the same time, Ondaatje's Villa Girolamo is made to suggest some the attributes of "smooth" space. The walls of the villa, rendered by the war into a porous ruin, are painted to represent different seasons, and its painted gardens on bombed-out walls are interchangeable with living gardens. Indeed, Hana is said to prefer being "nomadic in the house with her pallet or hammock" (13). As in the desert, even food and water are sparse. Representing a confusion of inside and outside, the villa is functionally irregular as well. Formerly a convent, then a bunker, then a hospital, it is now the nomad space of a small community of survivors bound together by their own exteriority to the institutional machinery of war, a community whose members, like those of the community of desert explorers, have shed the clothing of their countries only to find to themselves, in the end, back in costume, undermined by an act of incomprehensible barbarity perpetrated by "the West" against "the East." It is important to keep in mind, therefore, that the desert is not the embodied space of utopia, despite its challenge to "settled" forms of knowing and being. As Deleuze and Guattari point out, "smooth spaces are not in themselves liberatory; but the struggle is changed or displaced in them, and life reconstitutes its stakes, confronts new obstacles, invents new paces, switches adversaries. Never believe that a smooth space will suffice to save us."[17]

Hana's great dignity arises from the fact that she is her own self-creation: by opting out of the war machine and casting her lot with the English patient, she affirms the idea that "[t]enderness towards the unknown and anonymous . . . was a tenderness to the self," which is, surely, one of the primary truths of the novel (*EP*, 49). So "[a] man not of your own blood can break upon your emotions more than someone of your own blood. As if falling into the arms of a stranger you discover the mirror of your choice" (90). And, in fact, she has removed all mirrors from the villa, as if to be identical with one's self were a betrayal of some important truth. This is a lesson that Kip, too, has learned at the breast of his ayah:

> this intimate stranger from South India who lived with them, helped run a household, cooked and served them meals, brought up her own children within the shell of the household, having comforted his

older brother too in earlier years, probably knowing the character of all of the children better than their real parents did. . . . All through his life, he would realize later, he was drawn outside the family to find such love. The platonic intimacy, or at times the sexual intimacy, of a stranger. (226)

Hana, to Caravaggio, begins to assume the features of an ascetic, linking her to the tribe of Almásy.

Her ascetic face, which at first seemed cold, had a sharpness. He realized that during the last two months he had grown toward who she now was. He could hardly believe his pleasure at her translation. Years before, he had tried to imagine her as an adult but had invented someone with qualities moulded out of her community. Not this wonderful stranger he could love more deeply because she was made up of nothing he had provided. (222–23)

Hana "has made her face with her desire to be a certain kind of person" (300). And so, while Kip becomes the healer, Hana, rejecting the world of the fathers and the institution of healing, returns to the loving stepmother, a woman not of her own blood, to heal herself. Indeed, she is Almásy's true heir, for unlike Kip, who has made his peace with the sedentary, the proprietary, the familial, Hana, though back where she's "supposed" to be, "has not found her own company, the ones she wanted. She is a woman of honour and smartness whose wild love leaves out luck, always taking risks, and there is something in her brow now that only she can recognize in a mirror" (301). Letting her hair grow, she revokes the covenant with death and the "old world." Positioned or *re*positioned in "upper America," she remains homeless, but Almásy, it is suggested, transcends his positionality.

In the novel's most poignant plea for a universalist ethic, Almásy repudiates his "profession" of mapping the desert:

We die containing a richness of lovers and tribes, tastes we have swallowed, bodies we have plunged into and swum up as if rivers of wisdom, characters we have climbed into as if trees, fears we have hidden in as if caves. I wish for all this to be marked on my body when I am dead. I believe in such cartography—to be marked by nature, not just to label ourselves on a map like the names of rich men and women on buildings. We are communal histories, communal books. We are not owned or monogamous in our taste or experience. All I desired was to walk upon such an earth that had no maps. (261)

While calling to mind Axton's "global feeling," elicited by his pilgrimage to the Acropolis, and Brademas's desire to lose himself in a sea of the faithful at Mecca, Almásy's feeling of solidarity is far more compelling. The idea of being marked, rather than leaving one's mark, reflects Almásy's radical identification with the cosmos and humankind, and, indeed, a sense of Bataillian rupture and communication. It is, however, a reformulation of the modernist project of self-dismantling along postmodern lines, a project that envisions its subjects as incomplete and partial, constituted as much by each other as by themselves—an expatriate ethos, in other words, that aspires almost to global subjectivity, although in an entirely decentered way. Almásy's "credo" articulates the belief in and longing for such a global ethic, the more poignant because of its rapid annulment by the novel's central crisis, the dropping of the atomic bomb.

If Almásy comes to embody his ideal of namelessness, a variation on the theme of self-loss that the modernist expatriate narratives, particularly those of Bowles, tend to explore, Ondaatje will not leave the English patient unnamed. When he falls burning from the sky, losing not only the external indicia of identity, the face, and the official indicators of identity, identity papers, but also the internal indicator of identity, memory, it is left, finally, to others to name—or misname—him. The allied doctors name him the English patient; Caravaggio names him Count Almásy, the spy; and Kip identifies him with England even as his identity as an Eastern European is revealed. And yet Almásy, the unmade man, has presided over, has created, a kind of utopian community in the ruins of a convent. It fails; in the end, all naming and misnaming, all communal histories and communal books, are at the moment of reckoning subsumed in the essential positionality that separates East from West, and this calls a halt to any further transcultural experimentation between Hana and Kip, a younger generation of displacees who will not, cannot, remain expatriates. And yet, the text hints, they continue to inhabit one another in ways that are far more profound than their repositioning would suggest, ways that hark back to Almásy's credo. If *The English Patient* is a postmodern expatriate narrative that realigns subject and homeland, it is, nevertheless, with the idea of connection rather than rupture that the novel leaves us. For Kip and Hana, this connection is unimaginable; the narrative itself must do the work for them. It does so in the name—or under the sign—of Almásy and in a way that recapitulates the values of the modernist project even as it repudiates that project's structural underpinnings. In this double movement of annulment and preservation, of disavowal and exaltation, the figure of Almásy appears to leapfrog over the generation of post-modern expatriates to prefigure or illuminate an ethics of expatria-tion, generous in impulse and open to the world, that is as yet unrealizable.

With the Axtons, the Katharines, the Kips, and the Hanas, then, the ethics of expatriation that once focused on the self and its "work" now turn outward. At the same time, turning outward invariably means returning home, home itself having been trans-formed by a dialectic of imperialism. The population of the West comes more and more to resemble the "third world," while the geography of the third world comes more and more to resemble the West. Underwritten by postmodern notions of plurality, hybridity, and deterritorization, feeling global no longer requires going abroad; indeed, postcolonial theory suggests that staying put may well be the most "ethical" thing one could do. Some post-modern expatriate narratives, however, suggest otherwise. While *The Names* and *The English Patient* seem to tell us there is no avail-able narrative for the Western expatriate that is not hopelessly compromised, they show us otherwise through characters whose ethics of care, dialogism, and solidarity allow us to imagine new narratives and new ethical possibilities. *The English Patient* goes even one step further, suggesting that it is only from the ashes of the old, the discredited, the wholly compromised, the ashes of the man burnt beyond recognition, that is to say, Almásy's ashes, that such imaginings may spring.

It is one of the ironies of this study that the classically mod-ernist text more fully opens itself up to readings sponsored by thinkers associated with postmodernism, thinkers who at any rate contribute to the demise of the "grand narratives." Such texts embody the tension between subjects and systems. They stage the passion of the modernist hero whose flight from home is at once a liberation and a death of sorts. By the same token, the texts I call postmodern relegate that tension to its obsolescent modernist heroes. The postmodern hero's passion is an "antipassion"; it sig-nals his own inevitable acquiescence to the identity between him-self and the structures that on the one hand appear exterior to him, but on the other are the very tissue of his own interiority. This may be of little consequence to the enemies of the modern subject, but in terms of ethics the consequences are plangent. If the postmod-ern ethics of expatriation appear pallid and tentative, that is because they must tread lightly between the Scylla and Charybdis of essentialism and constructedness on the one hand, and universality and relativism on the other. If its cruelties are attenuated, so, by the same token, are its intimacies, its generosities. If *The Names*'s James Axton is small and somehow inconsequential, *The English Patient* returns us to the generosity of a self that exists to squander itself, to spend itself in feeling, in eroticism, in death.

Richard Rorty praises Foucault for exposing "how the patterns of acculturation characteristic of liberal societies have imposed on their members kinds of constraints of which older, premodern societies had not dreamed," but takes him to task because he is not "willing to see these constraints as compensated for by a decrease in pain, anymore than Nietzsche was willing to see the resentfulness of 'slave-morality' as compensated for by such a decrease."[18] Foucault, however, has shown how such constraints can in themselves be productive, by making us more attentive, first, to ourselves and then, one hopes, to others. Bruce Robbins argues that certain forms of global feeling, rather than opposing themselves to nationalism, can actually be

> continuous with forms of national feeling. This implies that, though the potential for a conflict of loyalties is always present, cosmopolitanism or internationalism does not take its primary meaning or desirability from an absolute and intrinsic opposition to nationalism. Rather, it is an *extension outward* of the same sorts of potent and dangerous solidarity. So understood, cosmopolitanism or internationalism cannot pretend to embody the interests of humanity itself or of universal reason. [My emphasis][19]

So Robbins opts for the idea of global *feeling*. In the same spirit of interrogation I would ask whether the attenuation of affect that postmodernity brings is likely to produce a "strong ethics," by which I mean to suggest not so much a moral code, but a cultivation of the sense, the conviction, that such a thing as ethics matters. I ask this question knowing full well that anything "strong" is bound to arouse suspicion, but maybe that is not a good enough reason to avoid it.

Conclusion

I HAVE TAKEN A DETOUR through postmodern or late twentieth-century expatriate narrative to explore changes in the way expatriate experience is represented and to reflect back upon a modernist ethics of expatriation from the perspective of an altered cultural landscape. If Sofia Coppola's recent film *Lost in Translation* is any indication of what "elsewhere" might look like as we move further into the twenty-first century, one thing becomes clear: we may live in a "post-"exotic world, but that does not make its inhabitants any more readable to one another. The modernist ethics of expatriation reflect a time before globalization brought the peoples of the underdeveloped world bodily into the developed one, a time when the "third world" looked distinctly "third world," rather reflecting back a mirror image of the "first."

A modernist ethics of expatriation follows the path of imperialism, not because imperialism opens up new "old" spaces in which to dwell, but because it introduces the Other into metropolitan discourse, giving rise to many of the myths and metaphors of modernism. Modernist cartographies would not exist without the "view from above" to penetrate and organize them and the armies to police them. At the same time, imperialism bears with it the whiff of death, the death of "ethnodiversity," to suggest an analogy with the term "biodiversity," and I do not mean here to elide or detract from the more devastating ills that imperialism leaves in its wake. Like certain species of plants and animals, certain lifeways are cut off by processes begun, for the most part, here in the West; they are cut off and simply disappear forever. It's hard to reconcile one's "nostalgia" for a diverse world, though, with the radical asymmetry in terms of natural resources, wealth, access to health care, education, and the like, which "ethnodiversity"—or a relatively static view of the term, at any rate—implies. I don't pretend to, but the ethics of expatriation require us to push the question. To whom are these quaint lifeways valuable? Do some areas remain in a permanent state of underdevelopment so that others can enjoy access to the "primitive"? The answers are, of course, beside the point. The processes of development move on independently of such considerations.

Lawrence, Durrell, and Bowles left the modern world, left it utterly. I have argued that they deserve greater consideration than postcolonial and postcolonial-related theory suggests might be due them. In their essence, the best expatriate narratives enact a self-questioning that I have analogized to Foucault's care of the self. Read together with—or against—the individual writer's biography, correspondence, and self-presentation in travel writing and autobiography, a greater density of ethical thought emerges. I'm reading figures here as well as individual texts, though it must be noted that my investigations and therefore my claims are limited to a particular period of time in each writer's life and the texts that in some way emerge from that experience. I don't pretend to be objective, and my ordering of the chapters is meant to contrast the relative lack of rigor that Durrell brings to bear upon the questions that concern me with the more troubled and contradictory stance of Lawrence and the even more ethically compelling work of Bowles. The chapters thus seek to represent a progressive complication of the ethics of expatriation.

What these expatriate writers tell us, first of all, is that something is deeply wrong with home, be it the organization of life under capitalism, the psychic ordering of "modern" subjectivity, the limitations of one's social identity, the constraints of life within a symbolic system—language—to which there is no outside. If the modern subject is characterized by its alienation, the expatriate is alienation personified. He is a lone figure, negotiating foreign landscapes and cultural systems. His supposed "weightlessness" bears down upon him in mysterious ways. These writers also tell us—and not in equal measure or to equal effect—that expatriate life is not lived in a vacuum and that the Other is not there merely to authenticate or to otherwise confirm the self, though that is part of it, but to call the self into question. Negotiating social space requires putting one's ambivalence—and one's desire—on the table.

Expatriates seek value in change, and they are particularly interested in exploring parts of the world that enable them—they think—to reach an outside to the systems in which they feel trapped. We have come to understand, with the help of Foucault and others, the extent to which we are both subjected and produced by those systems. I think Lawrence and Bowles intuited that and sought to represent modes of experience in which the self, by ceasing to be a self, could access that outside. What the innovative ethical thinkers tell us is that a radical shake-up is required if we are to live "beyond Oedipus." They cannot even fashion a language literal enough to represent what that might be. Expatriate narrative attempts to go there. And, as Bataille suggests, wherever "there" is, it is a place of bewilderment. If the figure of the colonizer or the "master of all he surveys" is emblematic of agency and power in operation against a human—and natural—landscape in need of cultivation, domestication, or naming, the figure of the expatriate comes on the scene bearing his wounds, castrated, open to the gaze of the native. This, as I have argued, has everything to do with the demands and counterdemands of masculine experience and self-definition. If to some extent it is the poverty of reason, or the problem of reason gone amuck, that motivates the expatriate's flight, it is also the case that, fleeing reason, the expatriate enters the domain of ethics. For it is (or may be) only in reason's absence—reason as the coercive, disciplinary engine of morality—that ethics are free to emerge as the essentially unmotivated and wayward acts of generosity. I speak in metaphor, of course, to elucidate the paradoxical sense that ethicality, for such thinkers as Connolly, Benhabib, and Bauman, does not emerge from rational discourse but from other registers of human experience that reason tends to disparage. But to say that ethics are free to emerge is not the same as saying that they do.

Of course, expatriate narrative tends to fall back upon stereotype—some more than others—and we have seen the extent to which Durrell seems content to "read" the native in terms that do not suggest a lot of the complicated processes Dennis Porter refers to when he distinguishes literary texts with their "self-interrogating density of verbal texture" from those nonliterary texts "that offer no internal resistance to the ideologies they produce."[1] The Greek figures who populate the travel books are little more than cartoon figures, while the Alexandrian characters seem like a deracinated and ethnically cleansed group of late-Romantic aesthetes minus the edginess. No doubt it was the nature of his own expatriate project that influenced his attitudes that in turn found their way into the texts. Durrell's correspondence, as well as his travel narratives, indicate that expatriation was not so much a quest, but a means to an end. *The Alexandria Quartet* seems to bear this out.

Once its narrator, Darley, is able to assert his authority as a writer and (as Boone argues) a lover, the sojourn to elsewhere can be terminated. The Other's demand, in the Durrellean oeuvre, is barely a whisper.

Taken as a whole, though, Durrellean texts, which are notoriously complex, do tend to call into question the discourses that authorize the imperial project. Durrell, as we saw, could readily articulate the contradictions in the British position on Cyprus even though he supported it. *The Alexandria Quartet*, too, with its stylistic sensorium and competing narratives calls into question much of the Enlightenment project. Unlike Lawrence and Bowles, however, Durrell invests art (and, perforce, the artist), with the supreme power to both order and redeem experience. This tends to close down the ethical project, for one cannot at the same time both affirm and call into question one's authority. Durrell's project is about becoming the writer. He documents this process in *The Alexandria Quartet*, where its hero must overcome various challenges to his masculinity and writerly authority. Besides this, the biographical subject calls out for self-consolidation, for the repair of an early and unforgotten wound: the loss of India. If Durrell showcases lack, it is to represent its overcoming. We have seen that the ethics of self-making or self-artistry are often in conflict with an ethics of care that requires sensitivity to particularity, the particularity of other selves. Lawrence and Bowles part company with Durrell in their capacity or willingness to consider the imagination as itself implicated in those very sructures of knowledge and understanding that they sought to overcome.

Stereotyping is, of course, antithetical to an ethics of care. It's interesting to read D. H. Lawrence's own reflections upon the Italian peasantry—the Other of his Italian narratives—against his representation of them in, say, *Aaron's Rod*. In both cases, the peasant embodies qualities of fixity and solidity, but in the individual portraits he is also seen as caught up in modernity's giant machine. Mostly, he is bound for America (like Gordimer's Abdu), while the observer from the modern world watches in dismay as traditional cultures disgorge their ancient inhabitants even as their lands—more ancient still—become repositories for architectural and cultural junk. Certainly we see in the figure of Ciccio a stereotypical rendering of the "Mediterranean man," macho and uncompromisingly antidomestic. He reserves his truest self for the piazza where the local men gather and share in a communal and public life. And yet we are given to understand that if there is to be a future for Alvina and Ciccio, it will likely be one of parity, or near parity, in America. Lawrence is up front about his ambivalence. He both desires and abhors the Italian—and here, as well, he makes certain assumptions about the quality of "Italianness," which he locates not in the Italian bourgeoisie, but in the working classes. In any case, Italy does not pose for us the same problems the colonies or former colonies do. The peasant may be Other to Lawrence, and like most Others, he is seen as authenticating, however imperfectly, Lawrence's "modern" identity, but their relations are not those of colonized and colonizer.

Lawrence's expatriate project, unlike Durrell's, is a quest, and his characters too are questors. The novels are quite explicit in their articulation of the disconnect between their protagonists and the world that engendered them. *Aaron's Rod*'s eponymous protagonist is desperately in search of a way to be himself. Italy, it is hoped, will provide a space in which to interrogate the failures of his life and to overcome his social identity, an identity bound up with what Kaja Silverman calls the dominant fiction. Like those marginal male subjectivities that she has studied, Aaron is a subject defined by his lack. Part of the ethics of expatriation is the exploration of masculine insufficiency; unlike Durrell's Darley, Aaron emerges from the narrative as the incarnation of a castrato, and this in contrast to the image of Michelangelo's David that he so admires. Undoing masculine privilege is perhaps the hardest work of the self, because the castrated self remains, precisely, a self. *The Lost Girl*, with its female protagonist, pushes the idea of self-overcoming much further than does *Aaron's Rod*. For Alvina Houghton, getting lost means much more than interment in a remote Italian village; it means foregoing one's identity as a self entirely. Alvina's terror and delight in submitting to Ciccio reflect the ambivalent pleasures of self-dismantling, the only true way out of the symbolic. The ethics of expatriation in these texts are in the nature of allegory; the work of the self goes hand in hand with the experience of being elsewhere, of getting lost.

In the work of Paul Bowles, getting lost is also literalized, but characters do not find their way back. The self is so compromised by its imbrication in language and culture that nothing short of wholesale destruction of the machinery of self is required. This leaves them, of course, incapable of meaningful action in the world. They are relegated to a realm about which philosophers such as Nietzsche, Bataille, and even Deleuze and Guattari can only allegorize. Bowles is so compelling because he dramatizes the face-to-face encounters of the expatriate and the native in ways that admit of no easy interpretation. And of course, he made his life in Tangier; he embodied the idea of "situatedness in displacement," staying on long after it became fashionable or even safe to do so and enjoying significant ties to the Moroccan community. In Bowles's imagination, the ethics of expatriation achieve a kind of complexity and urgency that is unique among the texts I have examined here. If the Lawrentian expatriate can be read as the incarnation of a castrated masculine subjectivity, the Bowlesian one is wholly torn apart, as made literal in Port's near-death hallucination. Self-overcoming was never so brutally and graphically imagined. At the same time, a text such as *The Spider's House* offers a salient critique of just the sort of expatriate attitudes and biases one might expect from an unself-critical xenophile who professes deep admiration for the culture in whose midst he has chosen to live but whose ability to see beyond the image he has constructed is severely limited.

More than do the expatriate protagonists of Durrell and Lawrence, the Bowlesian "anti-hero" drags behind him the legacy not only of a failed investiture in the dominant fiction, but of Western civilization itself. From "A Distant Episode" through *The Sheltering Sky* to *Let It Come Down* and even *The Spider's House,* it is evident that the work of the self involves both a reckoning with Enlightenment values, which takes the form of a repeated attack on the subject of reason, and an attempt, however flawed, to represent the confrontation, across boundaries of suspicion and desire, between self and Other. It is not from a position of mastery or power that the Bowlesian expatriate approaches Morocco. Far from "penetrating" the Arab world, he is himself penetrated. What is more, he desires such penetration and rushes toward danger as readily as another sort of character would turn and run. There is a certain arrogance in this courting of danger, and in this strange permutation of heroism we can read something of the Nietzschean tightrope walker. Against all received ideas concerning the easy life of the expatriate and the weightlessness of expatriate existence, the ethics of expatriation, and particularly those we can associate with Paul Bowles, tend to represent a much harsher aesthetic. Indeed, the expatriate of these texts is a child of the West, and the darkness of his story is perhaps the dark side of modernity itself.

In *Love's Knowledge,* Martha Nussbaum argues that "certain literary texts (or texts similar to these in certain relevant ways) are indispensable to a philosophical inquiry in the ethical sphere: not by any means sufficient, but sources of insight without which the inquiry cannot be complete" (23–24). For Nussbaum, the ethical inquiry is a "practical" one "that we undertake in countless ways when we ask ourselves how to live, what to be; one that we perform together with others, in search of ways of being together in a community, country, or planet" (24). The form of the question, however, is crucial to the ethics of expatriation. Asking "How should *one* live" is not the same as asking "How should *I* live." The former draws upon the norms and expectations of a particular community. And to the extent that conventional ethical concerns are essentially communitarian in nature— that is, they revolve around the individual's place in the world vis-à-vis other individuals, groups, life forms, and so on—the way "one" should live must resonate in some way beyond the merely personal "I." The search for the good implies some collective notions of what that good might be. The ethics of expatriation, however, are highly individualistic. They are rooted in a kind of exceptionalism. More than this, they are often deeply antagonistic to the values associated with domesticity, community, and the greater imagined community of the nation. To some extent, these reflect a modernist sense of alienation, but it is my belief that the modern world itself is imbued with an ethical darkness, the "other" of enlightenment values, if you will, that produces its own economy of negation, excess, and horror. This is nothing new, of course, but what I think my study reveals is that certain kinds of texts are, to use Nussbaum's word, "indispensable" to an illumination and interrogation of the radical negativity that philosophers such as Nietzsche and Bataille have sought to articulate. Indeed, their own work is a testament to the failure of conventional philosophical tracts to illuminate this harrowing and yet courageous path to places where reason no longer prevails. Expatriate narratives provide an essential dimension of this "ethical" quest, and we respond to them because we are beings of darkness, as well as light.

Bibliography

Abrams, M. H. *Natural Supernaturalism: Tradition and Revolution in Romantic Literature.* New York: Norton, 1971.

Aciman, André. *Out of Egypt: A Memoir.* New York: Riverhead, 1994.

Adorno, Theodor W., and Max Horkheimer. *The Dialectic of Enlightenment.* 1944. New York: Continuum, 1994.

Ahmad, Aijaz. *In Theory: Classes, Nations, Literatures.* London: Verso, 1992.

Ahmed, Leila. *A Border Passage: From Cairo to America—A Woman's Journey.* New York: Farrar, Straus and Giroux, 1999.

Alcalay, Ammiel. *After Jews and Arabs: Remaking Levantine Culture.* Minneapolis: University of Minnesota Press, 1993.

Anderson, Benedict. *Imagined Communities: Reflections on the Origin and Spread of Nationalism.* London: Verso, 1983.

Bakhtin, M. M. "Discourse in the Novel." In *The Dialogic Imagination: Four Essays by M. M. Bakhtin,* edited by Michael Holquist. Translated by Caryl Emerson and Michael Holquist. Austin: University of Texas Press, 1981. 259-422.

Barker, Stephen. *Strategies of the Self After Nietzsche.* New Jersey: Humanities Press, 1992.

Bartkowski, Frances. *Travelers, Immigrants, Inmates.* Minneapolis: University of Minnesota Press, 1996.

Bataille, Georges. *The Bataille Reader.* Edited by Fred Botting and Scott Wilson. New York: Blackwell, 1998.

———. "Chance." Translated by Bruce Boone. In *The Bataille Reader,* 37–54.

———. "The College of Sociology." In *Visions of Excess: Selected Writings, 1927–1939, Georges Bataille,* 246–53.

———. *Eroticism: Death and Sensuality.* 1957. Translated by Mary Dalwood. San Francisco: City Lights Books, 1986.

———. "The Festival, or the Transgression of Prohibitions." In *The Bataille Reader,* 248–52.

———. *Inner Experience.* 1954. Translated by Leslie Anne Boldt. New York: State University of New York Press, 1988.

———. "The Knowledge of Sovereignty." Excerpt from *The Accursed Share,* in *The Bataille Reader,* 301–12.

———. *Literature and Evil.* 1957. Translated by Alastair Hamilton. London: Marion Boyars, 1993.

———. "The Notion of Expenditure." In *Visions of Excess: Selected Writings, 1927-1939, Georges Bataille,* 116–29.

———. "The Object of Desire and the Totality of the Real." In *The Bataille Reader*, 264–70.

———. *On Nietzsche: The Will to Chance.* In *The Bataille Reader*, 330–42.

———. "Sacrifice, the Festival, and the Principles of the Sacred World." Excerpt from *Theory of Religion*, in *The Bataille Reader*, 210–19

———. "The Schema of Sovereignty." Excerpt from *The Accursed Share*, in *The Bataille Reader*, 313–20.

———. *Visions of Excess: Selected Writings, 1927–1939, Georges Bataille.* Edited by Allan Stoekl. Translated by Allan Stoekl with Carl R. Lovitt and Donald M. Leslie Jr. Minneapolis: University of Minnesota Press, 1985.

Bauman, Zygmunt. *Postmodern Ethics.* Oxford: Blackwell, 1993.

Baumeister, Roy F. *Masochism and the Self.* Hillsdale, N.J.: Lawrence Erlbaum, 1989.

Behdad, Ali. *Belated Travelers: Orientalism in the Age of Colonial Dissolution.* Durham: Duke University Press, 1994.

Benhabib, Seyla. *Situating the Self: Gender, Community, and Postmodernism in Contemporary Ethics.* New York: Routledge, 1992.

Benjamin, Jessica. *The Bonds of Love: Psychoanalysis, Feminism, and the Problem of Domination.* New York: Pantheon, 1988.

Bennett, Jane. *The Enchantment of Modern Life: Attachments, Crossings, and Ethics.* Princeton: Princeton University Press, 2001.

Bergonzi, Bernard. *Reading the Thirties: Texts and Contexts.* Pittsburgh: University of Pittsburgh Press, 1978.

Berman, Marshall. *All That Is Solid Melts into Air: The Experience of Modernity.* 1982. New York: Penguin, 1988.

Bernasconi, Robert, and David Wood, eds. *The Provocation of Levinas: Rethinking the Other.* London: Routledge, 1988.

Bersani, Leo. *The Culture of Redemption.* Cambridge: Harvard University Press, 1990.

Bhabha, Homi. *The Location of Culture.* London: Routledge, 1994.

Boldt, Leslie Anne. Introduction to *Inner Experience*, by Georges Bataille, ix–xxviii.

Bongie, Chris. *Exotic Memories: Literature, Colonialism, and the Fin de Siecle.* Stanford: Stanford University Press, 1991.

Boone, Joseph Allen. *Libidinal Currents: Sexuality and the Shaping of Modernism.* Chicago: University of Chicago Press, 1998.

Booth, Howard J. "Lawrence in Doubt: A Theory of the 'Other.'" In *Modernism and Empire*, edited by Howard J. Booth and Nigel Rigby, 197–223. Manchester: Manchester University Press, 2000.

Botting, Fred, and Scott Wilson. Introduction to *The Bataille Reader*, 37–54.

Bowen, Roger. "Closing the 'Toybox': Orientalism and Empire in *The Alexandria Quartet*." *Studies in the Literary Imagination* 24, 1 (Spring 1991): 9–18.

———. *Many Histories Deep.* Madison, N.J.: Fairleigh Dickinson University Press, 1995.

Bowker, Gordon. *Through the Dark Labyrinth: A Biography of Lawrence Durrell.* London: Sinclair-Stevenson, 1996.

Bowles, Jane. *"Everything Is Nice": The Collected Works of Jane Bowles.* New York: Farrar, Straus, 1966.

Bowles, Paul. *Collected Stories, 1939–1976.* Santa Rosa; Calif.: Black Sparrow Press, 1994.

———. *Conversations with Paul Bowles.* Edited by Gena Dagel Caponi. Jackson: University Press of Mississippi, 1993.

———. *Days: Tangier Journal, 1987–1989.* Hopewell, N.J.: Ecco, 1991.

———. "A Distant Episode." In *Collected Stories, 1939–1976.*

———. *In Touch: The Letters of Paul Bowles.* Edited by Jeffrey Miller. New York: Farrar, Straus and Giroux, 1994.

———. *Let It Come Down.* Santa Rosa, Calif.: Black Sparrow Press, 1992.

———. *The Sheltering Sky.* New York: Vintage Books, 1949.

———. *The Spider's House.* Santa Rosa, Calif.: Black Sparrow Press, 1988.

———. *Their Heads Are Green and Their Hands Are Blue: Scenes from the Non-Christian World 1963.* Hopewell, N.J.: Ecco, 1984.

———. *Without Stopping: An Autobiography.* New York: Ecco, 1972.

Bradbury, Malcolm. *The Modern British Novel.* London: Penguin, 1993.

Brantlinger, Patrick. *Rule of Darkness: British Literature and Imperialism, 1830–1914.* Ithaca: Cornell University Press, 198.

Briatte, Robert. *Paul Bowles: 2117 Tanger Soc Paris*: Plon, 1989.

Butler, Judith. *The Psychic Life of Power: Theories in Subjection.* Stanford: Stanford University Press, 1997.

Carter, Erica, James Donald, and Judith Squires, eds. *Space and Place: Theories of Identity and Location.* London: Lawrence and Wishart, 1993.

Cavitch, David. *D. H. Lawrence and the New World.* New York: Oxford University Press, 1969.

Célestin, Roger. *From Cannibals to Radicals: Figures and Limits of Exoticism.* Minneapolis: University of Minnesota Press, 1996.

Certeau, Michel de. *Heterologies: Discourse on the Other.* Translated by Brian Massumi. Minneapolis: University of Minnesota Press, 1986.

Chambers, Iain. *Migrancy, Culture, Identity.* London: Routledge, 1994.

Chase, Richard. *The American Novel and Its Tradition.* Baltimore: Johns Hopkins University Press, 1957.

Chow, Rey. *Writing Diaspora: Tactics of Intervention in Contemporary Cultural Studies.* Bloomington: Indiana University Press, 1991.

Clifford, James. *The Predicament of Culture: Twentieth Century Ethnography, Literatures, and Art.* Cambridge: Harvard University Press, 1988.

———. "Traveling Cultures." In *Cultural Studies*, edited by Lawrence Grossberg, Cary Nelson, and Paula Treichler, 96–112. New York: Routledge, 1992.

Connolly, William E. *Identity/Difference: Democratic Negotiations of Political Paradox.* Ithaca: Cornell University Press, 1991.

————. *Why I Am Not a Secularist.* Minneapolis: University of Minnesota Press, 1999.

Cooper, Artemis. *Cairo in the War: 1939–1946.* London: Hamilton, 1989.

Cowley, Malcolm. *Exile's Return: A Literary Odyssey of the 1920s.* New York: Viking, 1951.

Critchley, Simon. *The Ethics of Deconstruction: Derrida and Levinas.* Oxford: Blackwell, 1992.

Dasenbrock, Reed Way. "Lawrence Durrell and the Modes of Modernism." *Twentieth-Century Literature* 33 (1987): 515–27.

Deleuze, Gilles, and Félix Guattari. *Anti-Oedipus: Capitalism and Schizophrenia.* Translated by Robert Hurley, Mark Seem, and Helen R. Lane. Minneapolis: University of Minnesota Press, 1983.

————. *A Thousand Plateaus: Capitalism and Schizophrenia.* Translated by Brian Massumi. Minneapolis: University of Minnesota Press, 1987.

DeLillo, Don. *The Names.* 1982. New York: Vintage, 1989.

Dillon, Millicent. *You Are Not I: A Portrait of Paul Bowles.* Berkeley: University of California Press, 1998.

Dinesen, Isak. *Out of Africa and Shadows on the Grass.* 1938. New York: Vintage, 1985.

Douglas, Mary. *Purity and Danger: An Analysis of the Concepts of Pollution and Taboo.* 1984. London: Routledge, 1996.

Durrell, Lawrence. *Balthazar.* London: Faber and Faber, 1958.

————. *The Big Supposer: Lawrence Durrell, a Dialogue with Marc Alyn.* Translated by Francine Barker. New York: Grove, 1974.

————. *Bitter Lemons.* New York: Dutton, 1957.

————. *The Black Book,* New York: Dutton, 1963.

————. *Clea.* New York: Washington Square Press, 1960.

————. *The Durrell-Miller Letters, 1935–80.* Edited by Ian S. MacNiven. New York: New Directions, 1988.

————. Introduction to *Alexandria: A History and Guide,* by E. M. Forster. 1922. New York, Oxford University Press, 1986.

————. *Justine.* New York: Dutton, 1961.

————. "Landscape and Character." In *The Spirit of Place,* 156–63.

————. *Mountolive.* New York: Washington Square Press, 1958.

————. "Pied Piper of Lovers." In *The Spirit of Place,* 164–84.

————. *Prospero's Cell: A Guide to the Landscape and Manners of the Island of Corcyra.* 1945. London: Faber and Faber, 1962.

————. *Reflections on a Marine Venus: A Companion to the Landscape of Rhodes.* 1953. London: Faber and Faber, 1963.

————. *The Spirit of Place: Letters and Essays on Travel.* Edited by Alan G. Thomas. New York: Dutton, 1969.

Eagleton, Terry. *The Ideology of the Aesthetic.* Oxford: Blackwell, 1990.

Ehrenreich, Barbara. *The Hearts of Men: American Dreams and the Flight from Commitment.* Garden City, N.Y.: Anchor P/Doubleday, 1983.

Ely, John. "Intellectual Friendship and the Elective Affinities of Critical Theory." *South Atlantic Quarterly* 97, 1 (1998): 187–224.

Engels, Frederick, and Karl Marx. *The Communist Manifesto with Related Documents*. Edited by John E. Toews. Boston: Bedford St. Martins, 1999.

Feinstein, Elaine. *Lawrence and the Women: The Intimate Life of D. H. Lawrence*. New York: HarperCollins, 1993.

Fiedler, Leslie. *Love and Death in the American Novel*. New York: Criterion, 1960.

Finlayson, Iain. *Tangier: City of the Dream*. London: Flamingo, 1993.

Forster, E. M. *Two Cheers for Democracy*. New York: Harcourt, Brace, 1951.

Foucault, Michel. *The Care of the Self*. Vol. 3 of *The History of Sexuality*. Translated by Robert Hurly. New York, Pantheon, 1986.

———. "On the Genealogy of Ethics: An Overview of Work in Progress." In *The Foucault Reader*, edited by Paul Rabinow. New York: Pantheon, 1984, 340–72.

———. *Power/Knowledge: Selected Interviews and Other Writings, 1972–1977*. New York: Pantheon, 1980.

———. Preface to *Anti-Oedipus: Capitalism and Schizophrenia*, by Gilles Deleuze and Félix Guattari, xi–xxiv.

———. *The Use of Pleasure*. Vol. 2 of *The History of Sexuality*. Translated by Robert Hurly. 1984. New York, Vintage, 1990.

Freud, Esther. *Hideous Kinky*. Hopewell, N.J.: Ecco, 1992.

Fussell, Paul. *Abroad: British Literary Traveling between the Wars*. Oxford: Oxford University Press, 1980.

Gibson, Andrew. *Postmodernity, Ethics, and the Novel from Leavis to Levinas*. London: Routledge, 1999.

Gilroy, Paul. *The Black Atlantic: Modernity and Double Consciousness*. Cambridge: Harvard University Press, 1993.

Gordimer, Nadine. *The Pickup*. New York: Penguin, 2001.

Granofsky, Ronald. "Modernism and D. H. Lawrence: Spatial Form and Selfhood in Aaron's Rod." *ESC* 26 (2000): 29–51.

Green, Martin. *Dreams of Adventure, Deeds of Empire*. New York: Basic Books, 1979.

Green, Michelle. *The Dream at the End of the World: Paul Bowles and the Literary Renegades in Tangier*. New York: HarperPerennial, 1992.

Hamalian, Leo. *D. H. Lawrence in Italy*. New York: Taplinger, 1981.

Harpham, Geoffrey Galt. *The Ascetic Imperative in Culture and Criticism*. Chicago: University of Chicago Press, 1987.

———. *Shadows of Ethics: Criticism and the Just Society*. Durham: Duke University Press, 1999.

Hassan, Ihab. *Radical Innocence: Studies in the Contemporary Novel*. Princeton: Princeton University Press, 1961.

Herbrechter, Stefan. *Lawrence Durrell, Postmodernism, and the Ethics of Alterity*. Amsterdam: Rodopi, 1999.

Hibbard, Allen E. "Expatriation and Narration in Two Works by Paul Bowles." *West Virginia Quarterly* 32 (1986–87): 61–71.

———. *Paul Bowles: A Study of the Short Fiction*. New York: Maxwell Macmillan International, 1993.

Hite, Molly. *Ideas of Order and the Novels of Thomas Pynchon.* Columbus: Ohio State University Press, 1983.

Horton, Susan R. *Difficult Women, Artful Lives: Olive Schreiner and Isak Dinesen, in and out of Africa.* Baltimore: Johns Hopkins University Press, 1995.

Huxley, Aldous. Introduction to *The Letters of D. H. Lawrence,* ix–xxxiv.

Jameson, Fredric. *The Political Unconscious: Narrative as a Socially Symbolic Act.* Ithaca: Cornell University Press, 1981.

JanMohamed, Abdul R. "The Economy of Manichean Allegory: The Function of Racial Difference in Colonialist Literature." In *"Race," Writing, and Difference,* edited by Henry Louise Gates Jr., 78–106. Chicago: University of Chicago Press, 1986.

Jewinski, Ed. *Express Yourself Beautifully.* Toronto: ECW Press, 1994.

Jones, Carolyn M. "Male Friendship and the Construction of Identity in D. H. Lawrence's Novels." *Literature and Theology* 9 (1995): 66–84.

Kaplan, Caren. *Questions of Travel: Postmodern Discourses of Displacement.* Durham: Duke University Press, 1996.

Keeley, Edmund. "Byron, Durrell, and Modern Philhellenism." In *Lawrence Durrell: Comprehending the Whole,* edited by Julius Rowan Roper et al., 111–23. Columbia : University Press of Missouri, 1995.

Lash, Scott, and Jonathan Friedman. *Modernity and Identity.* Oxford: Blackwell, 1992.

Lawrence, D. H. *Aaron's Rod.* 1922. Edited by Mara Kalnins. New York: Cambridge University Press, 1981.

———. *The Letters of D. H. Lawrence.* Edited by Aldous Huxley. New York: Viking Press, 1932.

———. *The Lost Girl.* 1920. Edited by John Worthen. New York: Cambridge University Press, 1981.

———. *Mornings in Mexico and Etruscan Places.* London: Heinemann, 1956.

———. *Mr. Noon.* New York: Penguin Books, 1985.

———. *The Plumed Serpent.* New York: Vintage Books, 1926.

———. "The Spirit of Place." In *Studies in Classic American Literature,* 11–18.

———. *Studies in Classic American Literature.* New York: Doubleday, 1923.

———. *Twilight in Italy and Other Essays.* New York: Penguin, 1997.

Lears, T. J. Jackson. *No Place of Grace: Antimodernism and the Transformation of American Culture, 1880–1910.* New York: Pantheon, 1981.

Leask, Nigel. *British Romantic Writers and the East: Anxieties of Empire.* New York: Cambridge University Press, 1992.

LeFebvre, Henri. *The Production of Space.* Translated by D Nicholson-Smith. Oxford: Blackwell, 1991.

Levinas, Emmanuel. *Basic Philosophical Writings.* Edited by Adriaan T. Peperzak, Simon Critchley, and Robert Bernasconi. Bloomington: Indiana University Press, 1996.

———. *Totality and Infinity: An Essay on Exteriority.* Translated by Alphonso Lingis. Pittsburgh: Duquesne University Press, 1964.

Lillios, Anna. " 'The Blue of Greece': Durrell's Images of an Adopted Land." *Studies in the Literary Imagination* 24 (1991): 71–82.

Lowe, Lisa. *Critical Terrains: French and British Orientalisms.* Ithaca: Cornell University Press, 1991.

MacIntyre, Alasdair. *After Virtue.* Notre Dame, Ind.: University of Notre Dame Press, 1984.

MacKendrick, Karmen. *Counterpleasures.* Albany: State University of New York Press, 1999.

MacNiven, Ian S. *Lawrence Durrell: A Biography.* London: Faber and Faber, 1998.

Maddox, Brenda. *D. H. Lawrence: The Story of a Marriage.* New York: Norton, 1994.

Maier, John. *Desert Songs: Western Images of Morocco and Moroccan Images of the West.* Albany: State University of New York Press, 1996.

Manzalaoui, Mahmoud. "Curate's Egg: An Alexandrian Opinion of Durrell's Quartet." In *Critical Essays on Lawrence Durrell,* edited by Alan Warren Friedman, 144–57. Boston: G. K. Hall, 1987.

McAuliffe, Jody. "The Church of the Desert: Reflections on *The Sheltering Sky.*" *South Atlantic Quarterly* 91, 2 (1992): 419–26.

McClure, John A. *Late Imperial Romance.* London: Verso, 1994.

Morrison, Ray. "Mirrors and the Heraldic Universe in Lawrence Durrell's *The Alexandria Quartet.*" *Twentieth-Century Literature* 33 (Winter 1987): 499–514.

Morson, Gary Saul, and Caryl Emerson. *Mikhail Bakhtin: Creation of a Prosaics.* Stanford: Stanford University Press, 1990.

Mulhall, Stephen, and Adam Swift. *Liberals and Communitarians.* Second edition. Oxford: Blackwell, 1996.

Murphy, Peter. "Friendship's Eu-topia." *South Atlantic Quarterly* 97, 1 (1998): 169–85.

Nehamas, Alexander. *The Art of Living: Socratic Reflections from Plato to Foucault.* Berkeley: University of California Press, 1998.

———. *Nietzsche: Life as Literature.* Cambridge: Harvard University Press, 1985.

Nietzsche, Friedrich. *Beyond Good and Evil.* Translated by Marianne Cowan. Chicago: Henry Regnery, 1955.

———. *The Birth of Tragedy and the Genealogy of Morals.* Translated by Francis Golffing. New York: Doubleday, 1956.

———. *The Portable Nietzsche.* Edited and translated by Walter Kaufmann. New York: Viking Press, 1954.

———. *Thus Spoke Zarathustra.* In *The Portable Nietzsche,* 112–439.

———. *Twilight of the Idols.* In *The Portable Nietzsche,* 464–563.

Nussbaum, Martha. *Love's Knowledge: Essays on Philosophy and Literature.* New York: Oxford University Press, 1990.

Ondaatje, Michael. *The English Patient.* New York: Vintage, 1993.

———. *Running in the Family.* Toronto: McClelland and Stewart, 1982.

Patteson, Richard F. "Paul Bowles/Mohammed Mrabat: Translation, Transformation, and Transcultural Discourse." *Journal of Narrative Technique* 22, 3 (1992): 180–90.

———. *A World Outside: The Fiction of Paul Bowles*. Austin: University of Texas Press, 1987.

Pemble, John. *The Mediterranean Passion: Victorians and Edwardians in the South*. Oxford: Clarendon, 1987.

Perlès, Alfred. *My Friend, Lawrence Durrell*. London: Scorpion, 1961.

Pine, Richard. *The Dandy and the Herald: Manners, Mind, and Morals from Brummel to Durrell*. London: MacMillan, 1988.

———. *Lawrence Durrell: The Mindscape*. New York: St. Martin's, 1994.

Porter, Dennis. "Orientalism and Its Problems." In *Colonial Discourse and Post-Colonial Theory: A Reader*, edited by Patrick Williams and Laura Chrisman, 150–61. New York: Columbia University Press, 1994.

Pounds, Wayne. *Paul Bowles: The Inner Geography*. New York: P. Lang, 1985.

Pratt, Mary Louise. *Imperial Eyes: Travel Writing and Transculturation*. London: Routledge, 1992.

Praz, Mario. *The Romantic Agony*. Translated by Angus Davidson. London: Oxford University Press, 1933.

Richardson, Michael. *Georges Bataille*. London: Routledge, 1994.

Robbins, Bruce. "Comparative Cosmopolitanism." *Social Text* 31/32 (1992): 169–86.

———. *Feeling Global: Internationalism in Distress*. New York: New York University Press, 1999.

Rorty, Richard. *Contingency, Irony, and Solidarity*. Cambridge: Cambridge University Press, 1989.

Rossman, Charles. "D. H. Lawrence in Mexico." In *D. H. Lawrence: A Centenary Consideration*, edited by Peter Balbert, 180–209. Ithaca: Cornell University Press, 1985.

Said, Edward. *Culture and Imperialism*. New York: Knopf, 1993.

———. *Orientalism*. New York: Vintage, 1979.

Sawyer-Laúçanno, Christopher. *An Invisible Spectator: A Biography of Paul Bowles*. London: Paladin Grafton, 1990.

Sedgwick, Eve Kosofsky. *Between Men: English Literature and Male Homosocial Desire*. New York: Columbia University Press, 1985.

Seidel, Michael. *Exile and the Narrative Imagination*. New Haven: Yale University Press, 1986.

Seidler, Victor J. *Recovering the Self: Morality and Social Theory*. London: Routledge, 1994.

———. *Rediscovering Masculinity: Reason, Language, and Sexuality*. London: Routledge, 1989.

Showalter, Elaine. *Sexual Anarchy: Gender and Culture at the Fin de Siècle*. New York: Viking, 1990.

Siemerling, Winfried. *Discoveries of the Other: Alterity in the Work of Leonard Cohen, Hubert Aquin, Michael Ondaatje, and Nicole Brossard*. Toronto: University of Toronto Press, 1994.

Silverman, Kaja. *Masochism and Male Subjectivity*. New York: Routledge, 1992.

Soja, Edward W. *Thirdspace: Journeys to Los Angeles and Other Real-and-Imagined Places*. Cambridge: Blackwell, 1996.

Spera, Giovanna. *D. H. Lawrence's Dualistic Impulses in His Writings about Italy*. Galatina Le, Italy: Congedo, 1995.

Spivak, Gayatri Chakravorty. "Can the Subaltern Speak?" In *Colonial Discourse and Post-Colonial Theory: A Reader*, edited by Patrick Williams and Laura Chrisman, 66–111. New York: Columbia University Press, 1994.

———. *In Other Worlds: Essays in Cultural Politics*. New York: Methuen, 1987.

———. *The Post-Colonial Critic: Interviews, Strategies, Politics*. Edited by Sarah Harasym. New York: Routledge, 1990.

Spurr, David. *The Rhetoric of Empire: Colonial Discourse in Journalism, Travel Writing, and Imperial Administration*. Durham: Duke University Press, 1993.

Suleri, Sara. *The Rhetoric of English India*. Chicago: University of Chicago Press, 1991.

Taylor, Charles. *Sources of the Self: The Making of Modern Identity*. Cambridge: Harvard University Press, 1989.

Todorov, Tzvetan. *On Human Diversity: Nationalism, Racism, and Exoticism in French Thought*. Translated by Catherine Porter. Cambridge: Harvard University Press, 1993.

Tompkins, Jane. *West of Everything: The Inner Life of Westerns*. New York: Oxford University Press, 1992.

Torgovnick, Marianna. *Gone Primitive: Savage Intellects, Modern Lives*. Chicago: University of Chicago Press, 1990.

———. *Primitive Passions: Men, Women, and the Search for Ecstasy*. New York: Knopf, 1997.

Trinh, Minh-ha T. *Woman/Native/Other: Writing, Postcoloniality, and Feminism*. Bloomington: Indiana University Press, 1989.

Turner, Victor. *Dramas, Fields, and Metaphors: Symbolic Action in Human Society*. Ithaca: Cornell University Press, 1974.

Varadharajan, Asha. *Exotic Parodies: Subjectivity in Adorno, Said, and Spivak*. Minneapolis: University of Minnesota Press, 1995.

Weeks, Jeffrey. *Sexuality and Its Discontents: Meanings, Myths, and Modern Sexualities*. London: Routledge, 1983.

Williams, Raymond. *Marxism and Literature*. Oxford: Oxford University Press, 1977.

Wordsworth, William. "'The Prelude' Book Seventh, line 621." In *English Romantic Writers*, edited by David Perkins, 212–63. San Diego: Harcourt Brace Jovanovich, 1967.

Young, Robert. *White Mythologies: Writing, History, and the West*. London: Routledge, 1990.

Zahlan, Anne Ricketson. "The Destruction of the Imperial Self in Lawrence Durrell's *The Alexandria Quartet*." *Perspectives on Contemporary Literature* 12 (1986): 3–12.

Notes

In citing works in the notes, short titles are often used. Works cited frequently are identified in the text and notes by the following abbreviations:

AR   D. H. Lawrence, *Aaron's Rod*. 1922. Edited by Mara Kalnins. New York: Cambridge University Press, 1981.

BL   Lawrence Durrell, *Bitter Lemons*. New York: Dutton, 1957.

DE   Paul Bowles. "A Distant Episode." In *Collected Stories, 1939–1976*. Santa Rosa, Calif.: Black Sparrow Press, 1994.

EP   Michael Ondaatje, *The English Patient*. New York: Vintage, 1993.

GE   Michel Foucault. "On the Genealogy of Ethics: An Overview of Work in Progress." In *The Foucault Reader*, ed. Paul Rabinow. New York: Pantheon, 1984.

IE   Georges Bataille. *Inner Experience*. 1954. Translated by Leslie Anne Boldt. New York: State University of New York Press, 1988.

Let It   Paul Bowles, *Let It Come Down*. Santa Rosa, Calif.: Black Sparrow Press, 1992.

Letters   *The Letters of D. H. Lawrence*. Edited by Aldous Huxley. New York: Viking Press, 1932.

LG   D. H. Lawrence, *The Lost Girl*. 1920. Edited by John Worthen. New York: Cambridge University Press, 1981.

OA   Isak Dinesen, *Out of Africa and Shadows on the Grass*. 1938. New York: Vintage, 1985.

PE   Zygmunt Bauman, *Postmodern Ethics*. Oxford: Blackwell, 1993.

RMV   Lawrence Durrell, *Reflections on a Marine Venus: A Companion to the Landscape of Rhodes*. 1953. London: Faber and Faber, 1963.

SH   Paul Bowles, *The Spider's House*. Santa Rosa, Calif.: Black Sparrow Press, 1988.

SS   Paul Bowles, *The Sheltering Sky*. New York: Vintage Books, 1949.

Preface

1. Connolly, *Why I Am Not a Secularist*, 146.
2. Nussbaum, *Love's Knowledge*, 29, 390.
3. Lawrence, *Mister Noon*, 371.
4. Robbins, *Feeling Global*, 5.

Chapter 1. The Ethics of Expatriation

1. Spivak, "Can the Subaltern Speak?" 76.
2. Porter, *Orientalism and Its Problems*, 153.
3. Lowe, *Critical Terrains*, 5.
4. Kaplan, *Questions of Travel*, 2.
5. Bongie, *Exotic Memories*, 22.
6. Taylor, *Sources of the Self*, 456.
7. Taylor, "The State of Secularism," public dialogue sponsored by the Center for the Critical Analysis of Contemporary Culture, Rutgers University, 1 November 2000.
8. Bennett, *The Enchantment of Modern Life*, 7.
9. Pratt, *Imperial Eyes*, 4.
10. Harpham, *The Ascetic Imperative*, xiii, and 23, qtg. Peter Brown.
11. Foucault, "Genealogy of Ethics" 360, hereafter cited in the text as GE.
12. Foucault, *The Use of Pleasure*, 10–11.
13. Nehamas, *The Art of Living*, 6, 10.
14. Nietzsche, *Genealogy of Morals*, 226, 229.
15. Nietzsche, *Thus Spoke Zarathustra*, 228.
16. Nietzsche, *Beyond Good and Evil*, 196.
17. Ibid., 51.
18. Bataille, *Inner Experience*, 26–27.
19. Bataille, *On Nietzsche*, 331.
20. Bataille, *Inner Experience*, 3.
21. Ibid., 61.
22. Taylor, *Sources of the Self*, 462.
23. Bataille, "Knowledge of Sovereignty," 302.
24. Weeks, *Sexuality and Its Discontents*, 172
25. Foucault, Preface, xiii.
26. Deleuze and Guattari, *Anti-Oedipus*, 33, cited by page number in succeeding text.
27. Deleuze and Guattari, *A Thousand Plateaus*, 363, 360, xii.
28. Bataille, *Eroticism*, 11.
29. Bataille, *Literature and Evil*, 26, cited by page number in succeeding text.
30. Bataille, *Eroticism*, 13.
31. Bennett, *The Enchantment of Modern Life*, 62.
32. Jameson, *The Political Unconscious*, 236–37.
33. JanMohamed, "The Economy of Manichean Allegory," 84.
34. Bauman, *Postmodern Ethics*, 10, hereafter cited in the text as PE.
35. Silverman, *Masochism and Male Subjectivity*, 40, cited by page number in succeeding text.
36. Benjamin, *The Bonds of Love*, 170, cited by page number in succeeding text.
37. Seidler, *Recovering the Self*, 159, 8.
38. Deleuze and Guattari, *Anti-Oedipus*, 51, cited by page number in succeeding text.

39. Connolly, *Why I Am Not a Secularist*, 9, cited by page number in succeeding text.

40. Rorty, *Contingency, Irony, and Solidarity*, 39–40, cited by page number in succeeding text.

41. Weeks, *Sexuality and Its Discontents*, 175.

42. Benhabib, *Situating the Self*, 159, cited by page number in succeeding text.

43. Levinas, *Basic Philosophical Writings*, 16.

44. Ibid., 17.

45. Bennett, *The Enchantment of Modern Life*, 5, cited by page number in succeeding text.

Chapter 2. Lawrence Durrell and the Poet(h)ics of Imperialism

1. Durrell, *Bitter Lemons*, 35, hereafter cited in the text as BL.

2. Dasenbrock, "Lawrence Durrell," 520.

3. Bradbury, *The Modern British Novel*, 210.

4. Morrison, "Mirrors and the Heraldic Universe," 500.

5. Durrell to Henry Miller, November 1936, *Durrell-Miller Letters*, 27.

6. Durrell, *Clea*, 144, hereafter cited by title in the text.

7. Pine, *The Dandy and the Herald*, 171.

8. Bersani, *The Culture of Redemption*, 74.

9. Keeley, "Byron, Durrell, and Modern Philhellenism," 114.

10. MacNiven, *Lawrence Durrell*, 293.

11. Rorty, *Contingency, Irony, and Solidarity*, 39–40.

12. Lawrence, "The Spirit of Place," 16, cited by page number in succeeding text.

13. Nietzsche, *Beyond Good and Evil*, 152.

14. MacNiven, *Lawrence Durrell*, 37 (qtg. Durrell), 38.

15. Durrell, *The Big Supposer*, 26.

16. Durrell to George Wilkinson, *The Spirit of Place*, 30.

17. Bowker, *Through the Dark Labyrinth*, 127.

18. For a comprehensive history and analysis of the expatriate community of British exiles that flourished in wartime Egypt, see Bowen, *Many Histories Deep*.

19. Durrell to Sir Walter Smart, 5 December 1945, *The Spirit of Place*, 80.

20. Durrell to Henry Miller, c. October 1952, *Durrell-Miller Letters*, 263.

21. Ibid., April 1954, *Durrell-Miller Letters*, 277.

22. Ibid., 24 October [postmark] 1953, *Durrell-Miller Letters*, 272.

23. For a Greek view of Durrell's tenure as chief information officer, see *Deus Loci, The Lawrence Durrell Journal* NS3, 1994.

24. Bhabha, *The Location of Culture*, 151.

25. Durrell to Henry Miller, c. 27 January 1937, *Durrell-Miller Letters*, 52.

26. Lillios, " 'The Blue of Greece,' " 78, qtg. Durrell.

27. Durrell, *The Big Supposer*, 24–25.

28. Bowles, interview by Daniel Halpern, *Conversations with Paul Bowles*, 90.

29. Durrell, *Mountolive*, 51, hereafter cited by title in the text.
30. Bowker, *Through the Dark Labyrinth*, 21.
31. Durrell, *The Big Supposer*, 39.
32. Durrell, *Prospero's Cell*, 12, cited by page number in succeeding text.
33. Torgovnick, *Primitive Passions*, 15, 16.
34. Bataille, "The Notion of Expenditure," 117.
35. Durrell, *Reflections on a Marine Venus*, 17, hereafter cited in the text as *RMV*.
36. Bennett, *The Enchantment of Modern Life*, 10.
37. Durrell, *Bitter Lemons*.
38. Leask, *British Romantic Writers*, 23, qtg. Byron.
39. Dinesen, *Out of Africa*, 49, hereafter cited in the text as *OA*.
40. Horton, *Difficult Women, Artful Lives*, 7.
41. Ibid., 28.
42. Durrell, *Justine*, 64, hereafter cited by title in the text.
43. Jameson, *The Political Unconscious*, 237.
44. Bersani, *The Culture of Redemption*, 1.
45. Ibid.
46. Manzalaoui, "Curate's Egg," 155.
47. Durrell, Introduction to *Alexandria*, xvii.
48. Alcalay, *After Jews and Arabs*, 122.
49. Said, *Culture and Imperialism*, 156.
50. Ibid., 158–59.
51. Boone, *Libidinal Currents*, 365, cited by page number in succeeding text.
52. Silverman, *Masochism and Male Subjectivity*, 50, 54.
53. Durrell, *Balthazar*, 45–46, hereafter cited by title in the text.
54. Jameson, *The Political Unconscious*, 229, cited by page number in succeeding text.
55. Bowen, "Closing the Toybox," 17.
56. Jameson, *The Political Unconscious*, 236.
57. Durrell to Henry Miller, May 1944, *Durrell-Miller Letters*, 168.
58. Jameson, *The Political Unconscious*, 210.
59. Young, *White Mythologies*, 17.
60. Jameson, *The Political Unconscious*, 220.
61. Bennett, *The Enchantment of Modern Life*, 62–63.
62. Foucault, *Power/Knowledge*, 82.
63. For an alternate view of Durrell's engagement with gnostic philosophy and its ethical implications, see Herbrechter, *Lawrence Durrell*.
64. Bataille, *Literature and Evil*, 73.
65. Ibid., 74.

Chapter 3. Italy's Best Gift: D. H. Lawrence in the Mediterranean

1. Huxley, Introduction, xxxvi.
2. Ibid., xi–xii.

3. Nietzsche, *Beyond Good and Evil*, 132–33, cited by page number in succeeding text.
4. Taylor, *Sources of the Self*, 14.
5. Bennett, *The Enchantment of Modern Life*, 104.
6. Lawrence, "The Spirit of Place," 17.
7. Deleuze and Guattari, *A Thousand Plateaus*, 381.
8. Behdad, *Belated Travelers*, 75.
9. Robbins, *"Comparative Cosmopolitanism,"* 173.
10. Silverman, *Masochism and Male Subjectivity*, 2.
11. Ibid., 3.
12. Lawrence to Lady Ottoline Morrell," 1 February 1915, *Letters*, 224.
13. Nietzsche, *Beyond Good and Evil*, 194.
14. Ely, "Intellectual Friendship," 190, 188, cited by page number in succeeding text.
15. Lawrence, "Return Journey," in *Twilight in Italy*, 223.
16. Ibid., 224.
17. Lawrence, "The Lemon Gardens," in *Twilight in Italy*, 116.
18. Ibid., "San Guadenzio," in *Twilight in Italy*, 159.
19. Booth, "Lawrence in Doubt," 208.
20. Lawrence, "The Spirit of Place," 16–17.
21. Lawrence, *Aaron's Rod*, 145, hereafter cited in the text as *AR*.
22. Deleuze and Guattari, *Anti-Oedipus*, 315.
23. Rorty, *Contingency, Irony, and Solidarity*, 39–40.
24. Foucault, *The Care of the Self*, xiii.
25. Connolly, *Identity/Difference*, 32–33.
26. Bongie, *Exotic Memories*, 11.
27. Nietzsche, *Beyond Good and Evil*, 133.
28. Deleuze and Guattari, *Anti-Oedipus*, 381.
29. Lawrence to Edward Garnett, 17 April 1913, *Letters*, 120.
30. Deleuze and Guattari, *A Thousand Plateaus*, 383.
31. Lawrence, *The Lost Girl*, 2, hereafter cited in the text as *LG*.
32. Bataille, *Eroticism*, 11.
33. Eagleton, *The Ideology of the Aesthetic*, 53.
34. Ibid., 54.
35. According to John Worthen's footnote, this passage represents a revision made by Lawrence at the request of his publisher, Martin Secker, which appeared in the second-state and all subsequent English printings until the revised "Phoenix edition."
36. Deleuze and Guattari, *Anti-Oedipus*, 116.
37. Butler, *The Psychic Life of Power*, 28.
38. MacKendrick, *Counterpleasures*, 118.
39. Nietzsche, *Thus Spoke Zarathustra*, 127.
40. Huxley uses the phrase "mystical materialism" in Introduction, xx.
41. Bauman, *Postmodern Ethics*, 149.
42. Lawrence to Lady Cynthia Asquith, 23 October 1913, *Letters*, 150,
43. Lawrence, "John," in *Twilight in Italy*, 186.

44. Ibid.
45. Connolly, *Why I Am Not a Secularist*, 146.
46. Nietzsche, *Thus Spoke Zarathustra*, 228.
47. Lawrence to Robert Pratt Barlow, 30 March 1922, *Letters*, 548–49.
48. Booth, "Lawrence in Doubt," 218.
49. Spera, *D. H. Lawrence's Dualistic Impulses*, 13.
50. Lawrence, "The Spirit of Place," 16.
51. Ibid., 17.
52. Lawrence to Lady Cynthia Asquith, 30 April 1922, *Letters*, 552.
53. Lawrence, "The Lemon Garden," in *Twilight in Italy*, 117, cited by page number in succeeding text.
54. Deleuze and Guattari, *Anti-Oedipus*, 277.
55. Lawrence, *Mister Noon*, 371.

Chapter 4. The Dark Dream: Paul Bowles and the Quest for Non-Sense

1. Nietzsche, *Beyond Good and Evil*, 152.
2. Silverman, *Masochism and Male Subjectivity*, 65.
3. Ibid., 63.
4. Ehrenreich, *The Hearts of Men*, 18.
5. Boone, *Libidinal Currents*, 362.
6. Silverman, *Masochism and Male Subjectivity*, 63.
7. Hassan, *Radical Innocence*, 86.
8. Ibid., 88.
9. Bowles to Edouard Roditi, August 1931, *In Touch*, 86.
10. Bowles to Peggy Glanville-Hicks, 16 January 1948, *In Touch*, 189.
11. Lawrence, *LG*, 362.
12. Morson and Emerson, *Mikhail Bakhtin*, 50–51, qtg. Bakhtin.
13. Bowles, interview by Jeffrey Bailey, *Conversations with Paul Bowles*, 123.
14. Bowles to Aaron Copland, summer 1933, *In Touch*, 117.
15. Chase, *The American Novel*, 7.
16. Fiedler, *Love and Death*, xxiv, cited by page number in succeeding text.
17. Abrams, *Natural Supernaturalism*, 416, cited by page number in succeeding text.
18. Bowles to Bruce Morrissette, 7 January 1930, *In Touch*, 26.
19. Bataille, "The Notion of Expenditure," 116–17.
20. Bataille, "The Object of Desire," 269.
21. Ibid.
22. Bataille, "The Knowledge of Sovereignty," 305, cited in succeeding text by page number.
23. Bataille, "Sacrifice," 211.
24. Bataille, *Inner Experience*, 9, hereafter cited in the text as *IE*.
25. Dillon, *You Are Not I*, 173.
26. Bataille, *Eroticism*, 18–19.

27. Ibid., 24.
28. Bowles, "A Distant Episode," 39, cited hereafter in the text as DE.
29. Bataille, "Schema of Sovereignty," 317, 313.
30. Nietzsche, *Beyond Good and Evil*, 35.
31. Bowles, *The Sheltering Sky*, 6, hereafter cited in the text as *SS*.
32. Tompkins, *West of Everything*, 72, cited by page number in succeeding text.
33. Nietzsche, *Beyond Good and Evil*, 150.
34. Bataille, "Knowledge of Sovereignty," 308.
35. Bataille, "Schema of Sovereignty," 317–18.
36. Richardson, *Georges Bataille*, 37.
37. Boone, *Libidinal Currents*, 365.
38. Patteson, *A World Outside*, 62.
39. Bowles, interview by Michael Rogers, *Conversations with Paul Bowles*, 65–66.
40. Ibid., 66.
41. Bowles to James Leo Herligy, 30 April 1966, *In Touch*, 381.
42. Bataille, "The College of Sociology," 250.
43. Bowles, *Let It Come Down*, 20, hereafter cited in the text as *Let It*.
44. Maier, *Desert Songs*, 74, 149.
45. JanMohamed, "The Economy of Manichean Allegory," 94–95.
46. Bataille, "Schema of Sovereignty," 317–18.
47. Bataille, "Sacrifice," 214, cited in succeeding text by page number.
48. Botting and Wilson, Introduction, 8.
49. Richardson, *Georges Bataille*, 37.
50. Bataille, "Sacrifice," 214–15.
51. Ibid., 213
52. Maier, *Desert Songs*, 70.
53. Jane Bowles, "Everything Is Nice," 316.
54. Ibid., 320.
55. Bowles, *The Spider's House*, 195, hereafter cited in the text as *SH*.
56. Dillon, *You Are Not I*, 230.
57. Sawyer-Lauçanno, *An Invisible Spectator*, 294.
58. Dillon, *You Are Not I*, 216, 217.
59. Bowles to Aaron Copland, Summer 1933, *In Touch*, 117.
60. Dillon, *You Are Not I*, 216, qtg. Bowles.
61. Green, *The Dream*, 9–10.
62. Finlayson, *Tangier*, 185.
63. Ibid., 205.
64. Foucault, *The Use of Pleasure*, 20, cited by page number in succeeding text.
65. Bowles, interview by Jeffrey Bailey, *Conversations with Paul Bowles*, 142.
66. Patteson, "Paul Bowles/Mohammed Mrabat," 182.
67. Finlayson, *Tangier*, 346.
68. Certeau, *Heterologies*, 68.
69. Patteson, "Paul Bowles/Mohammed Mrabat," 181.

Chapter 5. Modern Expatriates and Postmodern Expatriate Narratives

1. McClure, *Late Imperial Romance*, 135.
2. DeLillo, *The Names*, 73, hereafter cited in the text as *Names*.
3. Pratt, *Imperial Eyes*, 34.
4. McClure, *Late Imperial Romance*, 136.
5. Ibid.
6. Harpham, *The Aesthetic Imperative*, 16.
7. Ibid.
8. Benhabib, *Situating the Self*, 159.
9. McClure, *Late Imperial Romance*, 135.
10. Ondaatje, *The English Patient*, 139, hereafter cited in the text as *EP*.
11. Ely, "Intellectual Friendship," 200, qtg. Bloch from Theodor Adorno, "Bloch's 'Traces': The Philosophy of Kitsch, *New Left Review* 121 (1980), 49, 53.
12. Murphy, "Friendship's Eu-topia," 171, cited by page number in succeeding text.
13. Deleuze and Guattari, *Anti-Oedipus*, 371, cited by page number in succeeding text.
14. Connolly, *Identity/Difference*, 44.
15. Fussell, *Abroad*, 134.
16. Deleuze and Guattari, *Anti-Oedipus*, 500, cited by page number in succeeding text.
17. Ibid.
18. Rorty, *Contingency, Irony, and Solidarity*, 63.
19. Robbins, *Feeling Global*, 6.

Conclusion

1. Porter, "Orientalism and Its Problems," 153.

Index